Divorce Law Reform In England

Contemporary Issues Series

B. H. LEE

Divorce Law Reform in England

PETER OWEN · LONDON

ISBN 0 7206 0252 1

PETER OWEN LIMITED

20 Holland Park Avenue London W11 3QU

First British Commonwealth edition 1974

© B. H. Lee 1974

Printed in Great Britain by
Bristol Typesetting Co Ltd
Barton Manor St Philips Bristol

To my wife

Contents

CONTENTS

Preface

This is a study of divorce reform legislation in England with special reference to the Divorce Reform Act 1969. The work is designed chiefly to tell the story of its background and its passage to the Statute Book.

The main part of the discussion is concentrated on the recent controversy over this age-old problem. Nevertheless, an attempt has been made to describe the treatment of marriage and divorce in England, and changes in the laws concerning divorce, in an historical context. But no legal case study is presented; strictly technical questions or interpretations of the law and of the role of the courts are also avoided.

Since the primary aim of the study is to give a narrative account, an effort has been made to avoid any direct moral or value judgment on the issues being discussed. However, the writer has endeavoured to deal with the problems synthetically, bearing in mind the many different factors—religious, sociological, legal and political—involved in a question of this kind. Particular attention has been paid to the part played by the Law Commission, the Church group, and the Divorce Law Reform Union; the interplay of roles between official and unofficial lawmakers—that is, Members of Parliament, Law Commissioners, members of pressure groups, and the public—has been examined. The procedure of the private member's bill is also examined, in the light of the increasing power of the Executive in modern governments. No attempt is made to make the story dramatic; all effort is focused upon giving an accurate description of the events.

It should be noted that, with the exception of various editorial changes and emendations which have been made subsequently, the manuscript of this book was completed in April 1971. To update it completely would involve revisions to the text that are not feasible without delaying publication still further.

Finally, the reader should be warned that greater space has been given to the activities of those who promoted the Bill than to those who opposed it. This is simply because the reformers were in general more active and better organized than their opponents, and the bias of the narrative as well as the repetitious debates between reformers and opponents thus reflect the pattern of events.

Lincoln College
Oxford

B.H.L.

Acknowledgments

I wish to take this opportunity to record my indebtedness to the numerous politicians, lawyers, scholars and students who have helped me in writing this manuscript. The outcome of this study was due to the combined effort of many people : their suggestions and information significantly contributed to whatever merit this work may have. To acknowledge them all would extend this acknowledgment unduly, but some should be mentioned here.

I owe a special debt of gratitude to Dr D. E. Butler, Fellow of Nuffield College, who generously guided and assisted me in writing this book, and who repeatedly read all of my typescripts. Equally, I am indebted to the following, who shared their recollections and opinions with me :

Mr Leo Abse, M.P.
Mr Daniel Awdry, M.P.
Mr R. V. Banks, Chairman, DLRU
Mr Bruce Campbell, Q.C., ex-M.P.
Lady Gaitskell
Lord Gardiner
Sir Arthur Irvin, Q.C., M.P.
Mr Peter Jackson, ex-M.P.
Mr T. Alec Jones, M.P.

Dr Mortimer, Bishop of Exeter
Mr Alastair Service
Mrs Renée Short, M.P.
Lord Stow Hill
Lady Summerskill
Dr Shirley Summerskill, M.P.
Dame Joan Vickers, M.P.
Dame Irene Ward, M.P.
Lady White
Mr William Wilson, M.P.

I owe much to two Law Commissioners, namely, Mr Gower and Sir Leslie Scarman. My thanks are also due to Professor J. N. D. Anderson, Chairman of the General Synod of the Church of England and who was also a member of the Church group appointed by the Archbishop of Canterbury; Mr William Latey, Q.C.; and the Archbishop of Canterbury.

I must also record my gratitude to the following : first, the late Sir Alan Herbert, M.P., who generously allowed me to cite his unpublished manuscript, *The Birth of an Act*, which is in the Senate Library of the University of London; secondly, Professor O. R. McGregor, author of *Divorce in England*; thirdly, Professor P. G. Richards, author of *Parliament and Conscience*, and its publishers, George Allen & Unwin; fourthly, Dr A. R. Winnett, author of *The Church and Divorce*, and its publishers, A. R. Mowbray, for their permission to quote from their works. I am also grateful to Mr P. S. C. Lewis, Fellow of All Souls College, Dr D. B. Goldey, Dean of

Lincoln College, Dr G. Marshall, Fellow of Queen's College, and
Professor P. A. Bromhead, University of Bristol, each of whom read
part or all of the manuscript, and offered thoughtful suggestions
and criticisms. Again I should like to express my gratitude to Mr
Abse, Mr Banks, Mr Campbell, Lord Gardiner, Mr Gower, Mr
Jackson, Mr Jones, Sir Leslie Scarman, Mr Service, Lord Stow Hill,
Lady White and Mr Wilson, for reading various sections of the
manuscript and helping me to correct errors of fact and judgment.
At the same time I must absolve them of any responsibility for
whatever shortcomings this book and the views herein expressed
may have. For those that remain, I alone am responsible.

Others whom I should thank for help in providing necessary
information include: the Law Commission, the Divorce Law Reform Union, and the Church of England.

My study in Britain was originally made possible by a Research
Fellowship (Rockefeller Grant) at the Institute of Advanced Legal
Studies and I owe thanks to Lincoln College for their financial aid.

B.H.L.

List of Tables

Chronology

1857 : The Matrimonial Causes Act

1906 : The Divorce Law Reform Union founded

1937 : The Matrimonial Causes Act

1951 : Mrs White's Bill, which contained a breakdown clause of seven years. The Bill was withdrawn on the Government's undertaking to appoint another Royal Commission.

1951 : The Royal Commission on Marriage and Divorce appointed

1956 : The Royal Commission Report 1951–5 presented to Parliament

1958 : Mr Deedes's Bill

1963 : Mr Abse's Bill : The Matrimonial Causes Act

21st June, 1963 : The Church group consisting of thirteen members appointed by the Archbishop of Canterbury

8th November, 1965 : The Matrimonial Causes Act

15th July, 1965 : The Law Commission set up

29th July, 1966 : *Putting Asunder* published

November 1966 : *Reform of the Grounds of Divorce: The Field of Choice* published

16th February, 1967 : *Putting Asunder* approved by the Church Assembly

21st July, 1967 : The Matrimonial Causes Act

29th November, 1967 : Mr Wilson's Bill presented

27th November, 1968 : Mr Jones's Bill presented

6th–17th December, 1968 : Second reading in the House of Commons

29th January–26th March, 1969 : Committee stage

25th April–12th June : Consideration on Report in the Commons

12th June : Third reading and passed in the Commons

16th June : The Bill brought from the Commons to the House of Lords

30th June : Second reading in the Lords

10th–24th July : Committee and report stage

13th October : Third reading and return to the Commons

17th October : Lords amendments accepted in the Commons

22nd October : Royal Assent to the Bill : The Divorce Reform Act 1969

PART ONE

PART ONE

Chapter 1

HISTORICAL BACKGROUND OF MATRIMONIAL LAW

I. *Christian Marriage and Divorce in England: 1857–1937*

The Church of England has long played the most important role in shaping the ideas on marriage and divorce in England, although the origins of Christianity in England are not known.[1] 'Until recent years Christian teaching has dominated all discussion of marriage and divorce and has determined the standard of accepted behaviour. Any examination of present-day conflicts about marriage and divorce must therefore begin with an understanding of the Christian position.'[2] Thus, before we deal with the fundamental change in divorce law, it is necessary to survey the teaching and practice of the Church of England relating to marriage and divorce, from the Reformation to the present day, and to illustrate the importance of the religious influence on the formation of English moral, social and legal standards of marriage and divorce.

The Church, at an early date, claimed jurisdiction over marriage and divorce, but it appears that the King's Court had some voice in deciding matrimonial causes until the middle of the twelfth century, and it was not until then that marriage and divorce were recognized as matters exclusively within the jurisdiction of the Ecclesiastical Courts. At first the various dignitaries of the Church exercised this jurisdiction in person in their principal churches, but, finding themselves unable to deal properly with such questions through lack of time and expertise, they were gradually forced to delegate their powers to ecclesiastical lawyers.[3]

By the middle of the twelfth century, the beliefs and jurisdiction of the Roman Church, dominating Western Christendom, which had previously been unsettled, hardened into established doctrine. From then until the Reformation the law of marriage was embodied in the law of the Church, the canon law, which was administered by the Church in its own Christian Courts. The civil law in England and Scotland had no official doctrine concerning jurisdiction over marriage and divorce. The law enforced by the Church derived its principles from the prevailing Christian fear of the pleasures of copulation.[4]

The Church has always prohibited marriage within certain prescribed degrees of consanguinity. Until the reign of Henry VIII,

3

the State did not interfere in the Church's authority in this matter, but in 1536 for the first time marriage within these degrees was forbidden by statute—in the Ecclesiastical Licences Act 1536, followed by the Marriage Act 1540, and confirmed by the Act of Supremacy in 1558—and this legislation can be seen as part of the process whereby Henry freed himself from the authority of Rome. The last fifty years have seen some changes in the list of degrees, but it is substantially the same as that laid down by the Catholic Church before the Reformation : intermarriage between persons within the third degree of kindred, or nearer, is forbidden. But Henry VIII's laws made marriage between first cousins legitimate, whereas before it had been necessary to obtain dispensation from the Pope for such a union.[5]

However, opinion on divorce and marriage in the Church of England had been acutely divided from the time of the Reformation onwards.

The continental reformers, in their opposition to the complexities of canon law, and to a system which 'failed miserably as guardian of the Holy Estate',[6] swept away the whole medieval catalogue of impediments to marriage other than those which they believed to have scriptural sanction. A marriage was no longer to be ended on the ground of some canonical flaw, but in general they were agreed that divorce, in the sense of a dissolution of the marriage-bond,[7] should be allowed for adultery and malicious desertion. Divorce for adultery was held to be permitted by Christ's teaching recorded by St Matthew, while divorce for malicious desertion was justified by reference to the Bible,[8] the deserter being on a par with the heathen or unbeliever. However, a few were prepared to allow divorce for a wider range of causes, although the Anglican reformers for the most part adopted the views of their more moderate continental brethren. Thus, the pendulum has swung between two major views depending upon the strength of each group at any one time : one view derived from the pre-Reformation Western tradition, according to which marriage is indissoluble if it is validly contracted; the other from the teaching of the continental reformers, which treated marriage as dissoluble on the grounds of unfaithfulness and desertion.[9] The failure of the proposed code of Canons known as the 'Reformatio Legum Ecclesiasticarum' to become law prevented the Church of England from adopting the practice of the Reformed Churches on the Continent, and the Canons of 1604 expressly disallowed *divorce a vinculo*. The Reformatio Legum admitted adultery, desertion, deadly hostility and prolonged ill-treatment of a wife by a husband as grounds for divorce.

When the 1857 Matrimonial Causes Bill was introduced,[10] churchmen revealed the difference of opinions which existed concerning divorce and remarriage.

> Of all the Bishops, Tait of London gave it the strongest support in the Lords : in his opinion it would mean no change in what had been the Church's practice during the previous one hundred years or more, and it had the merit of substituting a regular court procedure for the haphazard method of private Bills. A small group of bishops, led by Wilberforce of Oxford and Kerr Hamilton of Salisbury, opposed the Bill on the ground that marriage by our Lord's teaching admitted of no dissolution. The majority of Bishops, however, supported the Bill, but with some reluctance, which was due not to their holding marriage to be indissoluble, but to the liberty of remarriage which the Bill gave to the guilty party. . . . At the time the Divorce Bill was introduced the Tractarian or Oxford Movement had become an influential force in the Church, and John Keble, one of the leading Tractarians, opposed the Bill in two pamphlets, 'An argument for not proceeding immediately to repeal the Laws which treated the Nuptial Bond as indissoluble' and 'Sequel of the argument against immediately repealing the Laws which treat the Nuptial Bond as indissoluble'. Keble was among the first to realise that marriage meant two different things for the Church and for a State which was becoming increasingly secular.[11]

At the time of the Matrimonial Causes Act 1857 and until the end of the century, the majority of churchmen held that divorce was allowable within the limits of the Matthaean Exception, with the right of remarriage for the innocent party. This was the view of the great Tractarian, E. G. Pusey,[12] and it was apparently the view of such convinced high churchmen as Bishop Christopher Wordsworth,[13] William Bright[14] and Bishop Edward King.[15]

In 1853 the Commissioners[16] presented their Report, the main recommendations of which were as follows : that the distinction between *divorce a mensa et thoro* and *divorce a vinculo* should be maintained, that *divorce a vinculo* should be granted on the suit of a husband in the case of a wife's adultery; that 'in case of incest', bigamy or the like, it might be proper to give the wife the right to institute a suit for *divorce a vinculo matrimonii*; that a verdict at law and ecclesiastical sentence should no longer be required as conditions of obtaining a divorce; that causes relating to marriage and divorce constituted a civil tribunal, saving only that the ecclesiastical courts were to retain their jurisdiction in respect of the issue of marriage licences.[17]

The Commissioners did not regard themselves as innovating so

much as restoring the state of affairs in the latter half of the six-
teenth century, when in their opinion marriage was treated by the
Church as dissoluble. According to the historical survey with which
the Report opens the doctrine of indissolubility was not reinstated
until the celebrated case of Fuljambe in 1602, and the caution
against remarriage in the Canons of 1597 (and 1604) is not to be
interpreted as implying that such remarriage would have been held
invalid.[18] The Report was signed by all the members of the Commission except Lord Redesdale, who expressed his dissent on *divorce
a vinculo*. In his memorandum of dissent he disclosed that he had
changed his views since he was appointed to the Commission,
although he once held on the authority of St Matthew that divorce
might be granted for adultery and both parties allowed to marry
again. He claimed when once the principle of *divorce a vinculo* was
admitted, 'it is sure to degenerate into more extended abuse'. Lord
Redesdale's recommendations were 'that the law of England which
now holds the marriage-tie to be indissoluble should remain unaltered, and that the practice of passing exceptional laws in favour
of particular cases should henceforth be discontinued'.[19] Although
a clause was moved by the Bishop of Oxford, Bishop Wilberforce,
to prevent the remarriage of the guilty wife during the husband's
lifetime,[20] the Commissioners' recommendations were embodied in
a Bill which was introduced into the Lords in June 1854. However,
the Bill was soon withdrawn.[21]

When the Bill was reintroduced in June 1856, the opposition was
led by the Bishop of Oxford at the committee stage. While the
Bishop expressed his doubt as to the wisdom of the Bill, he admitted
the division of opinion in the Church from early times and said in
his opinion Christ taught that marriage might be dissolved for
adultery. He feared the proposed grounds for *divorce a vinculo*
would 'open the floodgates of licence upon the hitherto blessed
purity of English life', and preferred the continuance of the existing
practice of maintaining the principle of indissolubility and granting
divorce only by special legislation in cases which could not be
resisted.[22] The Bishop of St David's feared that the Bill would pave
the way for future concessions until divorce was brought within the
jurisdiction of the County Courts and made cheap and easy of
access to the lowest classes of society, which was actually accomplished through the Legal Aid and Advice Act 1949 after ninety-
three years of struggle.

On the motion to omit clauses 19–24 of the Bill, which dealt with
divorce a vinculo and remarriage, the Bishop of Oxford said that in
his opinion the alteration of the law would do more evil than good
by 'shaking the foundation of society and endangering its purity'.

He admitted the exception made by Christ in case of adultery but 'objected to the provisions by which a wife might divorce her husband for adultery with aggravating circumstances : this was contrary to the New Testament, which allowed a husband to divorce a wife but not a wife a husband. Adultery was as sinful in a man as in a woman, but in a woman it was a "social crime of different magnitude".'[23]

As Dr Winnett pointed out in the same book, from the standpoint of belief in the absolute indissolubility of marriage a protest was made against the Bill by the Bishop of Salisbury (Kerr Hamilton). According to his argument, the New Testament allows no dissolution of marriage except separation for adultery on the ground of St Matthew. Before the Bill was withdrawn again, the Bishop of Oxford successfully carried an amendment forbidding a guilty party to marry a partner in guilt.[24]

In February 1857, the Bill was introduced for a third time, and when it came up for its second reading in the Lords in March 1857, the Bishop of Exeter (Philpotts) moved the postponement of the second reading so that a Commission might be appointed to examine leading divines as to the doctrine of the Church concerning marriage and divorce. He emphasized a need to go back before Rome to the purer days of the Early Church, and urged the abolition of *divorce a mensa et thoro* as unknown to the Church except under the domination of Rome. The motion was supported by the Bishop of Oxford with the opinion that the Bill 'would shake everything and settle nothing'.[25] However the motion was defeated; the Bill received its second reading and was brought into the Lords again in May 1857. According to Bishop Wilberforce, opinion among the bishops was again divided, which reflected the division of opinion on divorce in the Church. The following note is to be found in his journal :

Discussed sporadically the law of marriage. The Archbishop said he had no doubt that it was contrary to the law of God to allow of the remarriage of divorced persons. It was allowable to dissolve the marriage but not to remarry. The Bishop of London (Dr Tait), Carlisle (Dr Villiers) and Ripon (Dr Bickersteth) rather in favour of the Bill. The Bishop of Winchester silent. The Bishop of Salisbury strong against the Bill.[26]

The Archbishop of Canterbury, J. B. Sumner, said in the ensuing debate that by divine law marriage was designed to be indissoluble, save only for the one cause of unfaithfulness. The question here was narrowed down to whether remarriage should be allowed by the Bill. However, the Bishop of Salisbury again upheld the indissolubility of marriage as the teaching of the New Testament and of the Church from the early centuries, and said that by the providence of God no alteration was made in the law of England at the time of the Reformation.[27] The Bishop appealed to the House to resist any change in the divorce law, and continued by saying that the House had granted Acts of Divorce by way of privilege to the wealthy, but so far from extending them to the poor they should abolish them altogether. The Bishop of Oxford warned the House and the nation that the Bill would not only create difficulties for churchmen but might change the whole moral aspect of the nation and cause the temper of the people to deteriorate.[28] Thus the division of opinion among churchmen was obvious and the second reading was carried by 47 votes to 18. The Bishop of Oxford expressed his unease in his journal: 'Sad, the debate of last night. The division of the Bishops, and especially the Bishop of London's tone[29] pained me deeply. What is to be the end of it but that of a house divided against itself.'[30]

The bishops were divided: ten supported the Bill, while five voted against it.[31]

The third reading of the Bill took place on the 27th June, 1857, and Lord Nelson reintroduced his amendment providing that the remarriage of divorced persons should take place only before a registrar. The amendment was rejected, the Bishop of Oxford supporting it and the Bishop of Exeter opposing it. The opposition to the Bill in the House of Commons was led by Mr Gladstone, who declared that the Bill was 'fraught with danger to the highest interests of religion and the morality of the people' and argued at length from the Scriptures and from the teaching of the Church for the absolute indissolubility of marriage.[32]

The proposed Divorce Reform Bill also led to the publication of two sermons on the subject of divorce by Canon Christopher Wordsworth, of Westminster, afterwards Bishop of Lincoln. In April 1854 the first, 'On Divorce', was preached in Westminster Abbey, while the second, 'On Marriage with a Person Divorced', was preached in the Abbey in July 1857. In his sermon 'On Divorce' Wordsworth argues that Christ declared marriage indissoluble except in the single case of fornication on the part of the wife, where he admitted that Christ 'does not forbid a man to put away his wife in that one predicament'.[33]

After passing through these agonizing but to some extent interesting paths of debate, the Bill became the Matrimonial Causes Act 1857, despite the fact that a petition was sent to the Queen from a number of clergy and laity in 1857 requesting Her Majesty to refuse the Royal Assent to the Divorce Bill on the ground that it was inconsistent with the teaching of the Prayer Book marriage service.[34]

In February 1858 the Convocation of Canterbury was marked by the presentation of petitions protesting against the Matrimonial Causes Act 1857.[35] According to Winnett, however, the Convocation of York which took place in 1861, did not discuss the question of divorce.

In any case, the Matrimonial Causes Act 1857 brought pain to some of those who were against it, while it offered considerable relief to those who suffered because of precarious ecclesiastical rule in the name of God and the high cost of a private act. The debate between the two divisions of the Church group on divorce and marriage continued and the people under the control of the Church were compelled to obey the law of God while the interpretation of that law was solely in the hands of churchmen. The law of the land made by Parliament sometimes stood for Church opinion and at other times against it, but the people had no choice once the law was made by Parliament and it is conceivable that many have suffered between the teachings of the Church and the law of the land. Public opinion on divorce was shaped by these two divisions of Christian thinking, and by the outcry from people who felt the divorce law to be unjust.

In 1912, the Royal Commission, after an exhaustive examination of Christian principles concerning the dissolubility of marriage, found that opinions were maintained in favour of each of the following principles : 'That all marriages are indissoluble. That Christian marriages are indissoluble. That marriage is dissoluble on the ground of adultery only. That marriage is dissoluble on the ground of, (i) adultery, (ii) desertion. That marriage is dissoluble on particular serious grounds, based upon the necessities of human life.'[36] The majority report was unable to

find any general consensus of Christian opinion which would exclude any of the questions stated above from being freely considered. In view of the conflict of opinion which has existed in all ages and in all branches of the Christian Church . . . and the fact that the State must deal with all its citizens, whether Christian, nominally Christian, or non-Christian, our conclusion is that we must proceed to recommend the legislature to act upon an unfettered consideration of what is best for the interest of the State, society and morality and for that of parties to suits and their families.[37]

This majority report, signed by the Archbishop of York, Sir

William Anson and Sir Lewis Dibdin, agreed in substance with most of the majority's recommendations but, whilst accepting additional grounds of nullity, emphatically rejected the proposals to extend the grounds for divorce.

Contrary to the early continental reformers in the Anglican Church who regarded marriage as dissoluble, the Roman Catholic Church has always stressed the indissolubility of marriage as a principle. This all too frequently has been the extent of its teaching about marriage, although there were some who believed this negative approach was insufficient. There was a need now, widely recognized, for more constructive teaching dealing with all the aspects of marriage. Without this teaching some marriages were bound to fail, for man and woman could not understand the nature of the union they were forming. Meanwhile, the Lambeth Conference produced resolutions on divorce and remarriage with which we shall deal later in detail.

> At the beginning of the present century, significant changes occurred in Anglican opinion on divorce and remarriage, and took the form of strengthening the indissolubility position. Many factors contributed to this. New Testament criticism questioned the Exceptive Clause in St Matthew (not found in St Mark) as an authentic word of Jesus. The Anglo-Catholic movement, with a moral theology largely derived from Roman sources, had gained ground among the clergy. Divorce, moreover, was no longer an exceptional occurrence, but had come to be regarded as a major challenge to the Christian conception of marriage demanding an uncompromising stand on the part of the Church.[38]

An illustration of the change was provided by the 1908 Lambeth Conference, which not only reaffirmed the resolution of the 1888 Conference, that the remarriage of a guilty party should not receive the blessing of the Church, but also declared it undesirable. A further illustration of the change is afforded by a comparison of Bishop Gore's book, *The Question of Divorce* (1911), with his earlier work, *The Sermon on the Mount* (1895).[39]

In 1920, the Lambeth Conference, in its resolution on marriage, affirmed 'our Lord's principle and standard of marriage, a lifelong and indissoluble union'. This was the first occasion when the word 'indissoluble' was used in such a resolution. It did, however, admit the right of a national or regional Church to make its own rules in respect of cases falling within the scope of the Matthaean Exception. In 1930 the Lambeth Conference went further and recommended that no marriage of a divorced person[40] with a partner living should be celebrated with the rites of the Church, and that where an innocent party had remarried and desired to receive Holy Communion, the case should be referred to the Bishop for consideration.[41]

In 1932 the Joint Committees on Marriage of the Convocations of Canterbury and York began their sessions under the chairmanship of the Bishops of Salisbury (Donaldson) and Sheffield (Burrows), and their report was issued three years later in 1935. The Majority Report of the Joint Committees, 'The Church and Marriage', affirmed unequivocally the principle of indissolubility of marriage : marriage not only ought not to be dissolved but also involved a moral and spiritual bond which cannot be finally terminated save by death.[42] However, the Minority Report, signed among others by Dr Barnes, Bishop of Birmingham, declared that the indissolubility of marriage was *not a law* but *an ideal*, and that the mind of Christ would approve of legislation on the part of His Church which, while keeping ever in view the divine ideal, had compassionate consideration for the troubles arising from failures to live up to that ideal, and which might be changed from time to time to meet the requirements of changing conditions. It also recommended that the Church should accord generous treatment to an undoubtedly innocent party, while it should be free to forbid the use of its buildings for the marriages of divorced persons.[43]

In June 1938, after the passage of the Herbert Act, and after prolonged discussion of the Joint Committees' Report, both the Convocations of Canterbury and York passed resolutions to the effect that marriage is a personal union, for better or for worse, of one man with one woman, exclusive of all others on either side, and indissoluble save by death; that remarriage after divorce during the lifetime of a former partner always involves a departure from the true principle of marriage as decided by Christ.[44]

Thus, the Church has been preaching the indissolubility of marriage as the union prearranged by God and many people have been and are still under the influence of the Church. Yet public sentiment in favour of easier divorce has been growing steadily. It may be said here that public sentiment on divorce in England still depends upon the osmosis of Christian doctrine of marriage into the British social life. However, Professor McGregor[45] pointed to the confusion which surrounds much thinking on this subject :

All Christians agree that God intended marriage as a monogamous, indissoluble union but Christians also differ irreconcilably concerning the rules of behaviour imposed by this general principle. The concept of 'Christian marriage' is so variable as

B

between different churches that it provides criteria for personal behaviour and public control only to those who adhere to particular dogmas. These present-day confusions are only aggravated by the claim, common to Christians and agnostics alike, that their particular rules will ensure the stability of the family and thus embody the good of society. There is, beyond all dispute, a widespread rejection in the country of religious and therefore denominational interpretations of marriage and divorce, and legal rules based on them no longer command general respect.

To sum up: as Flood said,[46] matrimonial law in England has undergone a complicated history. In Anglo-Saxon times the Canon law of the Catholic Church and that of the State were one. The State was in the fullest sense Catholic; then after the Conquest the Ecclesiastical Courts were separated from the Court of Common law, and this separation continued even as the Court of Equity developed under the Chancellors who, till Sir Thomas More, were ecclesiastic.

At the time of the Reformation the new Established Church retained its own courts and jurisdiction in matrimonial causes. This lasted until the nineteenth century when the Established Church lost this jurisdiction to the State—the civil courts. Since then marriage has been the province of the State law and considerable deviations from the other Christian doctrines have taken place.

All through, the Catholic Church has stood firm to retain the marriage law as expressed in its Canons. None the less, the Church of England has been a dominant figure in almost every sense; in particular, its influence on moral and social issues has been immense, although the influence it exerts is declining.

II. *Summary of the Divorce Law in England and Wales: 1857–1937*

Over the last hundred years, the divorce law has been reviewed three times by Royal Commissions. The first of these was appointed in 1850, the second in 1909 and the third in 1951. They reported in 1853,[47] 1912,[48] and in 1956[49] respectively. On the other hand, numerous laws relevant to the institution of marriage have been made and amended by Parliament since the enactment of the Matrimonial Causes Act 1857. The main legislative landmarks are the Matrimonial Causes Acts of 1937 and 1950, the Divorce Act 1958 and the Divorce Reform Act 1969.

1. PRE-1857

The sources of English Divorce Law lie in Roman and Ecclesiastical Law.[50] The exclusive jurisdiction of the Ecclesiastical Courts over all matters relating to marriage and its dissolution was established at an early date; and appeal came from the courts to the Pope in Rome. However, in the reign of King Henry VIII the problem of a royal divorce occasioned a transformation of the relationship between Church and State. The Supremacy of the Crown in both Church and State was established and by the Statute of Appeals in 1533 the right of appeal from the Ecclesiastical Courts to Rome was abolished.

After the Reformation these courts continued to exercise matrimonial jurisdiction and the principal relief granted included decrees of nullity, decrees for restitution of conjugal rights in cases of desertion, and decrees of *divorce a mensa et thoro* (which we should now call decrees of judicial separation) on the grounds of adultery, cruelty and unnatural offences. The courts had, however, no power to grant divorce as the term is understood today; that is to say, by making a decree dissolving the marriage. It appears that by the beginning of the seventeenth century the earlier view prevailed that the courts had no power to dissolve marriages, although in the years immediately following the Reformation parties regarded themselves, in some cases, as entitled to marry again with (or possibly even without) a decree of *divorce a mensa et thoro*. From then until 1857, the only means of setting aside a valid marriage was by Private Act of Parliament—a practice which developed at the end of the seventeenth century. This process was both slow and expensive, and over the period 1715 to 1852 the total number of dissolutions was, according to the Report of the Royal Commission of 1850, only 244,[51] less than two a year.

These arrangements on divorce continued unchanged until the middle of the nineteenth century. The Report of the Royal Commission of 1909 summarizes the situation as it existed in 1850 as follows :

> . . . according to common law as well as Ecclesiastical law and practice, divorce remained unrecognized; but the Legislature recognized it, in the case of a wife's adultery and, in case of a husband's when his adultery was accompanied by aggravating circumstances, by giving a remedy . . . through what was in form a legislative, but in substance a judicial, proceeding, which was open, with sufficient evidence, to anyone who was rich

enough to pay for it. The cost and inconvenience were however, so great, that the remedy was obviously beyond the means of the great bulk of the community.

2. THE MATRIMONIAL CAUSES ACT 1857

The Matrimonial Causes Act of 1857, based on the Report of the Royal Commission, made a decisive break with the past and established the basis of present jurisdiction and procedure by abolishing the jurisdiction of the Ecclesiastical Courts in matrimonial matters and setting up a new court—The Court for Divorce and Matrimonial Causes—to exercise that jurisdiction.[52] The Matrimonial Causes Act 1857 transferred all jurisdiction, at that time exercised in matrimonial matters by the Ecclesiastical Courts in England, to a new Court for Divorce and Matrimonial Causes.[53] It abolished *divorce a mensa et thoro* and substituted decrees for judicial separation. The most important provision of the Act was the introduction of the petition for the dissolution of marriage. This could be presented by the husband on the ground of adultery by his wife. However, the wife was treated differently and the grounds for divorce were her husband's (i) incestuous adultery, (ii) bigamy with adultery, (iii) rape, (iv) sodomy, (v) bestiality, or (vi) adultery, coupled either with desertion for two years or upwards, or with cruelty, while in the husband's petition simple adultery sufficed. The more rigorous conditions attached to a petition for divorce in the instance of a woman were not new, but carried forward a practice which had grown up under the procedure for dissolution by Private Act of Parliament. In contrast, in earlier times, the Ecclesiastical Courts appear to have granted[54] decrees of *divorce a mensa et thoro* on the same grounds—the adultery of either spouse—to husband and wife alike. After the abolition of the matrimonial jurisdiction of those courts by the Matrimonial Causes Act 1857, the corresponding relief of judicial separation was to be granted without distinction to a petitioner of either sex.[55]

The main and most important object of the Act of 1857 was to create a new Divorce Court and to make the civil system of divorce, established by the House of Lords in 1697, more widely available. It altered the procedure for obtaining divorce and changed the court, but introduced no new principles. The Attorney-General, Sir Richard Bethell, later Lord Westbury, emphasized this during the debates on the Bill, as follows :

The Bill had excited great anxiety and even alarm in the country at large. It had been said by some, and believed by others, that the Bill was an attempt to introduce new laws and new principles

... the Bill only involved long-existing rules and long-established principles, and it was intended only to give a local habitation to doctrines that had been long recognized as part of the law of the land, and for a century and a half administered in a judicial manner, although through the medium of a legislative assembly. Its object was to remove the inconvenience of that practice, but in all other respects the law of England upon the subject of divorce would remain what it was now.[56]

However, the Court was given the power to pronounce a decree of *divorce a vinculo matrimonii* on the above-mentioned grounds.

In the years following, further Acts relating to matrimonial causes were passed, dealing with ancillary questions relating to property and maintenance, custody of children, and various procedural matters. Then, by the Judicature Act 1873 all jurisdiction formerly exercised by the Court for Divorce and Matrimonial Causes was assigned to the High Court of Justice and has since then been exercised by the Probate, Divorce and Admiralty Division.[57]

Following these developments, a further review of the divorce law was carried out by the Royal Commission[58] on Divorce and Matrimonial Causes, which was appointed in 1909. The Commission by a majority (the minority including the then Archbishop of York) recommended that the grounds for dissolving marriage should be (i) adultery, (ii) wilful desertion for three years and upwards, (iii) cruelty, (iv) incurable insanity after five years' confinement, (v) habitual drunkenness found incurable after three years from the first order of separation, and (vi) imprisonment under commuted death sentence. The Commission also recommended that the law should be amended so as to place the two sexes on an equal footing as regards the grounds on which divorce might be obtained; and that certain additional grounds of nullity should be introduced.[59]

A quarter of a century elapsed before any one of the main recommendations of the Royal Commission for the introduction of additional grounds of divorce was given legislative effect. Between 1912 and 1937 unsuccessful attempts to implement various recommendations of the Commission were made by many prominent people, including Lord Gorell (son of the Chairman of the Royal Commission), Lord Buckmaster and Mr Holford Knight, M.P. After the First World War, a major social issue on which public attention was focused was the removal of women's disabilities, and this was reflected in the sphere of matrimonial law by the passage in 1923 of an Act[60] (sponsored by Lord Buckmaster) which empowered a wife to present a petition for divorce on the ground of simple adultery by her husband. After 1923, further changes did

not come until 1937 when a private member's bill, sponsored by Mr
A. P. (later Sir Alan) Herbert, received enactment.

3. THE HERBERT ACT : THE MATRIMONIAL CAUSES ACT 1937

For eighty years since the Matrimonial Causes Act 1857, there had
been continuous agitation for divorce law reform by people who
felt that the Act did not give sufficient opportunity of relief to
those who found their marriage state intolerable and wished to
change it. After three years of study, the 1909 Royal Commission
(Gorell Commission) produced its Report in 1912, but none of its
recommendations were carried into effect until the Herbert Act had
been passed.

In 1935, after being elected to the House of Commons as Junior
Burgess for Oxford University, Mr A. P. Herbert proposed a
Divorce Reform Bill in his maiden speech in the first session and,
with the assistance of Mr Rupert De la Bère, successfully presented
the Matrimonial Causes Bill.[61] The Bill was originally the 'Holford
Knight Bill' which had never had the good fortune to get enough
support to become an act.[62] Mr Herbert did not draft[63] the Bill, but
with the help of Lord Kilbracken and Mr Claud Mullins, the
Metropolitan Magistrate, made a number of improvements to the
original.

The preamble[64] of the Act written by Herbert, was significant
evidence of the anxieties inside and outside Parliament at that time.
Mr Herbert justified his Bill to the House of Commons by quoting
as representative of public opinion, a speech by the Archdeacon of
Coventry to a Diocesan Conference.

> The limitation of the grounds of divorce to the one ground of
> adultery, had resulted in a state of affairs which was disastrous
> and prejudicial to public morality. As the law stands at present,
> those who wished to bring an end to the marriage were forced
> to take one of two alternatives—either one must commit adultery
> or one must commit perjury.[65] The law as it stands is a definite
> incitement to immorality. It was the duty of the Church to
> press for and not merely to acquiesce in any reform of the exist-
> ing marriage law; reform could be found in extension of the
> grounds for divorce which did not necessarily mean making
> divorce more easy.[66]

Certainly, Mr Herbert's skilful handling of the Bill was of major
importance in securing its passage, but public recognition of the
necessity for change also played its part. To quote the Lord Chief
Justice (Lord Hewart) :

Changes in the substantive law of divorce appear to be quite inevitable. As for procedure, by way of diminishing difficulties and inequalities, especially as between rich and poor, it is conceivable that 19 divorce cases out of 20, with all their puzzles, may perhaps before very long, be heard and determined gratis by those diligent and accomplished gentlemen, the stipendiary magistrates, the county-court judges, and the Chairmen of the quarter sessions who happen to be lawyers.[67]

Thus the public and the Court[68] were fully aware of the defects of the old Matrimonial Causes Act and the change of Church opinion can be seen in the following resolutions discussed (and later carried) by the Upper House (in other words, the Bishops of the Convocation of Canterbury) :

That this House, recognizing that full legal enactment of the Christian standard of marriage may not always be possible in a State which comprises all sorts and kinds of people, including many who did not accept the Christian way of life, or the means of grace which the Church offers its members, is of opinion that some amendment of the State Law relating to grounds of divorce may be demanded by the circumstances of the day, and that the Church should be prepared to give consideration to proposals for such amendment, provided that any proposed amendment does not tend to make marriage a temporary alliance or to undermine the foundations of family life.[69]

However, it was by no means an easy task to propose divorce reform in public. It was clearly too risky for the Members of Parliament who were from constituencies where there were dominant Catholic influences.

There are, I believe, only 2,000,000 Catholics in the kingdom, but they seem to dominate it. Other members had had matrimonial troubles of their own, and naturally shied away. Some were put off by the Five Years' Clause, and among those, I suspect, was Mr Winston Churchill, who had half-promised his powerful aid. Not all who signed[70] were happy about that. A few said frankly, why don't you leave things alone? The rich can get a divorce easily enough by bogus adultery; and, as for the poor, it is a good thing that there should be one law for the rich and another for the poor.[71]

The Matrimonial Causes Act 1937 introduced into the law the following additional grounds for divorce : (i) wilful desertion for three years and upwards, (ii) cruelty, (iii) incurable insanity after

five years' confinement. At the outset, the Bill provided for the introduction of habitual drunkenness and imprisonment under commuted death sentence as additional grounds, but these clauses were
dropped.[72] It introduced new grounds of nullity—wilful refusal to
consummate the marriage, that either party was at the time of the
marriage of unsound mind or a mental defective or subject to recurrent fits of insanity, or epilepsy, and that the respondent was at
the time of marriage suffering from venereal disease in a communi-
cable form, or was pregnant by some person other than the petitioner. The Act permitted the Court to make a decree of presump-
tion of death or dissolution of marriage where reasonable grounds
exist for supposing that a party to a marriage is dead. The Statute
also enlarged the jurisdiction of the Court where the husband has
changed his domicile after desertion or deportation. Thus, early
attempts to give effect to recommendations of the Gorell Commission[73] bore fruit in 1937 and the same Act introduced, in substance, the additional grounds of nullity which the Gorell Commission had recommended.

These were the grounds on which divorce could be obtained from
1938 to 1970, although the earlier laws were consolidated, with
corrections and improvements, by the Matrimonial Causes Act
1965. The grounds for divorce in English Law—adultery, cruelty,
desertion for three years, and incurable insanity—had remained the
same since 1937, but the courts had perceptibly enlarged the definition of cruelty and made 'constructive' desertion easier to establish.

As social life—standards of behaviour and ways of thinking—
changes, so do the attitudes of the public and the courts alter as to
what conduct should, or should not, be tolerated in marriage. The
grounds of divorce have been changed and extended, regardless of
the pertinacious opposition by Church groups. However, once it
was true to say (and perhaps still is) that many men and women
took each other for better or for worse, and the 'indissolubility' of
marriage was the first principle of Christian marriage, although
even the Bible presupposes divorce while preaching that the wife
should not separate from her husband and the husband should not
divorce his wife.[74]

The advocates of divorce law reform claimed that it was hypocrisy to pretend that husbands and wives should be expected to accept
whatever the marriage may bring, when there was the right for certain people to divorce if the worse prevails over the better. The question was not only where the line should be drawn—that is to say,
how far the grounds for divorce should be allowed to extend—but
how to eliminate inequality and injustice caused by the existing
Matrimonial Causes Act which gave the rich the possibility of

divorce while making divorce difficult, if not impossible, for the poor. How much misery should one partner be allowed to inflict on the other? How far should the law perpetuate a marriage which has outlived its usefulness and is no longer anything but a burden to both husband and wife?

The English moral climate demanded a compromise which recognizes the personal rights of the parties and yet preserves as far as possible the ideal of the sanctity and indissolubility of marriage. Consequently, there should not be, in principle, divorce for mere incompatibility, and the idea of a matrimonial 'offence'—adultery, cruelty and desertion, etc.—as a ground for divorce has prevailed until very recently.

4. SOCIAL BACKGROUND

As we have seen above, the history of divorce legislation in England has been the history of a long and stubborn fight to force easier conditions of divorce upon the Christian Churches which did not want and still do not want to recognize any divorce at all, while public sentiment in favour of an easier divorce law has been growing steadily.

As the advocates of divorce reform legislation pointed out in their arguments in the Royal Commission Report, changing public attitudes to divorce, accelerated by social change, and the doctrinal schisms within the Church of England, have been the main causes of divorce controversy in England. The period which saw the passing of the Matrimonial Causes Act 1857 was a period when the voice of utilitarianism and individualism prevailed. After Jeremy Bentham's death, John Stuart Mill's *On Liberty* was published, in 1859, *Considerations on Representative Government* in 1861, *Utilitarianism* in 1863, and the *Subjection of Women* in 1869. It was a period when Britain had acquired the command of the seas throughout the world and the international markets by her successful Industrial Revolution. Accordingly, the growing number of middle class and the industrial labourers became a considerable voice not only in national politics but in social affairs. Against this background, the Matrimonial Causes Act 1857 was born.

Then attention should be focused on the late Victorian and Edwardian era, and the character of the Victorian family which cannot be described without reference to its changing occupational and class setting. With the acceleration of industrial development it was the middle-class family which became the exemplar of morals in the decade after the Great Exhibition, compelling conformity from above, attracting aspirants from below. Growing industry and the development of mass communication brought rapid change in the life of almost every family in England. Consequently, there came demands not only for equal rights and social justice in terms of politics, law and economics, but in terms of sex and family life as well.

A brief survey of social legislation since the beginning of the century indicates the direction of social change. Already the extension of the franchise in 1867, and the Education Act 1870, were steps on the way to greater political equality. A series of Acts between 1901 and 1911, including Factory and Workshops (1901), Unemployed Workmen (1905), Trade Disputes (1906),[75] Labour Exchanges (1909) and National Insurance (1911), improved the conditions and economic security of workers, and gave them powerful bargaining power. Further Education Acts, of 1902 and 1912, raised the school-leaving age to fourteen. Provision of school meals (1906, 1914) and pensions for the elderly, widows and orphans (1906, 1925, 1929), were attempts to further social justice; and greater attention to maternity and child welfare (Midwives', 1902; Children's, 1908, 1918, 1926) show increased concern for the weaker members of society. Along with better education and the improved economic position of the family came advancement in the status of women, and this was crucial to the later reform of the divorce laws. The Representation of the People Act 1918 first gave the vote to women over thirty. The Sex Disqualification (Removal) Act 1919 abolished disqualification by sex or marriage for entry to the professions, universities and the exercise of any public function. The Matrimonial Causes Act 1923 empowered a wife to present a petition for divorce on the ground of simple adultery by her husband, thus making the conditions for both sexes equal. The Guardianship of Infants Act 1925 gave equal rights to mothers to apply to the Court if the parents disagreed on the questions relating to the custody or upbringing of children. In 1926 the New English Law of Property provided that both married and single women may hold and dispose of their real and personal property on the same terms as a man. And finally the Representation of the People (Equal Franchise) Act 1928 introduced a uniform qualification for men and women and gave all women over twenty-one the right to vote.

The social legislation of these years thus reflects trends towards greater social, political and sexual equality : there was a trend which was no longer prepared to accept one law for the rich and one for the poor, one law for men and another for women; a society too, which had shown its concern to protect the interests of its weaker members. A better educated public became increasingly aware of the contradictions and inadequacies in the divorce law.

NOTES

1 D. P. Flood, *The Dissolution of Marriage* (1961), p. 2.

2 O. R. McGregor, *Divorce in England* (1957), p. 101.

3 *Rayden on Divorce* (11th ed. 1971), p. 1.

4 McGregor, op. cit., p. 1. It should not be overlooked, however, that the whole attitude derived from more profound social and biological reasons based on the needs of children.

5 M. Puxon, *The Family and the Law* (1967), p. 18.

6 T. A. Lacey, *Marriage in Church and State* (1947), p. 137.

7 A. R. Winnett, *The Church and Divorce* (1968), p. 10.

8 See 1 Corinthians 7 : 15 *et seq.* and 1 Timothy 5 : 8.

9 See A. R. Winnett, *Divorce and Re-Marriage in Anglicanism* (1958), p. 1.

10 See below.

11 Winnett, *The Church and Divorce*, pp. 5–6.

12 This is implied in a letter to Pusey from Gladstone who refers to Pusey's disagreement with Keble on the remarriage of the innocent party. *Letters on Church and State,* ed. D. C. Lathbury (1910), pp. 136–7.

13 *Occasional Sermons,* Series IV, Preface to Sermon L; Misc. III, pp. 202–3.

14 *Selected Letters of William Bright,* ed. J. B. Kidd (1903), pp. 9–11.

15 G. W. E. Russell, *Edward King* (1912), p. 280.

16 Its members were Lord Campbell, Dr Lushington, Judge of the Consistory Court of London, Lord Beaumont, Lord Redesdale, Mr E. P. Bouverie, the Rt Hon. S. H. Walpole, and Sir William Page Wood, appointed in 1850. See the Royal Commission on Divorce 1850, col. 1604.

17 Ibid., pp. 21–2.

18 Ibid., p. 6.

19 Ibid., pp. 24–6.

20 In addition to the move, the Bishop of Ossory (O'Brien) and St David's (Thirlwall) voted for the clause, but it was defeated.

21 Parliamentary Debates, 3rd Series, CXXXIV (June-July 1854), cols 935–47.

22 Ibid., CXLII (May-June 1856), cols 1979-83.

23 Winnett, *Divorce and Re-Marriage in Anglicanism*, p. 136.

24 PD, CXLIII (June-July 1856), cols 230-51.

25 PD, CXLIV (Feb.-March 1857), cols 1698-1707.

26 R. G. Wilberforce, *Life of Bishop Wilberforce*, II (1881), p. 343.

27 However, the divine theory in which he so strongly believed was in doubt even when he was fighting against the Bill, and 'the law of God' has been changing through changes in the law of the land, by Members of Parliament, and by members of the Judiciary.

28 PD, CXLV (Apr.-June 1857), cols 523-31. However, contrary to his prediction, 'the whole moral aspect of the nation' changed before the law of God was changed by men.

29 The Bishop of London was Dr Tait, who supported the Bill.

30 See Wilberforce, op. cit., p. 343; Davidson and Benham, *Life of Archibald Campbell Tait* (1891); and PD, CXLV (Apr.-June 1857), cols 531–3.

31 The ten bishops, including the Archbishop of Canterbury, were: the Bishops of London, Winchester (Sumner), Bangor (Bethnell), Bath and Wells (Lord Auckland), Carlisle (Villiers), Kilmore (Beresford), Llandaff (Ollivant), Ripon (Bickerteth), and St Asaph (Short). The five opponents were: the Bishops of Chichester (Gilbert), Durham, Lincoln, Oxford and Salisbury.

32 For the attitude of Mr Gladstone towards divorce reform, see *Letters on Church and State*. The Bill passed the Lords by 21 votes. Among those who entered protests against the third reading were the Bishops of Oxford, Salisbury and Exeter.

33 C. Wordsworth, *Occasional Sermons*, Series V (1850–9), Sermon XL, pp. 203–4. He writes: 'But in no case is a woman allowed the liberty of putting away her husband and marrying another.'

34 While the Divorce Bill was being discussed in the Houses, a declaration was drawn up and received the signatures of nearly 9,000 of the clergy, who expressed their earnest desire that no facilities unauthorized by the Scripture and the law of the Church should be granted for the dissolution of Holy Matrimony. The petition continued: 'Remembering also, that it is declared in the Word of God, that marriage with a divorced woman is adulterous, we fervently pray that the clergy of this realm may never be reduced to the painful necessity of either withholding the obedience which they must always desire to pay to the law of the land, or else of sinning against their own consciences, and violating the law of God by solemnising such marriages as are condemned as adulterous in His Holy Word.' See Winnett, *Divorce and Re-Marriage in Anglicanism*, p. 153.

35 The Canterbury Convocation held its first meeting in 1854 and that of York in 1861. However, there is no record of the Canterbury Convocation having considered the subject of divorce while the Bill was before the Parliament, but after the Bill was passed it spent several years discussing the subject.

36 Report of the Royal Commission on Divorce and Matrimonial Causes 1912, Cmd 6478, p. 30.

37 Loc. cit.

38 Winnett, *The Church and Divorce*, p. 7. The reasons for the Church's move toward a stricter marriage discipline in the early years of the present century are outlined by Archbishop Fisher, *Problems of Marriage and Divorce* (1955), p. 18.

39 See *The Question of Divorce*, pp. 23–7; *The Sermon on the Mount*, p. 75. See Winnett, *The Church and Divorce*, p. 8.

40 However, in April 1971, forty-one years after the 1930 Lambeth Conference, an important event took place: the remarriage of divorced people in church—which the law allows and the Church of England condemns— was supported by a commission set up in 1968 by the Archbishop of Canterbury in a report entitled 'Marriage, Divorce and the Church: the Report of the Commission on the Christian Doctrine of Marriage' published on 22nd April, 1971. The Bishop of Kingston, speaking at a conference in London to introduce the Report, said his personal opinion was that the Church would support the findings, although the Church Union was quick

to voice its disapproval of the Report, which was to be discussed at the General Synod of the Church of England in November 1971.

41 See Winnett, *The Church and Divorce*, pp. 7–8.

42 See the Report of the Joint Committees, *The Church and Marriage*, p. 18.

43 See Ibid., pp. 34–8.

44 Winnett, *The Church and Divorce*, p. 9.

45 Op. cit., p. 195.

46 See *The Dissolution of Marriage*, pp. 2 *et seq.*

47 Col. 1604, 1852–3.

48 Cmd 6478.

49 Cmd 9678, 1951–5.

50 For a short history of the practice and procedure in the Ecclesiastical Court, see the Historical Introduction to *Rayden on Divorce*.

51 See note p. 245, below.

52 Report of the Royal Commission on Marriage and Divorce 1956, Cmd 9678, p. 4; and see also McGregor, *Divorce in England*, pp. 17–18.

53 See W. S. Holdsworth, *A History of English Law* (paperback ed., 1969), Vol. I, p. 624.

54 Divorce, including divorce by mutual consent, appears to have been generally recognized in England and Wales in Anglo-Saxon times. See Holdsworth, *A History of English Law*, Vol. II (3rd ed., 1923), p. 90 and T. P. Ellis, *Welsh Tribal Law and Custom in the Middle Ages*, Vol. I (1926), pp. 414 *et seq.*

55 Report of the Royal Commission, Cmd 9678, p. 4.

56 Hansard, Vol. 147 (1857), cols 718–19.

57 Since 1967 by the County Courts, and will soon be exercised by the Family Division.

58 Generally known as the Gorell Commission.

59 Cmd 6478, pp. 4–5.

60 Lord Lyndhurst's original proposal waited sixty-six years before reaching the Statute Book in 1923. See Hansard, Vol. 145 (1857), cols 496 *et seq.*

61 Actually, on the 4th December, 1935, 'like an ass' he made his maiden speech and the ballot for places for private members' bills was held on the 6th February, 1936. However, Mr Herbert's drawn number was 81. In the second session again, Mr Herbert was not lucky enough to draw an early number and had to ask Mr Rupert De la Bère (Conservative), a new member like Mr Herbert, who luckily had place number 2, for help. See Herbert, *The Ayes Have It* (1937), pp. 33 *et seq.*

62 Ibid., pp. 53 *et seq.*

63 See Herbert, op. cit., pp. 53–4: 'Who drafted it, I have never been able to discover, much of it was Greek to me, not being a practising lawyer, and this year when the Law Officers looked at it at last, they found some clauses that were out of date or undesirable, and one or two that seemed to be meaningless. Still, it was all based on the Royal Commission; and it would be foolish for a new fellow to tamper with their main proposals. But I wanted to make a few alterations. For example, I had boldly announced in my Election Address that whatever else is done or not done, I should abolish

the cruel system of the decree nisi, which (like the King's Proctor) is not found necessary in Scotland.'

64 'Whereas it is expedient for the true support of marriage, the protection of children, the removal of hardship, the reduction of illicit unions and unseemly litigation, the relief of conscience among the clergy, and the restoration of due respect for the law, that the Acts relating to marriage and divorce be amended. . . .'

65 To that extent it was a false and hypocritical law. See M. I. Cole, *Marriage Past and Present* (1939), pp. 137–8 : 'If Lord Desart some years ago was correct in saying that seventy-five per cent of divorces were divorces by consent, i.e. cases of collusion which were not discovered, it is a monstrously lying law. And a lying law is a bad law.'

66 Hansard, Vol. 317 (1937), col. 2082.

67 *Daily Telegraph* (22nd Oct., 1935).

68 See Report of the Royal Commission, Cmd 6478, p. 12. Mr Justice Maule's famous satirical judgment in Regina *v*. Thomas Hall, which is printed in Cole, op. cit., pp. 55–7, and in McGregor, *Divorce in England*, pp. 15–17.

69 Herbert, op. cit., pp. 64–5.

70 Sponsors of the Bill.

71 Herbert, op. cit., pp. 67–8.

72 The Royal Commission wanted habitual drunkenness and imprisonment for life under a commuted death penalty to be grounds for divorce. This has not yet been secured, although Clause 2 (1) (b) and (e) will cover the situation eventually.

73 After Lord Gorell's death in 1913, his son introduced a bill into the House of Lords to give effect to those recommendations upon which majority and minority had agreed. The Bill was withdrawn because it was too late in the session to find time for adequate discussion. Before it could be reintroduced the Kaiser's war had carried discussion of divorce to temporary oblivion and the second Lord Gorell to his death at Ypres. See McGregor, op. cit., p. 29.

74 See 1 Corinthians 8 *et seq*.

75 This is the year that the Divorce Law Reform Union (DLRU) was founded by Mrs M. L. Seaton-Tiedemann (1858–1948); it was incorporated in 1914.

Chapter 2

1938–1965

I. *Subsequent Changes*

After the Herbert Act, there was little change in the law. The Matrimonial Causes (War Marriages) Act 1944 effected a further enlargement of the jurisdiction of the Court where the husband was at the time of the marriage domiciled abroad. In 1946, after the Second World War, a Committee on Procedure in Matrimonial Causes was appointed under the chairmanship of Mr (now Lord) Justice Denning. The Committee reported that 'the existing assize system is a failure', and, whilst stressing the importance of retaining the High Court's jurisdiction, recommended extensive administrative changes. The important result was the proposal that judicial strength should be increased by appointing Special Commissioners, mainly from the ranks of County Court judges. This recommendation was accepted and Commissioners, with all the authority of High Court judges, now sit in London and thirty-eight provincial towns to hear divorce petitions.[1]

A far-reaching change was effected by the Law Reform (Miscellaneous Provisions) Act 1949,[2] and by the Legal Aid and Advice Act 1949, which was the result of recommendations made by the Committee on Legal Aid and Legal Advice. When under wartime conditions the old Poor Persons' Procedure proved hopelessly inadequate, the work was handed over to the Law Society which established a Service Divorce Department financed by the Treasury. After this, the Committee on Legal Aid and Legal Advice was established under Lord Rushcliffe, and it reported that it was impossible to return to the old system. Its recommendations led to the Legal Aid and Advice Act 1949, which provided a considerable measure of equality before the law; the legal aid provisions came into operation in the autumn of 1950,[3] although as Professor McGregor has pointed out in his book, *Divorce in England*, it was no more than a paper aspiration. At any rate, in 1949 the wife was given the right to apply to the High Court for maintenance on the ground of her husband's failure to provide reasonable maintenance for herself or the children.

The statutes relating to matrimonial causes in the High Court were consolidated in the Matrimonial Causes Act 1950.

25

II. *Mrs White's Bill*

On 9th March, 1951, a Matrimonial Causes Bill was introduced by Mrs White (Labour, Flint East), later Baroness White. As she made clear in the Commons, she was a happily married woman and had no personal interest in divorce law, but Mr Marcus Lipton had persuaded her that it was a worth-while measure, and she had agreed to introduce the Bill. There had been little time for reflection, as she had to announce her intention of introducing the Bill on the same day as the result of the ballot was announced. Eventually, after detailed discussion with Mr Lipton, she introduced the Bill to add a new ground of divorce to those already established. Her main proposal was that, when spouses had been living apart for seven years without reasonable prospect of reconciliation, it should be open to either to petition for divorce without having to prove a matrimonial offence by the other. As had been expected, the Catholic and Anglican Churches strongly opposed the measure; in particular the Mothers' Union vehemently attacked the Bill, although the press reaction in general was favourable.

Like Mr Herbert and Mr De la Bère, Mr Lipton and Mrs White encountered strong traditional resistance. The Labour Government, through Mr Herbert Morrison, pressed Mrs White to withdraw the Bill. However, she refused the request and continued to campaign for reform with Messrs Marcus Lipton and Martin Lindsay. Her private member's bill was well received, being given its second reading in the Commons by 131 votes to 60, a majority of 71. The Ayes included : Mr Crosland, Mr Crossman, Mr Michael Foot, Mr Jenkins, Miss Jennie Lee, Mr Maudling, Mr Mikardo, Mr Stewart, and Mr George Strauss. The Noes included : Mr Boyd-Carpenter, Mr Edward Heath, Mr J. Profumo, and Miss I. Ward.

However, after the second reading Mrs White could no longer resist mounting pressure from the Government, and decided to accept its offer of a Royal Commission in return for withdrawing the Bill. Some observers still maintain that the Bill could have got through if she had decided not to withdraw, but recently Lady White has said emphatically that there was no chance of its going through, as the Government would have done everything to kill it. In any case, 'the Bill would have introduced new principles, repugnant to the "religious" attitudes, by enabling one "guilty" partner to dissolve a marriage against the will of the "innocent" spouse, and have destroyed the ecclesiastically derived doctrine of the matrimonial offence'.[4]

In September 1951, a Commission of nineteen members, under the chairmanship of Lord Morton[5] of Henryton, was appointed by Royal Warrant

> to enquire into the law of England and the law of Scotland concerning divorce and other matrimonial causes and into the powers of courts of inferior jurisdiction in matters affecting relations between husband and wife, and to consider whether any changes should be made in the law or its administration, including the law relating to the property rights of husband and wife, both during marriage and after its termination (except by death), having in mind the need to promote and maintain a healthy and happy married life and to safeguard the interests and well-being of children; and to consider whether any alteration should be made in the law prohibiting marriage with certain relations by kindred or affinity.[6]

III. *The Royal Commission on Divorce: 1951–5*

In September 1951 a Royal Commission, the so-called 'Morton Commission', was appointed following the withdrawal of Mrs White's Bill. The private members' bills such as Mrs White's and Lord Mancroft's[7] were the immediate causes of the Commission's appointment.

Of the nineteen members of the Commission who signed the final Report in 1955, eight were lawyers representing all branches of the profession in England and Scotland, two were Justices of the Peace, one a barrister's wife. There were also two schoolmasters, a Director of Education, two doctors and a retired trade-union official,[8] although the numbers of the Commissioners varied from time to time as a consequence of deaths and resignations.[9]

The scope of inquiry by the Commission was 'very wide, embracing not only the law relating to divorce and other matrimonial proceedings but also the administration of that law in all courts, and the law governing the property rights of husband and wife.'[10] The Report consists of sixteen parts, plus the conclusion—summaries of recommendations for England and Scotland, and notes and appendices extending over 405 pages.

The form of the Report is described by the Commission Report itself as follows :

> We have not been able to reach agreement on all the questions which were before us. This is not, perhaps, surprising when regard is had to the nature of the matters under discussion and

to the wide differences of opinion revealed among those who gave evidence. In general, differences of view within the Commission have been set out in the body of the Report. It seemed to us that this would enable us to present more fairly the two sides of questions raising issues of wide social and moral significance.[11]

The Morton Commission, having carefully considered the principle underlying Mrs White's proposal (which it called the 'doctrine of the breakdown of marriage' in contradiction to the received 'doctrine of the matrimonial offence'), reported[12] in March 1956 on the most controversial proposal, namely whether there should be a new ground of divorce founded on the complete breakdown of the marriage. Nine members of the Commission voted in favour and nine against, while one, Lord Walker, wished to see the notion of the matrimonial offence banished altogether from the law and the notion of breakdown established in its place.[13]

THE SUGGESTED NEW BASIS FOR DIVORCE

In England the divorce law was until 1970 founded on what is called, for brevity, the 'doctrine of the matrimonial offence'. Certain acts, which are termed 'matrimonial offences', are regarded as being fundamentally incompatible with the undertakings entered into at marriage; the commission of these acts by one party to the marriage gives to the other party an option to have the marriage terminated by divorce.[14]

Public attitude to divorce was sharply divided : some people strongly supported the retention of the matrimonial offence as the determining principle of the divorce law; others argued that the time had come to recognize a new principle—namely, that the basis of granting divorce should be that the marriage had irretrievably broken down.[15] According to the Report, there were in the main three proposals for the introduction of the principle of breakdown of marriage.

  (i)   Breakdown of marriage as a comprehensive ground of divorce;
  (ii) Divorce by consent;[16] and
  (iii) Divorce at the option of either spouse after a period of separation.[17]

As for the proposal (i),

some witnesses considered that the existing divorce law should

be re-framed on the basis of this new principle, which, for con-
venience, we call the 'doctrine of breakdown of marriage'. They
recommended that the existing grounds of divorce should be
abolished and their place taken by a single, comprehensive
ground which would allow divorce to be granted if it could be
proved that the marriage had irretrievably broken down. . . .
The majority of those witnesses favoured the addition to the
present law of one or both of the following new grounds : (i)
divorce by the mutual consent of husband and wife; (ii) divorce
at the option of either spouse after a period of separation.[18]

The essential feature of the various proposals for 'divorce by
consent' is that husband and wife should be entitled to come before
a judge and ask for a divorce simply on the ground that they both
seriously desired their marriage to be dissolved, and the judge
should be given the right to grant divorce if he were satisfied that
the consent had been freely given.

The advocates of proposals on these lines argued that if a marriage has irretrievably broken down it is in the interests of the
parties to the marriage, of any children of the marriage, and of
the community, that the marriage should be ended by divorce,
and the parties set free to enter into new marriages, if they so
wish. They pointed out that without such freedom illicit unions
are formed, and illegitimate children often begotten.[19]

It was argued that the parties to the marriage are in the best position to know if it has failed, and that it follows from the concept
of the individual as a free and responsible person that husband and
wife should be allowed to terminate their marriage if they both
wish to do so.

VIEWS OF THE COMMISSION

With one exception,[20] all the members of the Commission agreed
that the present base of the doctrine of the matrimonial offence
should be retained. They differed, however, on whether or not it
would be in the interests of the community as a whole that an
additional ground should be introduced based on the principle that
there should be dissolution of a marriage which has irretrievably
broken down. 'Nine members of the Commission are opposed to the
introduction of the doctrine of breakdown of marriage, in any
form, because they consider that it would be gravely detrimental to
the well-being of the community. . . . We believe that the consequences of providing the "easy way out" afforded by divorce by

consent would be disastrous to stability in marriage.'[21] Ironically, both groups, the nine supporting and the nine opposing the new ground of divorce, based their view on the belief that it was not only in the interests of the husband and wife concerned and the children of the marriage but also of the community as a whole. The opponents believed that there was no widespread desire in the country for any material change in the grounds of divorce, and said, 'we believe that most people consider that the present facilities are sufficient'.[22]

The nine members who supported the introduction of a new ground of divorce founded on the complete breakdown of the marriage, believed that

(i) . . . it is no longer in the best interests of the community that the remedy of divorce should, in principle, only be available if what is called a matrimonial offence has been committed, (ii) it is unnecessary to examine closely the sources of this doctrine. Though divorce was recognized in pre-Christian eras, and in Roman law and exists generally today in non-Christian communities, there seems little doubt that so far as England and Scotland are concerned modern divorce law developed from views founded on religious sanctions as to conduct justifying *divorce a mensa et thoro* (judicial separation) as distinguished from *divorce a vinculo*. With certain possible exceptions into which it is unnecessary to enter, it may be said that *divorce a vinculo* both here and on the continent dated from the Reformation.[23] Divorce for adultery and desertion is recognized in and forms part of The Westminster Confession of Faith, (iii) under the stress of changes in society and the waning influence of religious thought on the pattern of social habits, divorce has tended to be regarded as a measure of relief granted to a spouse from considerations of individual hardship, though the general description of grounds of divorce as matrimonial offences and the habit of treating the parties to a divorce, one as the innocent party and the other as the guilty party, can no doubt be traced to the conception of divorce as a penalty for breach of matrimonial offence. There is, however, no obvious reason why a matrimonial offence should be the only ground of divorce, although as we have said, for historical reasons it may have come to provide the ruling principle in divorce in England and Scotland and to appeal to legal minds accustomed to discourse in a world of legal rights and wrongs. Yet in many countries and in many religions, divorce is not based essentially on any code of matrimonial offences, but is allowed for a variety of grounds thought to be inimical to a realistic marriage state. In England and Scotland this point of view has already received recognition in allowing divorce for incurable insanity . . . (vii) we think that the time has come to recognize that matrimonial offences are in many cases merely symptomatic of the breakdown of marriage, and that there should also be provision for divorce in cases where, quite apart from the commission of such offences, the marriage has broken down completely.[24]

The Commission was thus irreconcilably divided on the crucial issue reflecting the state of unsettled English public opinion on divorce. With the exception of Lord Walker who maintained that 'the doctrine of the matrimonial offence ought to be abandoned as the basis for divorce and replaced by a provision that marriage should be indissoluble unless, having been living apart for no less than three years, either party shows that the marriage has broken down. . .',[25] all other members expressed their wish to retain the matrimonial offence as the basis for divorce law. Four of those nine members who supported the new basis for divorce, however, 'considered that it would be desirable to widen the scope of the new ground, in order to allow a husband or a wife to obtain a dissolution of the marriage, notwithstanding the other spouse's objection, if he or she could satisfy the court that the separation was in part due to the unreasonable conduct of the other spouse'.[26]

Finally, a word about the purpose and competence of a Royal Commission. The Royal Commission may be formed by the Government to investigate any subject the Government thinks fit, and in fact the reports of these Commissions have led to such important legislation as the Matrimonial Causes Act 1857, which we have already discussed.

> Strictly speaking these reports should be regarded as efforts to gather all the materials needed for the understanding of various subjects, together with the considered views of a representative selection of thinking people upon that material. The material and recommendations should weigh heavily with the Government and with the country as a whole, but they should certainly not be regarded as binding upon anyone. They indicate weighty opinion, but they do not necessarily show conclusively that the country is ready for any of the particular reforms suggested. . . . The Committee and Commission system is sometimes said to be the British way of ensuring that nothing is done, but that is unjust.[27]

As McGregor commented on the Royal Commission on Marriage and Divorce:

> The Report consequently contributes nothing to our knowledge, and fails even to clarify and define opposing viewpoints or to

facilitate public discussion. Instead of the traditional division into majority and minority Reports, the Commission presented its readers with a luxuriant confusion of footnotes indicating the agreement or disagreement of different Commissioners with this or that proposition or paragraph. It is a matter of opinion whether the Morton Commission is intellectually the worst Royal Commission of the twentieth century, but there can be no dispute that its Report is the most unreadable and confused. Fifty years ago, in a social atmosphere less favourable to clear thinking on such problems, the Gorell Commission served as an agent of clarification. The Morton Commission has proved a device for obfuscating a socially urgent but politically inconvenient issue.[28]

IV. *Mr Leo Abse's Bill: The Matrimonial Causes Act 1963*

Despite the shortcomings of the Morton Commission there resulted, in consequence of the Report, a new set of Rules, supplemented by various directions; a longer period between decree nisi and decree absolute; the Maintenance Agreements Act 1957, enabling certain agreements to be varied by the Court; an extension of the scope of small maintenance payments; and the Matrimonial Causes (Property and Maintenance) Act 1958, enabling the Court (i) to make orders for permanent alimony, maintenance and secured provision at any time after a decree, (ii) to set aside dispositions of property made for the purpose of defeating a wife's claim for financial relief, (iii) after the death of a party to a marriage which has been dissolved or annulled to make provision out of the deceased's estate in favour of the other party, and (iv) to give more extensive relief under the Married Women's Property Act 1882. Further changes came with the Divorce (Insanity and Desertion) Act 1958, the Maintenance Orders Act 1958, the Matrimonial Proceedings (Children) Act 1958, the Legitimacy Act 1959, the Marriage (Enabling) Act 1960,[29] the Matrimonial Proceedings (Magistrates' Courts) Act 1960[30] and the Magistrates' Courts (Matrimonial Proceedings) Rules 1960.

Early in 1963, under the Conservative Government, the substance of Mrs White's proposal was again brought before the Commons by Mr Leo Abse (Labour, Pontypool). His Matrimonial Causes Bill proposed that divorce should be obtainable (a) at the suit of either the innocent or the guilty party where a matrimonial offence has been committed, after seven years' separation, or, (b) by consent, after seven years' separation. According to Mr Abse's proposed second ground for divorce, there need have been no matrimonial offence committed by either party. His Bill contained measures to

permit reconciliation as well, and to ensure the passage of these he
eventually withdrew the controversial clauses. Subsequently an
amendment, which would have had the effect of restoring them,
was moved in the Lords by Lord Silkin, but failed.

It was in the course of an important debate on that amendment,
on the 21st June, 1963, that the Archbishop first disclosed his intention of forming[31] the Church group to review the law of England
concerning divorce and

> recognizing that there is a difference in the attitudes of the
> Church and State towards the further marriage of divorced
> persons whose former partner is living, to consider whether the
> inclusion of any new principle or procedure in the law of the
> State would be likely to operate, (1) more justly and with greater
> assistance to the stability of marriage and the happiness of all
> concerned including children, than at present; and (2) in such a
> way as to do nothing to undermine the approach of couples to
> marriage as a lifelong covenant.[32]

Six months later he appointed the group consisting of the thirteen
members.[33]

The motives behind Mr Abse's proposals were those of humanity.
He quoted figures to show that about one-third of all illegitimate
children were born to cohabiting parents who were apparently living in permanent union though unmarried.[34] These illicit unions,
he maintained, had all the potentialities of permanent and happy
marriages, but were denied the seal of legality because at least one
of the parents in the relationship was already married to someone
else who was not prepared to divorce the erring partner.

Sir Jocelyn Simon, the President of the Probate, Divorce and
Admiralty Division of the High Court, was a spokesman for the
opposite viewpoint and stated in a speech to a branch of the Magistrates Association that to permit any form of divorce by consent
would be tantamount to society disclaiming its concern in the endurance and stability of marriages. Marriage, he said, was an institution of society, under which children gained legal, moral and
social rights. Wives, he continued, were not infrequently brought
under a quite cruel and relentless pressure to divorce their husbands
who wished to remarry when they themselves desired a reconciliation and resumption of married life. Therefore, divorce by consent
would increase the scope for such grievous situations and consensual
divorce would be a dangerous thing, even in those cases where marriages had been irreparably broken. To quote Sir Jocelyn's actual
words, as reported in *The Times* on 8th April, 1963 :

> Is it consonant with our ideas of justice that a husband who has enjoyed the services of his wife during her springtime and summer, should be able to cast her away in the autumn and claim that the marriage has irretrievably broken down because he has certainly no intention of returning to a woman who has lost all attraction for him. . .? The truth is that many marriages break up—irretrievably, if divorce is available—for no other reason than that the wife has lost her sexual attraction before the husband has lost his.

Similar but stronger opposition to Mr Abse's proposals was voiced by many leaders of the Anglican, Roman Catholic and Free Churches,[35] and many M.P.s of the two major parties felt that to open the doors to divorce by consent would lead to a major change in the whole basis of marriage which ought not currently to be permitted.

However, Mr Abse stated that the result of failure to reform was that the law was still choked by humbug and pretence. He believed that the true significance of marriage lay not in the ceremony in church, synagogue or registry office, but in cohabitation in love and affection in the home and family. Therefore, he said, the position remained that where the bond had been broken irretrievably, the marriage might yet have to continue in name, while a suburban housewife, married for years and with several children, would give her husband a ground for divorce if in a moment of madness she had a quarter of an hour's adultery with the milkman.

Nevertheless, the House of Commons made it clear that to insist on the retention of any clause of this nature—divorce by consent—in the Bill, would ensure the defeat of the whole measure. Consequently, Mr Abse reluctantly withdrew the clause altogether, and a later attempt to revive it in the House of Lords met with little success, as has already been mentioned.

However, the Matrimonial Causes Act 1963 followed Mr Abse's attempt to make divorce possible in certain circumstances after a period of seven years' separation. This attempt failed, but the Act made fundamental changes in the law of condonation, providing that adultery which has been condoned shall not be capable of being revived, the idea being to encourage attempts at reconciliation. After Mr Abse's 1963 Act had been largely emasculated by its strong opponents,[36] a Bill was introduced in the House of Commons by Mr John Parker in 1964,[37] but without success. His bill attempted to add a further ground to the existing ones : that after a five year separation one of the partners could obtain a divorce even if the other partner did not consent to it.

Thus, the 'forties were a relatively quiescent period for the divorce reform issue, but in the 'fifties Mrs White's Bill and the appointment of the Royal Commission again aroused public discussion. Although both events took place under a Conservative majority, as did Mr Abse's Bill in 1963, the tide of public and legislative opinion was slowly becoming more favourable to reform. Then in October 1964 Labour moved into Downing Street, though with a majority of only five.

V. *The Matrimonial Causes Act 1965 and After*

Following the Matrimonial Causes Act 1963, the Married Woman's Property Act 1964,[38] and the Administration of Justice Act 1964,[39] were the most notable pieces of legislation until the Matrimonial Causes Act 1965 was passed. This Act, which was a consolidating statute repealing and re-enacting almost the whole of the statute law previously scattered over the Matrimonial Causes Act 1950, and five other Acts, was a welcome measure for the advocates of divorce reform legislation.

Thus, the ground for reform had been prepared by each new attempt to introduce new grounds for divorce and still more by social change. Between 1937 and 1965, the Matrimonial Causes Act 1950, the Matrimonial Causes Rules 1957, the Maintenance Agreement 1957, the Matrimonial Causes Act 1963, and the Matrimonial Causes Act 1965 were important landmarks in divorce legislation.

In March 1966 Labour won the election and came back to Downing Street with a comfortable majority. During this period under the Labour Government a number of controversial private members' bills were introduced and indeed many of them reached the Statute Book.[40]

As a result of these persistent activities by the advocates of divorce reform legislation, *Putting Asunder* was published in July 1966 by the group appointed by the Archbishop of Canterbury in 1964.[41] On 3rd August, within a week after *Putting Asunder* was published, the Vice-President of the DLRU, the Earl of Balfour, introduced his 'Strengthening of Marriage Bill'[42] along the lines proposed by the DLRU, to enable a further marriage to be contracted by either spouse when a separation has existed for five years.

Then, on 25th October, 1966, Mr Abse, under the Ten Minute Rule procedure, introduced his Matrimonial Causes Bill to test opinion in the House. He used the opportunity to make sure that the time was ripe to attempt divorce law reform, and attacked the opponents[43] by saying :

> On two occasions when Bills were presented to the House—in 1951 . . . and in 1963 . . . the House has given a Second Reading to Bills which were designed to introduce into our law a new ground of divorce. . . . On each occasion the expressed wishes of the House were subsequently frustrated : on the first occasion by the appointment of a Royal Commission which, after a very long period of deliberation, gave an ambiguous and divided Report which stemmed the tide of reform, and on the next occasion, in 1963, by the effective manipulation of procedural stratagems by a cabal in this House prompted by Church opposition.

The Bill was supported by Mr John Parker, Mr Nicholas Ridley, Mr Emlyn Hooson, Dr Michael Winstanley, and Mr Iorwerth Thomas.

In November 1966 the Report of the Law Commission, *The Field of Choice*, was published by the Lord Chancellor's Office, and it, together with *Putting Asunder*, was presented to the House of Lords. On 23rd November, the Bishop of Exeter, Dr Mortimer, rose to call attention to the divorce laws with special reference to the two above-mentioned reports. The House received the reports favourably, although several peers, and particularly Lady Summerskill, who had already made clear her opposition to any divorce law reform without adequate financial protection for deserted wives, expressed their opposition. Dr Mortimer frequently stood against Lady Summerskill and defended *Putting Asunder*.[44]

On 26th June, 1967, the Earl of Balfour withdrew his Bill which was still awaiting a second reading. He said : 'How splendid it would be if the Putting Asunder Committee and the Law Commission could reach agreement ! I should not want to take any action which might conceivably make such agreement more difficult.' Then the Lord Chancellor, Lord Gardiner, said significantly : 'My Lords, I think, if I may say so, that the noble Earl is acting wisely in asking leave to withdraw this Bill. Discussions in this field are going well, and it is sometimes a mistake to try to rush things. To those who are concerned to see this branch of our law reformed I would only say that I do not think they need be unhopeful.'[45]

NOTES

1 See McGregor, op. cit., p. 32.

2 It provided that the Court should have jurisdiction where the wife had been ordinarily resident in England for three years and the husband was not domiciled in the United Kingdom, Channel Islands or the Isle of Man. It also prevented legitimate children of subsisting voidable marriages from being bastardized by annulment decrees.

3 After thirty-eight years of delay, an attempt was made to implement the principle of the Royal Commission Report of 1912 that no person should be denied access to the Divorce Court by reason of poverty.

4 McGregor, op. cit., p. 127.

5 For a further discussion on the Morton Commission see McGregor, pp. 126 *et seq.*

6 See the Report of the Royal Commission, Cmd 9678, p. 1.

7 Lord Mancroft introduced a private member's bill in the House of Lords in 1949, which proposed to treat a divorced spouse as a deceased spouse, as far as the statutory exceptions from prohibited degrees of relationship were concerned. The Bill was strongly resisted by all the Churches which gave evidence to the Morton Commission. See Royal Commission on Marriage and Divorce, *Evidence* (1953), 6th Day, p. 142.

8 'The only apparent principle behind this choice appears to have been the importance of securing a preponderance of lawyers. The Commission was not representative in any general sense, save perhaps of professional lawyers, doctors and schoolmasters; in social composition it was heavily biased towards upper- and middle-class outlooks. The personnel of the Commission suggests two comments. Firstly, the absence of known opponents and advocates of changes in the divorce laws is striking. The explanation lies probably in present doctrinal schisms within the Church of England.' (McGregor, op. cit., p. 179.)

9 Cmd 9678, pp. iii–iv.

10 Cmd 9678, p. 3.

11 Ibid. However, the criticism of the role of the Royal Commission, its character and the content of the Report varies. See McGregor, op. cit., pp. 177–93.

12 Report of the Royal Commission on Marriage and Divorce 1951–5, Cmd 9678.

13 Cmd 9678, Chap. 2, and 'Statement of His Views by Lord Walker', pp. 340–1.

14 'With one exception (that of insanity, to which special considerations apply), all the present grounds of divorce, being conduct of a grave nature which cuts at the root of marriage, conform to this principle.' (Report of the Royal Commission, Cmd 9678, p. 12.)

15 Ibid.

16 'It was said that among the divorces granted under the present law many are in fact divorces by consent, since, in an undefended case, it is very difficult for the court to detect whether there has been collusion, and further, ground for divorce may be provided by one party in circumstances which do not amount to legal collusion. . . . The introduction of divorce by consent

would therefore not make divorce any easier than it is at present (since it would merely allow people to do openly what they now do by subterfuge) and, in the view of the witnesses, it would result in an "honest" divorce law which would command the respect of the public.' (Ibid., p. 13.)

17 The suggestions ranged from two to seven years' separation.

18 Report of the Royal Commission, Cmd 9678, p. 13.

19 Ibid.

20 Lord Walker, whose views are set out in the Report, pp. 340–1.

21 Cmd 9678, p. 14.

22 Ibid., p. 22.

23 As we have indicated earlier, divorce, including divorce by mutual consent, appears to have been generally recognized in England and Wales in Anglo-Saxon times.

24 Cmd 9678, pp. 22–3.

25 Ibid., p. 341.

26 See Ibid., pp. 14 and 25.

27 D. C. M. Yardley, *The Future of the Law* (1964), p. 38.

28 McGregor, op. cit., p. 193.

29 This Act enables a man to marry sister, aunt or niece of his former wife, whether living or not, or the former wife of his brother, uncle or nephew, whether living or not. The Marriage Act 1949 was amended by this Act. Under the Marriage Act 1949, a marriage between persons either of whom was at the date of the marriage under the age of sixteen years is void. See the same Act, § 2.

30 Magistrates' Courts have more extensive matrimonial jurisdiction under this Act, which replaced the Summary Jurisdiction (Separation and Maintenance) Act 1895 to 1949, and under this Act both the wife and the husband can apply for an order.

31 *Putting Asunder*, p. 5; and see Hansard, Vol. 298, col. 1547: 'My Lords. . . . Indeed, I am asking some of my fellow churchmen to see whether it is possible to work at this idea, sociologically as well as doctrinally to discover if anything can be produced.'

32 *Putting Asunder*, p. ix.

33 See p. 58, note 2, below.

34 See pp. 213 and 256, below.

35 See Report of the Royal Commission, Cmd 9678, p. 344, and Yardley, op. cit., p. 133.

36 Indeed, the Anglican and Roman Catholic archbishops, and the Moderator of the Free Church Federal Council, had joined together to oppose Mr Abse's Bill. See *The Guardian* (29th July, 1966), and pp. 36 *et seq.*, above.

37 Mr Parker again introduced a Bill in 1966.

38 Under this Act if any question arises as to the right of a husband or a wife to money and property derived from the housekeeping allowance, it shall be treated as belonging to husband and wife in equal shares.

39 This Act regulates the composition of courts for domestic proceedings.

40 See p. 168, below.

41 See p. 43, below.

42 Hansard (House of Lords), Vol. 276, col. 1311.
43 Hansard, Vol. 734, cols 834 *et seq*.
44 Hansard (House of Lords), Vol. 278, cols 239–347.
45 Ibid., Vol. 284, cols 8–9.

PART TWO

Chapter 3

PUTTING ASUNDER AND THE CHURCH OF ENGLAND

I. *Putting Asunder*

As has already been pointed out, until little more than a century ago the Church of England was the sole guardian of matrimonial law in England, and enjoyed jurisdiction over marriage and divorce. For centuries, the Church alone had performed the rites of matrimony, and exercised its authority through the Ecclesiastical Court over matrimonial disputes. Until the reign of Henry VIII, the State did not interfere in the Church's authority in this matter. It was the Matrimonial Causes Act 1857 which finally abolished the Ecclesiastical Court.

Since then, the Church of England has been a major opponent, particularly through its bishops[1] in the House of Lords, of any reform which might make divorce easier. The voice of the Church in this matter was firm, and prevailed; it continues to exert considerable influence through its teaching and institutions. The history of divorce law reform in England may thus be seen as a history of long struggle between the authority of the Church of England and the demands of reformers. The gulf between the principles of Christian marriage and the practical aspects of matrimonial life has made it necessary to reform the law of divorce and remarriage on several occasions since 1857.

In a society where divorce and remarriage are recognized by both law and social morality, the Church of England had to consider her position with regard to the present law and possible future reforms. In order to bridge the gap between the practice of the State and the principles of Christian marriage, and with the purpose of maintaining the Church's own discipline, Dr Michael Ramsey, the Archbishop of Canterbury, appointed the group 'mainly but not exclusively drawn from members of the Church of England',[2] in January 1964. The main purpose was to review the law of England regarding divorce.

The Report was published by the Society for Promoting Christian Knowledge under the title *Putting Asunder: A Divorce Law for Contemporary Society*.[3] It recommended that 'the doctrine of breakdown of marriage should be comprehensively substituted for the doctrine of the matrimonial offence as the basis of all divorce'.

In short, this Church group made a recommendation for a new divorce law for modern British society. Under the chairmanship of Dr Robert Mortimer, the group concluded that the 'present law' of divorce was unjust, 'superficial', 'remote from matrimonial reality' and 'quite simply, inept'. The group, in the light of its assessment, made a far-reaching recommendation : the arresting character of the proposal was underscored by the fact that no jurisdiction in the Anglo-American world embraces the principle of breakdown exclusively.

The Mortimer Report, *Putting Asunder*, was an important and impressive step taken by a Christian group. The *Observer* commented (31st July, 1966) : 'It is by any standard a significant social document. It is anything but another theological tract written by theologians for the Church's communicants and by implication a code for the citizenry of a Christian country with an established Church.' The group worked for two years, discussing a great variety of proposals respecting the importance of divorce law. They met[4] mainly at the Institute of Advanced Legal Studies in the University of London, where Professor Anderson, who was a member of the group, was the Director.

Viewed as a statement by eminent persons whose work was sponsored by a Church with a conservative heritage, it came as a breath of fresh air in England and an important step. The Report starts by questioning their terms of reference and their background with the proposition : '. . . how the doctrine of Christ concerning marriage should be interpreted and applied within the Christian Church is one question; what the Church ought to say and do about secular laws of marriage and divorce is another question altogether.'

It was the second question with which the Committee concerned itself. The Report made it clear by : 'Our own terms of reference make it abundantly clear that our business is with the second question only. We have therefore confined our attention to the law of the State exclusively, in order to see if there is any amendment or reform of that law we can recommend in the interests of the nation as a whole.' Thus the Report was not a statement about the Christian view of marriage and divorce. But it was 'one of the most controversial of its kind published and could well lead to allegations against the Church of England that it is setting double standards, if not actually facing both ways'.[5] It emphasized that the group was concerned solely with the secular side of marriage, with advising the secular society with regard to the secular law; and that the secular legislation on divorce must not derogate from the Church's freedom to treat the marriages of its own members in accordance with its doctrine and rules, upon which no recommendations were made.[6] Its main aim was to advise the State of those changes in the secular law of divorce which would be expedient, wise and just. The group pointed out, however, that 'by reason of its legal establishment the Church of England has both a special interest in what happens to the secular matrimonial law and a special duty to concern itself with that law's improvement'.[7]

At a press conference to introduce the Report, Dr Mortimer also emphasized that it was not an official report of the Church of England, but the conclusion of a group set up on the initiative of the Archbishop of Canterbury, to whom the Report would be presented.[8] But the advice given generated controversy and exerted substantial influence on the framing of the 1969 Act, although the Act exceeded the original bounds suggested by *Putting Asunder*. In any case, the Report contained a bold recommendation and gave official recognition to the difference in the attitude of Church and the State towards divorce.[9]

However, the Committee's main conclusion regarding the present divorce law was that 'it would not be an improvement but the reverse to introduce the principle of breakdown of marriage into the existing law in the shape of an additional ground for divorce'— additional, that is, to the existing matrimonial offence. Accordingly, they found themselves faced with a choice, on which there could be no compromise, of abandoning the matrimonial offence entirely and substituting the principle of breakdown for it, or maintaining the strict doctrine of the matrimonial offence, without adding to it grounds incompatible with it. Their study of the 'matrimonial offence system . . . elicited little to its credit and nothing at all to make us want its perpetuation'. On the other hand, the Committee members

> were persuaded that a divorce law founded on the doctrine of breakdown would not only accord better with social realities than the present law does, but would bear the merit of showing up divorce for what it essentially is—not a reward for marital virtue . . . and a penalty for marital delinquency . . . but a defeat for both, a failure of the marital 'two-in-oneship' in which both its members, however unequal their responsibility, are inevitably involved together.[10]

Consequently, they came to their central recommendation that 'the doctrine of breakdown of marriage should be comprehensively substituted for the doctrine of matrimonial offence as the basis of all divorce'. At the same time, the Report emphasized that the substitution of the new principle of breakdown of marriage for the existing one of matrimonial offence would give greater prominence to the matter of reconciliation.

The group then faced three questions about the procedure which they had recommended : firstly, 'Is breakdown a triable issue?' Their answer was 'yes', since actions and conduct which under the present law constitute matrimonial offences would still be valuable as evidence for breakdown, even though no longer in themselves grounds for a decree. Other facts now treated as irrelevant could also be taken into account. But the procedure would have to be changed. They recognized that the Court could not be expected to reach true conclusions about the state of matrimonial relationships unless the existing accusational procedure were abandoned and something like procedure by inquest substituted for it. However the group later dropped this provision at the bargaining table with the Law Commission,[11] when Dr Mortimer, Professor Anderson, Canon Bentley and Miss Rubinstein met[12] the members of the Law Commission to see whether differences between them could be bridged. The Law Commission and the Lord Chancellor pointed out that a judge's inquest in every case was impracticable. In the event, the Law Commission accepted from the Church group that breakdown of marriage should be the sole ground of divorce, while the Church group accepted from the Law Commission that it would not be practicable to hold a full inquest in every case, but that various matrimonial situations must be recognized as providing *prima facie* evidence of breakdown.[13]

The second question which the group faced was : 'Would it be fair for marriage to be dissolved against the will of an unoffending spouse?' The answer was 'No, but it is inevitable.' To demand that a divorce law allow no one to be hurt is to ask the impossible. The law and the courts are faced with trying to uphold distributive justice in situations which, by their very nature, exclude wholly just solutions. The third question was : 'How could maintenance and costs be assigned under the new system?' For these purposes it was decided that the court would still need to have regard to the conduct of the spouses and to make a comparative estimate of their responsibility for the breakdown of the marriage. That estimate would be distinct, however, from judgment on the state of the marriage.

In the Report there are six chapters and six appendices. As Mr Christopher Driver pointed out[14] the six appendices contained some of the most interesting reading. The agencies for matrimonial reconciliation were surveyed and it was concluded that the amount of money which the Government and local authorities grant for the training and supervision of counsellors was ludicrously small in relation to the need and in comparison with the initial cost of divorce. The Report recommends that the grants be substantially increased. Society, since it cannot be without divorce, should be prepared to pay for making the administration of it as good as can be contrived.

The sociological essay by Donald MacRae, Professor of Sociology in the University of London, observed:

> Divorce statistics can mislead if the greater life-expectancy of marriage is forgotten, and the fact that the termination of marriage is now in all classes 'de jure' and not just a 'de facto' rupture unremarked by law . . . less than 5 per cent of marriages seem likely to end in divorce. Of these probably about 60 per cent will be marriages where there is either only one child or no child.[15]

The appendix on psychological considerations pointed out the haphazardness with which the community treats marital problems:

> General medical practitioners, for instance, tended to treat neurotic symptoms with palliative medicines or with simple direct advice like 'have another baby' or 'leave home'. Solicitors, asked for legal advice, may not think of trying to look behind the requests to the client's motive for making it. Clergymen and ministers often even take a moralistic line, or offer counsel of a stereotyped kind.[16]

It is also observed:

> Setting up *ménages à trois*, taking mistresses or lovers, may represent lasting or transitory endeavours to satisfy personal needs which the marital relationship has failed to meet. When such experiments prove transitory and the situation is restored by an act of forgiveness, the marital relationship may sometimes even be enhanced in consequence. It is important to stress the point that divorce is only one of the possible resolutions of a marital situation felt to be intolerable.[17]

The *New Law Journal* later criticized this aspect of the Report:

> The committee's investigation of the nature and aetiology of marriage breakdown (as opposed to their belief in its usefulness as a basis for divorce) is a rather superficial one, and this is very unfortunate because the nature and aetiology of breakdown are so profoundly relevant to an understanding of such matters as marriage counselling and reconciliation attempts on which the

committee express strong views. But it is an especially unfortunate omission in relation to the question of what kind of courts ought to administer the proposed new divorce jurisdiction, and what their procedure ought to be. It is true that the committee recommend, rather tentatively, that there should be a new series of regional courts exercising jurisdiction in the whole of what has come to be called 'family law'. . . . If the causes of marriage breakdown are to be properly investigated and determined, psychological and emotional factors of great complexity will have to be gone into. Unfortunately the committee's consideration of how this is to be done is superficial. It is perhaps significant that the sociological and psychological aspects of the subjects are dealt with in separate chapters appearing near the end of the report, not welded into the report itself. Inevitably they appear as something of an afterthought. . . . To some extent the timidity of the committee's procedural proposals—so sharply contrasting with the originality of their substantive recommendations—may arise from their concern to dissociate the principle of marriage breakdown from 'divorce by mutual consent'.[18]

II. *Reactions to Putting Asunder*

The group's Report received plenty of publicity. The *Solicitors' Journal* said :

> The Church of England is in a particularly responsible position here, since little more than a century ago, she was the sole architect of matrimonial law in this country. Whatever this group should advise was bound to be received with deep interest and respect by all interested in divorce law reform; in fact the report turns out to be a most searching review of the failings of the present law, with some quite revolutionary suggestions for change.[19]

The *New Law Journal* described *Putting Asunder* as 'one of the most important documents of this century',[20] and *The Times* with the headline 'A New Light on Divorce' contributed an editorial (29th July, 1966) to the Report :

> It is doubtful whether there has been published in recent times a more persuasive, thoughtful, or constructive plea on behalf of the breakdown of marriage doctrine, or a more effective condemnation of the present methods of divorce only upon the grounds of a specific offence. . . . But the report raises large questions, and puts the onus of reply upon the conservatives.

So on the same day did *The Guardian*, the *Daily Telegraph*, and

other major newspapers, an editorial in *The Guardian* concluding :
'The issue must now be taken up by the Law Commission—and
ultimately by the Government.'

However, the Rev. Evelyn Garth Moore, Chancellor of Durham,
Gloucester and Southwark, described the report in the *Church
Times* (29th July, 1966) as a revolutionary change in law which
would mean divorce by consent. The *Church Times'* editorial under
the headline 'An End to Marriage?' confirmed this by saying that
Chancellor Garth Moore's word 'revolutionary' 'was certainly not
too strong a word to describe the suggestion made in the report',
and supported the Chancellor's suggestion that the Church ought
now to take a fresh, long look at its own theology of marriage. It
called attention to two questions : Is it expedient for a Christian
group to give advice to the State which, to say the least, contradicts
the Church's whole view of marriage as a Christian institution,
when all the odds are that popular opinion will fail to appreciate
the subtle distinction and seize on the recommendations as representing the Church's own view of what is right? The risk of such
misunderstandings is so great as to make it almost a certainty. Can
the popular newspapers really be blamed too much for coming out
with headlines declaring that 'the Church favours divorce for incompatibility' or 'divorce by consent'? Secondly : 'Can it be right
for the Church to recommend a course of action which is so dia-
metrically opposed to its own convictions as to be pronounced
wrong by the Christian conscience?'

Mr Leo Abse said that on learning details of the Report, he
planned to introduce a Ten Minute Rule Bill in October 1966[21]
proposing that a marriage breakdown after five years' separation
should be an additional ground for divorce. 'I tried to introduce
marriage breakdown into my Bill in 1963 but this was savagely
attacked by the Church and I was forced to throw it out. I agree
with the report that ideally breakdown should be the only cause
for divorce, but there are not enough judges, lawyers or social
workers to conduct the exhaustive inquisition that would be
needed.'[22] Many bishops, including the Bishop of Carlisle, Dr
Thomas Bloomer, the Bishop of Liverpool, the Rt Rev. Stuart
Blanch, and the Bishop of Manchester, Dr John Wilson, praised the
Report and considered that the existing law led often to hypocrisy
and collusion.[23]

In an editorial (4th Aug., 1966) the *Methodist Recorder* also welcomed the Report :

Acute observers will have noticed that in recent years a change
has come over ecclesiastical pronouncements on controversial

questions. Not so long ago it could be taken for granted that ninety-nine out of a hundred would be so cautious that no one need be either greatly offended or greatly interested. Nowadays one in three come boldly off the fence. There can be no doubt that *Putting Asunder* is one of the new and welcome type.

However, the official Anglican opposition to divorce remained unaltered. The Bishop of Birmingham represented the voice of the Church by saying that the Church must uphold the sanctity of marriage and must try to effect reconciliations. The recommendations, if adopted, would make this more likely.[24] Most of the leading Catholics firmly upheld the principle of indissolubility of marriage.

Nevertheless, on 16th February, 1967, the general principle of breakdown was affirmed by the Church Assembly of the Church of England by a large majority. In July 1967 the Methodist Conference affirmed the principle of breakdown as against matrimonial fault.

III. *Mutual Consent:*
Arranged Divorce and the Community's Interest

Thus, the Report recommended a controversial new ground for divorce and raised an important question for public discussion. Ironically, it also more or less acknowledged the existence of divorce by mutual consent by recognizing the fact of divorce by collusion,[25] although the Report firmly denies the principle of divorce by consent. However, the Rev. Garth Moore of Durham wrote in the *Church Times* (29th July, 1966):

> . . . divorce by consent is already a reality, though a reality thinly veiled under the present law by the necessity of one of the parties' going through the motions of committing a 'matrimonial offence' in order to provide the only ground (other than insanity) on which the court can pronounce a decree.

The Archbishop of Canterbury also recognized the fact:

> It is clear that many divorce cases are virtually divorce by consent—thus, those who are upholding the present law unaltered can fairly be called the upholders of a system of divorce by consent; and also in the operation of the present divorce laws it is clear that already the judge makes decisions not strictly on the principle of an offence but by employing tacitly a principle of breakdown.[26]

The Mortimer group 'emphatically' rejected the notion of divorce by mutual consent on two grounds. The idea would virtually repudiate the community's interest in the stability of marriage, because a judge (the community representative) would take no effectual part in the proceedings. Further, if a marriage can be ended by mutual consent, the intention of the covenant to marry would no longer be 'lifelong'. Neither point carries much weight, as most people who marry today are well aware that divorce is available if the marriage does not work, but few intend anything other than a lifelong relationship, at least at the moment of the ceremony.

Does divorce by mutual consent teach the citizens that marriage is unimportant and encourage them to take it lightly? There is little evidence to suggest that the ease of legal divorce increases the number of marriages which break down (as opposed to increasing the number of divorce decrees). Surely it has long been easy enough to obtain a divorce in almost all American states and the American rate of divorce has remained relatively stable for over twenty years —if one allows for a short-lived increase immediately after the Second World War.[27] The same short-term increase is to be found in England, but there has also been a steady rise in the divorce-rate all through the 1960s. In Japan, where there is divorce by mutual consent, the rate of divorce has remained stable for decades. The reasons for divorce and marital breakdown, as the Mortimer group itself recognized, lie deep in the culture and the personalities it has produced, not in the provision of a statute.

Sir Jocelyn Simon has suggested[28] that divorce by consent should be allowed if there are no dependent children, but that no divorce at all should be permitted if the couple have children in need of care and upbringing. But as Professor Paulsen has said, even this attractive and seemingly reasonable limitation on the principle of divorce by consent appears unsound to many people.[29] And as the parliamentary debates pointed out, married couples with children can find life unbearable and joyless. Many would agree that such a situation cannot be a happy one for children, nor is such a marriage educative or helpful for their future. Most people today would agree that the community has an interest in promoting stable and happy family life in which children can grow and flourish. The question is how this is to be achieved. As the Report suggested and recommended, the law can safeguard a child's economic interest to the extent that family resources permit or that the Government can afford. The provision for care and custody of children may be carefully reviewed and guaranteed by the law; but the law cannot preserve the home. The State or the Court can refuse to break the bonds of matrimony, but neither the State nor the law nor the

Church can bind the spouses to love each other or to live together happily.

'Mutual consent' grounds exist in Australia, New Zealand, Japan, Mexico and in some American states in the form of statutes granting divorces after a period of separation of two, three or five years. As has been seen, divorce by consent in England had been achieved by manipulation of the other grounds for divorce, and this would still be possible under the new ground recommended by the Report. It could even be easier than previously as the couple would simply have to convince the judge that the marriage had irretrievably broken down. Of course how the Court would interpret the term 'irretrievably broken down' is open to question, but it is understood that it might recognize adultery or cruelty or desertion as evidence of 'irretrievable breakdown'. Furthermore, the judge might well agree to granting divorce in cases where both parties had lived apart for a certain period or either party had committed a serious breach of marital obligation. The Lord Chancellor, Lord Gardiner, said : 'Surely our common sense tells us that adultery, desertion and bad conduct at home, are often symptoms of matrimonial collapse, rather than the disease itself.'[30] If the courts should interpret the term 'irretrievably broken down' along the lines suggested by the Lord Chancellor, there would certainly be easier divorce, perhaps even divorce by consent, although some believed that divorce would be more difficult under the new law.

In so far as the Mortimer Committee hoped to avoid 'arranged' divorce, it seems clear that they were unsuccessful despite their good intentions. Decrees can be 'arranged' under the new basis as well as under the old law. The facts adduced to show breakdown can be carefully selected. The consenting spouse can eagerly seek out conciliation services in order to establish unsuccessful attempts at reunion. The new arrangements will, of course, extend delay and add expense.

The Mortimer Committee, was, of course, concerned most deeply with the troubled, unfortunate couples involved, and it is precisely in relation to these cases that the doctrine of marital breakdown is thought most civilized and beneficial. Neither party would have to blacken the other with distorted, false allegations of adultery, desertion or cruelty. Neither would 'divorce' the other and neither would stand innocent or guilty; the decree would merely pronounce 'dead' that which had already died. The aim was doubtless admirable, but it was neither new nor an invention of the group.[31]

The point to which attention must be drawn is that the main issue which the proposal presents is hidden in the Report. The draftsmen ask, 'Is the issue of breakdown triable?' Clearly, in one sense the answer is 'yes'. Judges often employ legal standards rather than rules and decide issues of degree. A judge could take the standard suggested and come to a conclusion. Indeed, quite often he would be right, at least when he granted the decree. The main point is not, however, whether a judge can arrive at a decision in a reasonable way but whether it is wise and expedient that he should do so.

The plan of the Mortimer Committee envisages a situation in which a judge might properly refuse a divorce to an established couple both of whom earnestly desired release from the burden of marriage, because the judge has not been convinced of 'breakdown'. A single act of adultery, a course of cruelty, even a substantial period of desertion, would no longer suffice in themselves as reasons for granting a decree of divorce. Such matters would be sufficient only if the marriage had 'broken down'. The Report does list them as evidence of breakdown, and members of the Committee could easily suppose that most judges would grant a decree to the offended spouse on the grounds of breakdown. However, the proposal does allow for the exercise of judgment and discretion, knowing that in such matters, men, even judges, are apt to judge only in the light of their deepest personal conviction.

As has already been pointed out, the Mortimer group vigorously rejected the idea that 'breakdown' should be added to the list of grounds for divorce, principally for the reason that, in the group's view, the principle of the matrimonial offence and the principle of breakdown are mutually inconsistent, and the incompatibility, the Report asserts, would be 'glaringly obvious', creating an unfortunate anomaly. This point carries weight only if the State chooses one principle as the exclusive one, and then adds grounds which are justified on the other principle. But, one may ask, why should an exclusive choice be made? One principle can serve the case of the spouse who has committed serious offence. The other can serve the spouse in respect of whom no glaring misconduct can be identified, and the spouse who seeks divorce against the will of a relatively innocent partner. The difficulty can perhaps be overcome by making the new ground, 'breakdown of marriage', serve for all of these cases. However, it must not be forgotten that the legal system frequently chooses different principles to dispose of distinguishable situations. It is also obvious that a combination of both approaches (i.e. offence and breakdown) would clearly have made the law of divorce easier rather than better.

As Professor Paulsen raised the question, we may inquire whether the Report did not really signal a change in the Church's attitude towards marriage, divorce and remarriage, despite what some

Church members claimed. If it did not signal change, at least in the long run, the Report is indeed a curious document. *Putting Asunder* would then appear to give man advice about divorce while forbidding him to practise it.

Another important point is that the Report is considered to represent the opinion of the Church of England,[32] although the Archbishop of Canterbury, in his Preface to the Report, was careful not to express approval, but only to commend it for study. However, it should be remembered that the Archbishop also considered the Report's suggestion as a lesser evil than the old law and practice of divorce in England.

IV. *The Report and the Church of England as a Pressure Group*

Although the genesis of the group was not in doubt, the motive of the Church of England in producing the Report must also be scrutinized. What was the main aim of the Archbishop in setting up the group? Why was the Church so concerned over the reform of the State law on divorce? There may be many reasons, but the instinct of self-preservation of the Church in this permissive society must not be overlooked. The Church of England has considered itself for many centuries the guardian of morality in England, whereas in many other countries the signs of the declining authority of the Church are now all too obvious. Furthermore, it is still true that the majority of marriage ceremonies are conducted by the Churches, which retain their economic and religious interest in psychological influence on the matrimonial life of English people.

Divorce has always troubled the Church of England deeply, ever since, in fact, it broke from Rome at the time that its temporal head, Henry VIII, was trying to divorce his wife. On the other hand the Catholic Church was far less disturbed by divorce. The simple reason was that Catholics do not recognize divorce : there is no divorce at all for Catholics, at least in theory. However, promoters of divorce law reform point out that in Catholic countries there are millions of people living in sin, producing millions of illegitimate children in unblessed union just because of this principle.

For Moslems, in theory, divorce is not too much of a problem. For Buddhists and Jews, the problem is less serious as they recognize divorce and there is not much gap between the spirit of the State laws and the religious teachings. In Britain, there are a number of minority groups, for example Jewish people, but they have little voice over the law of the land, although they are legally allowed to marry according to their own customary rules. However, there is no exception in the case of divorce; they have to follow the English divorce law procedure if they want to obtain divorce. When various marriage rituals are recognized, the enforcement of a uniform divorce procedure is arguable, although a prominent member of the Church of England has said : 'This country happens to be a democracy !'

Thus the basic principles of English divorce law were laid down by the early Christians and still prevail in England, however shaky they may be. Indeed, keeping pace with rapid social change has been the problem of the Churches for years; the fact of change in matrimonial life and in the attitude of the Court—easier divorce, virtually divorce by consent—forced the Church to reconsider the divorce law. As Dr Ramsey said in the *Sunday Times*, 'to bring honesty and compassion into the English Divorce Law has for long been the aim of the reformers'.[33] In 1964, as a consequence of Mr Leo Abse's Divorce Bill, he invited the Bishop of Exeter with a group of distinguished experts to consider how best this could be achieved.[34]

As the Archbishop of Canterbury clearly stated in his Preface to the Report, *Putting Asunder*, their motive was not only the need to discover a new ground for the divorce law of the State, but the desire to preserve the principles of Christian marriage. It seems that the latter objective was the greater concern of the Church of England. The Archbishop confirmed his concern over the issue by saying : 'If there were to be legislation on the lines of what is suggested in this Report, I believe that the Churches would still maintain their own pastoral discipline.' The Church of England therefore discovered through the group a reasonable ground on which to take a stand and decided not to oppose the reform so long as this stand could be maintained, allowing the bishops to vote freely, each according to his conscience, in the House of Lords. In other words, the Church wanted to avoid the kind of divorce law reform which would make divorce easier, and hoped to discover a safeguard by which they could stop the law becoming too permissive. Professor Anderson perhaps best described the attitude of the Church in this respect in the debate at the Church Assembly :

... I am convinced that changes in our law of divorce will come. There is a mounting pressure in many different areas and among many different groups. In the past, the Bishops, in the House of Lords, and other Church leaders have stood, if I may say so, rather like Canute trying to prevent the tide coming in. I am sure that changes in the law of divorce are going to be imposed on us, and it therefore seems to me to be imperative that the Church, instead of merely saying 'No, no, no', should apply its mind to what would be a more satisfactory civil law of divorce than the present law—I am not pleading for any change in our attitude to divorce, but that we should realise that we have a responsibility to the nation not merely to say 'no' and then accept whatever law comes, but to make constructive and suitable suggestions.[35]

The result was a compromise reflecting the division of opinion on divorce not only in the Church but in England. But at least the former rigid attitude of the Church of England had given way to the pressure of time.

Finally, a serious question which must be raised here is, what was the role of the Church of England as a pressure group and what influence had the Mortimer group's Report? As the Lord Chancellor said in his speech at the Annual Conference of the National Marriage Guidance Council at Brighton, on 5th May, 1967, *Putting Asunder* recommended 'the sweeping away of all existing grounds of divorce and their replacement by the single ground of the breakdown of the marriage'. The proposed ending of the matrimonial offence was a big breakthrough, although it would still be used as evidence of breakdown. *Putting Asunder* was not merely a recommendation of a new ground for divorce. It was a cautious but constructive and persuasive report, at least for many English people, which resulted from a careful study by a group which included a number of distinguished clergymen, judges, legal practitioners, social workers and a lady writer on Christian ethics. On 31st July, 1966, Professor McGregor wrote in the *Sunday Times*:

. . . *Putting Asunder* is a document of major importance less for its detailed proposals than for the new impetus and direction it will give to the search for an acceptable divorce law. The willingness of the group to urge the Church of England away from old positions will help to release the log jam which has obstructed the shaping of a new divorce law which will be respected because accepted as reasonable by most citizens. The group has done invaluable service by creating a new atmosphere for the consideration of the proposals for reform already promised by the Law Commission.

The Church Assembly of the Church of England took a significant step in approving the general principle of the recommendation in *Putting Asunder*; for the first time in its history the Church of England appeared to be for the reform of the law of divorce, and this was largely owing to the efforts of the Mortimer group.

The evidence of the documents and the result of a number of interviews with responsible members of the Church of England suggest that the opinion of the group was not too much ahead of that expressed by the Church Assembly. The Report was based on carefully collected evidence, as well as being the product of the beliefs and personal backgrounds of members of the group. Most of the members, being also members of the Church of England, were certainly in a better position to understand the attitude of the Church and its concern over the doctrine of Christian marriage and divorce than was the public at large. None the less, the Report did represent a compromise of opinion[36] both within the Church of England and between the Church and the public, although its original recommendation was impracticable and it could not solve the problems which had been accumulating for decades. It was later watered down by the effort of the Law Commission, as we have already seen, and the final decision was left for the legislators.

The Report was received favourably by the press and public in general. Credit must be given to *Putting Asunder* and the press reports for bridging the gap between public and legislative opinion, and for bringing the recommendation into Parliament. Despite the fact that there were many critics, as was only to be expected in a case of national importance, *Putting Asunder* strengthened the cause of the reformers and received the approval of the House of Lords. It demonstrated the way in which the attitude of the Church of England on social and moral issues is still important in British politics. The role of the Churches in other non-Catholic Christian countries, such as the United States, is not comparable. A Buddhist or Moslem group, in countries where these faiths are predominant, might well be capable of producing an equally influential document, but might be expected to take a quite different stand on the specific question of divorce. Misunderstanding created by press reports, which reported *Putting Asunder* as the opinion of the Church of England, also helped the reformers who fully exploited the mistake.

Once the Church Assembly of the Church of England had approved by a large majority the general principle of the recommendation, the Church of England ceased to be a pressure group against reform. It could therefore no longer be counted as the greatest strength of the opponents. Thus the royal road towards the reform of divorce law was opened by the Church group appointed by the Archbishop of Canterbury three years after Mr Leo Abse's Bill. The Report of the Archbishop's group spurred the reformers into new action. As far as the reform itself was concerned, the crucial test was left with the official lawmakers. All depended upon the strength of the reformers in Parliament and the attitude of the Government in providing time in the coming session.

NOTES

1 At present there are two archbishops and twenty-four bishops in the House of Lords. Of course, opponents were not only the Church of England, but the Roman Catholics, the Free Churchmen, and even some agnostics who opposed the reform on various grounds.

2 The Lord Bishop of Exeter as Chairman, and twelve other members were appointed in January, but in November Mr E. W. Short, Labour M.P., resigned, having been appointed Government Chief Whip. The vacancy was filled in March 1965 by A. J. Irvine, Q.C., Labour M.P. (now Sir Arthur Irvine), but he resigned in November of that year after attending one meeting. The reason, he said, was that most of the evidence had already been collected and the hearing was over. Sir Arthur Irvine was to become Solicitor-General and attended most of the debates on Mr Jones's Bill in the Commons. The Report, therefore, was made by the following twelve members: Dr Mortimer, Bishop of Exeter, former Regius Professor of Moral and Pastoral Theology, and Lecturer in Early Canon Law, at Oxford; Professor J. N. D. Anderson, Barrister and the Director of the Institute of Advanced Legal Studies in the University of London; the Rev. G. B. Bentley, Canon of Windsor; Viscount Colville of Culross, Barrister and President of the National Council for the Unmarried Mother and her Child; Lord Devlin, Lord of Appeal; the Rev. G. R. Dunstan, Minor Canon of Westminster Abbey; Quentin Edwards, Barrister; Professor D. MacRae, Professor of Sociology in the University of London; Lady Oppenheimer, writer on Christian ethics; the Hon. Mr Justice Phillimore, Justice of the High Court of Justice; Dr D. A. Pond, Consultant Psychiatrist; Miss Joan S. Rubinstein, a partner in a firm of London solicitors. . . . Professional representation consisted of ten men, two women, six lawyers, one of them being Lord of Appeal, three reverends, and one M.D. consultant psychiatrist, one writer and one sociologist. Thus the legal profession was heavily represented.

3 172 pages, including a Preface by the Archbishop of Canterbury.

4 The full group met eighteen times between May 1964 and March 1966, on one occasion at the London School of Economics, on all the others at the Institute of Advanced Legal Studies. Eight of the meetings extended to two days. In addition three sub-committees—theological, legal and sociological—prepared material for discussion and inclusion in the Report.

5 *The Times* (29th July, 1966).

6 For the Church's discipline with regard to the remarriage of divorced persons, see *Marriage, Divorce and the Church*, the Report of the Commission on the Christian Doctrine of Marriage.

7 *Putting Asunder*, p. 13.

8 *The Times* (29th July 1966).

9 See the Report, pp. 4, 6, 12–24, and the Preface to the Report by the Archbishop.

10 *The Christian and Christianity Today* (29th July, 1966).

11 See pp. 71 *et seq.*, below. A member of the group said that what they did was to agree that it was impossible to apply the procedure.

12 The credit for arranging this meeting should be given to Canon Bentley who actively participated.

13 *Sunday Times* (18th Feb., 1968): Professor Anderson's reply to the article by the Archbishop of Canterbury in the *Sunday Times* of 11th Feb., 1968.

14 *The Guardian* (29th July, 1966).

15 *Putting Asunder*, pp. 163 *et seq.*

16 Ibid., pp. 146 *et seq.*

17 Ibid., p. 143.

18 4th Aug., 1966, pp. 1152–3.

19 Vol. 110, No. 30, (20th July, 1966).

20 4th Aug., 1966, p. 1153.

21 See p. 36, above.

22 *Daily Mail* (29th July, 1966).

23 Ibid.

24 Ibid.

25 *Putting Asunder*, para. 48, p. 34. It is certainly arguable—if both parties recognize that a marriage has broken down, is this collusion?

26 The Church Assembly, *Report of Proceedings*, Vol. XLVII, No. 2 (Spring Session 1967), p. 250; and see also his article in the *Sunday Times* (11th Feb., 1968).

27 It should be noted, however, that according to the US Census Bureau, the national divorce-rate climbed 33 per cent in the last decade.

28 'The Seven Pillars of Divorce Reform', *Law Society's Gazette* (June 1965), p. 344. Sir Jocelyn, now Lord Simon of Glaisdale, was Solicitor-General in the Macmillan Government. Lord Simon became Lord of Appeal in Ordinary in succession to Lord Hodson, who retired at Easter 1971.

29 See *New Society* (4th Aug., 1966).

30 On 5th May, 1967 at Brighton, when opening the Annual Conference of the National Marriage Guidance Council.

31 Mutual consent as a ground for divorce exists in many countries, and Mrs White's Bill had contained a breakdown clause of seven years which was fully discussed in the Report of the Royal Commission (1951–5), Cmd 9678, Chap. 2, and 'Statement of His Views by Lord Walker', pp. 340 *et seq.*

32 But see *Putting Asunder*, p. 6: '. . . we have thought it right to consider rather carefully and thoroughly the nature and the basis of the Church's attitude to secular matrimonial law, and the justification it may claim for tending advice to the State in the matter.'

33 11th Feb., 1968. See also Archbishop of Canterbury, Church Assembly, *Report of Proceedings*, Vol. XLVII, No. 2, p. 250.

34 See p. 43, above.

35 Church Assembly, *Report of Proceedings,* Vol. XLVII, No. 2 (Spring Session 1967), p. 239.

36 The approval of the Church Assembly and the results of the Opinion Polls taken in 1965 and 1967 support this interpretation.

Chapter 4

THE LAW COMMISSION

The Law Commission was set up for the purpose of promoting the reform of the law of England and Wales.[1] Its establishment was a unique event in England, although, as Sir Leslie Scarman has said,[2] the United Kingdom cannot claim to be the first in having such an institution to review and reform the law, since law reform or revision agencies have been an integral part of the legal scene in the United States for years. Many other countries which possess a civil law system, have this kind of institution; in some countries, including those with common law systems, a Ministry of Justice is the chosen instrument of such activities, while in others an independent advisory agency, comparable with the two British Law Commissions,[3] is used.

The Law Commission for England and Wales is only five years old and there is, as yet, no comprehensive study of its role in the process of policy formation and law reform. However, since 1965, the work of the law reform in Britain has advanced at an unprecedented pace, and for that much of the credit must be given to the Law Commission. The mechanics of this process are complicated just as its social and political significance is immense. Although the ensuing account may be an oversimplification, it provides a summary of the origin, purpose, structure and activities of this increasingly important body.

I. *The Debut of the Commission*

It was not until the Law Commissions Act 1965 that the movement for law reform in England became institutionalized and the reforming tendencies of the then Lord Chancellor, Lord Gardiner, and his personal and public contribution to the divorce legislation are accordingly of especial interest. Any study of this kind will find it necessary to take some account of the personal background of the figures who play a large part in the drama, since it is often in the earliest years of a man's life that the genesis of his later attitudes is to be found. Sociological and psychological influences and the whole process of political socialization provide a fascinating illumination of the official personality, but it is as well to remember that factors which may appear to be decisive in one situation may have little or no effect in another. As Ron Hall comments :

> Factors in political socialisation have a cumulative influence, and in England often operate in a single direction. . . . By studying the influence of factors, either individually or in combination, it is possible to make significant statements about the probability that a group of individuals will act in a certain way politically . . . probabilities, however, they cannot be accurate in every instance; all individuals exposed to similar social experiences do not respond identically.[4]

In any case, it is no more easy to estimate the influences which make a man a reformer than it is to identify those which make another a supporter of the *status quo*.

In the case of Lord Gardiner the interest in reforming the laws relating to marriage began before he, as a bachelor, joined the Divorce Law Reform Union. Educated at Magdalen College, Oxford, and a sensitive Protestant, he joined the Inner Temple and later became Chairman of the Society of Labour Lawyers, and a progressive outlook was from his earliest youth a feature of his character. His immediate objectives on reaching the Woolsack were fourfold[5]—to secure the abolition of capital punishment, to establish the Law Commission, to reform the system of Assizes and Quarter Sessions and to alter the Divorce Law. In the five years following the Law Commissions Act 1965, all these aims were accomplished, the Divorce Reform Bill finally being passed in 1969. Lord Gardiner was also responsible for the transfer of jurisdiction over undefended matrimonial causes to the County Courts from the High Court.[6]

Since the passing of the 1965 Law Commissions Act the process of law reform has become a deliberate and continuing activity in the English legal system.[7] 'The First Programme of the Commission, which was for the examination of 17 subjects with a view to reform, was submitted on 19th July.'[8] It was laid before Parliament on 27th October, after receiving the Lord Chancellor's approval with some amendment on 20th September, 1965. On 7th July the Lord Chancellor officially requested the Commission to prepare a comprehensive programme for consolidation and statute law revision.[9]

II. *The Structure of the Law Commission*

The Law Commission for England and Wales consists of five full-time Commissioners[10] and forty-eight other full-time staff members :

the Secretary, four draftsmen and sixteen other lawyers, together with twenty-seven clerical and administrative staff. They also have the help of draftsmen from the Parliamentary Counsel's Office in Whitehall and the part-time services of four other lawyers.

That Lord Gardiner was able to appoint all five Law Commissioners on 16th June, 1965, the day after the Royal Assent was given to the Law Commissions Act, is a significant[11] indication of the degree of careful consideration and preparation which had been given to the problem behind the scenes. The Law Commission with their staff have clearly demonstrated the immense political role which this new institution may play in England, and its participation in the cause of divorce law reform is a singularly good illustration of this. As the Chairman of the Commission has said, law reform is not exclusively a legal topic but also a social, political and moral problem. 'It is no longer possible to think of the law as an esoteric and technical discipline, whose values are safe in the hands of the Judges and the profession.'[12]

The Commission has also undertaken a great deal of work relating to the repair of the legal framework. The expansion of its province has meant that more staff have been required, but this has enabled it to develop its skill in appraising the variety of problems involved in its comprehensive activities. It is perhaps a measure of its success that it is now widely esteemed[13] both inside and outside of the legal profession as a source of informed legislative opinion. For this unique union of professional expertise and ideological stimulus, much of the credit is due to the close relationship between the Lord Chancellor's Office and the Law Commission.

III. *The Role of the Law Commission*

The Law Commission, however, is not a lawmaking body, but a purely advisory institution. In this respect it differs from the courts and Parliament. 'In the field of law reform the Commission is an advisory body possessing a right of initiative. Action in this field remains the responsibility of Parliament and the Government.'[14] In other words, the Commission neither makes final judgment over legal cases nor makes laws; the final decision—action—must be taken by Parliament and the Government to change any law of the land. Yet in the exercise of its statutory duty to keep the law under review with regard to its systematic development and reform, and in the preparation of further programmes, the Commission has always to be planning ahead.[15] The Chairman of the Commission described its members' duties as follows :

Their function is to watch the law in its social and economic context and to prepare proposals for any reforms which in the exercise of their independent judgement they believe to be necessary. . . . The Commissions[16] are exclusively legal bodies, their membership limited to the legal profession (including the academic, as well as the practising branches of the profession). The legal character of their membership determines their working methods.[17]

Sir Leslie, in a speech at the University of Bristol on 18th March, 1966, favoured evolutionary change rather than radical innovation.[18] This approach towards the reform of the law reappeared as a motto of the Law Commission in the Commission's *First Annual Report 1965–66*, which states: '. . . haste is the enemy of sound law reform and . . . law reform must concern itself as much with the form, arrangement and procedures of the law as with its substance. All too often quick law reform can only be achieved at the sacrifice of research and consultation.'[19] Thus in the words of the Law Commission itself, the ultimate goal of the venture is 'the development and reform of the English law as a whole. We must build brick by brick; but each brick must fit into a coherent structure.'[20]

However, in a series of lectures delivered at the University of Keele in November 1967, seventeen months after the Commission's *First Annual Report*, Sir Leslie called for a 'revolution' in English lawmaking procedures[21] which might make way for a new revolutionary era of law reform. Indeed, the very establishment of the Law Commission was itself something of a revolution, although its subsequent successes were largely the result of effective groundwork.

On the one hand, since the Act does not require that all law reform must be achieved exclusively through the Law Commission, other devices such as a widely representative Royal Commission, departmental committee or other inquiry body are available to those who wish to find an outlet for reformist opinions. On the other hand, the Law Commission is a permanent and a principal architect of law reform in England and has been since it was set up.

The main tasks of this institution may be divided into the planning of law reform, research, consultation, submission of law reform proposals, the drafting of bills and the giving of technical assistance in their passage into law.[22] In a word, the duty of the Law Commission is to adopt a comprehensive approach to reform and to take care to relate its proposals to the developing pattern of the law as a whole.

Sir Leslie Scarman says that once the programme is approved by the Lord Chancellor, the Commission's judgment as to its solution is completely independent and its own. The requirement that any proposed reform must be reported to the Lord Chancellor for his approval means that the Commission's programme is effectively under the firm control of the Government. In other words, if necessary, the Government or the Lord Chancellor can exercise their power of veto over the Law Commission's activities under section 3(1)(b), (c) and (d).[23] Nevertheless, the most important function of the Law Commission in parliamentary legislation lies with the proposals which they present. The Commission's recommendations are carefully selected and scrutinized, both by experts and by bodies and persons representative of public opinion as a whole. 'This is no substitute for subsequent parliamentary scrutiny, but should ensure that proposals submitted to Parliament are properly prepared so as to reveal the true issues for decision by the legislature. Unnecessary or bogus controversy can be avoided, if Parliament so wishes, by this consultation based on the working-paper.'[24] When a report or recommendation is submitted to the Lord Chancellor, it is usually accompanied by a draft bill prepared by parliamentary counsel attached to the Commission. The following table gives an indication of their output to the end of 1970 :

1. Working Papers published 33
2. Command Papers 40
3. Implementation of the Law Commission's Proposals 24[25]

Thus the work done by the experts carries considerable weight even in Parliament and in fact many M.P.s use the name of the Law Commission or its reports as compelling data, in the knowledge that few opponents will argue with the Law Commission's carefully worded documents.

It appears that the determination and conviction of Lord Gardiner and Sir Leslie Scarman were the key factors in mobilizing the full capacity of the Law Commission in support of divorce law reform.

In the operation of any public organization such as the Law Commission, the personality of the head of the institution is of vital importance. In the process of divorce reform it was doubly significant owing to the little publicized but central work of the Law Commission in this field. Thus the appointment of Sir Leslie Scarman as Chairman of the Commission was applauded by those who favoured an alteration in the law. He was educated at Brasenose College, Oxford, and shared Lord Gardiner's outlook and his rejection of the principle of the indissolubility of marriage. His practical experience as a lawyer has enabled Sir Leslie to bridge the

gap between theoretical principles and reality in order to make the
law more consonant with the interests of the community. His dedi-
cation to the public service and his idea of the proper function of
the Commission comes over clearly in his speeches. When he described the statutory character of the Commission and its relationship to the machinery of Government in his lecture at the University of Keele in 1967, he also commented : 'Parliament has made a
take-over bid in a field of activity which has been for centuries the
traditional reserve of the courts and the legal profession. The terms
of the bid are to be found in the Law Commission Acts 1965. . . .
The Act has established the machinery for the purpose of promoting the reform of the law.' However, it is important to notice that
the Law Commission itself has also to some extent made a take-over
bid in a field of activity which has been for centuries the traditional
reserve of the lawmakers in Parliament. The Law Commission, in
selecting its materials and in the preparation and presentation of its
proposal and reports, has virtually appropriated an important
aspect of the lawmakers' business and its voice probably carries far
greater weight than the Commissioners claim. Almost all their proposals have been accepted and as the Chairman himself recognized,
the process of law reform has speedily gathered momentum.

IV. *The Law Commission and Divorce Law Reform*

As early as March 1966 Sir Leslie Scarman, in a carefully worded
speech at the University of Bristol, had expressed his view on 'the
law relating to divorce and an unsatisfactory feature of the law
relating to the financial support of the broken family'.[26] The objectives of family law he listed as

> first and foremost, the preservation of family life; secondly, if
> and when family life breaks down, that divorce should be avail-
> able in relief of human suffering, and that, whether divorce
> follows or not, matrimonial breakdown with its inevitable splin-
> tering of the family group—man, woman, children—should be
> met by proper arrangements for the care and upbringing of the
> children and the support of the spouse who is not the bread-
> winner. . . . After a fashion these objectives are more or less
> achieved in the framework of existing law. . . . By its artificialities
> English law manages to provide divorce in most, though cer-
> tainly not all cases, in which it is wanted.[27]

The necessity for reform existed largely because of the gap which
could be seen to exist between the law and reality. Firstly, even
though divorce actions were only justifiable in the High Court,

there were some 40,000 divorces being granted each year. An un-defended suit would cost a little over £100 although account must be taken of the subvention which the legal aid scheme supplies for divorce actions at a cost of about £4 million a year to the tax-payer.[28] The community thus gets what it wants by a number of fictions, artificialities and subsidies to an extent which is often breathtaking. Three fictions may perhaps be mentioned in relation to divorce. First, while divorce was ostensibly a remedy available only in the High Court, in practice the great majority of un-defended suits and some defended suits were before 1967 handled by the County Court Bench,[29] whose judges suffered an ephemeral elevation to the High Court so that the formalities might be ob-served. Another fiction was that the Court would in theory inquire minutely into the facts of an undefended suit. But the delay which this course would entail meant that in practice this was rarely done. Finally there existed the embarrassing fictions of the discretion state-ment and of the doctrine of the matrimonial offence. It was little wonder that Sir Leslie Scarman remarked, 'the law emerges looking silly and out of touch', when so many undefended suits were con-sensual. The deficiencies of the law in this respect were all too obvious. The great majority of divorces were granted after a hear-ing of ten minutes or so before a commissioner in which usually only one of the spouses, the petitioner, would give evidence. Sir Leslie asked, 'Is this a genuine judicial process, or does it mean that, whatever the theory of the law, there has in practice, in the great majority of cases, been submitted a rubber stamp for a genuine trial and finding by a judge? Is the undefended suit a mockery of the judicial process?' The answer given to these questions was that, although there were not enough lawyers, the problems might be solved by the full working of the judicial process; in a word, 'the law, though it creaks, works'. His ultimate judgment was therefore tolerant towards the existing arrangements and he opposed the idea of divorce by administrative process; he suggested that it was in the interest of society to restrict the ability to grant divorces to judicial decision. He also mentioned the idea of establishing family courts at regional centres under a Family Division of the High Court,[30] or by a Family Division of the Court of Appeal, which would enable justice to be dispensed quickly and cheaply throughout the country. However, decentralization and devolution of the administration of justice in divorce cases could be achieved only in the context of complete reorganization of the machinery of justice in England and Wales.

In conclusion, he called for serious attention to the following eight points:[31]

1. the establishment of a Family Division of the Supreme Court;

2. the establishment of regional family courts;

3. the elimination of domicile as a basis of jurisdiction in divorce actions and the substitution of habitual residence of either spouse;

4. the modernisation of the relief . . . ;

5. while retaining the matrimonial offence as a ground for divorce, the addition of irretrievable breakdown evidenced by separation over a period of years, whatever the cause of the separation;

6. the Court should be in no case feel obliged to grant a divorce unless satisfied that there was no reasonable chance of reconciliation and that proper arrangements were being made, not only for the care and upbringing of the children, but for the financial support of the members of the family exposed to risk by the destruction of the family unit;

7. the encouragement for consensual arrangements for divorce, when there is family breakdown;

8. the establishment of a personal file for each individual maintained in some central registry so that orders for the support of mothers and children can be effectively enforced.

Coincidentally or not, *Putting Asunder* and other important reports later embodied his ideas[32] expressed in 4, 5 and 6.

Although the Lord Chancellor made it clear during the debate in the House of Lords[33] that the Law Commission would not get involved in any question of party politics or in any controversial social questions, particularly any with religious aspects, the Commission did play, in a brilliant if necessarily cautious manner, a substantial role in achieving a reform which must inevitably affect the social, moral and religious opinions of the English people.

In fact, in July 1965, when the Law Commission had drawn up its first programme, and nine months before Sir Leslie made his speech at Bristol, the Commissioners clearly stated their desire to review the existing matrimonial law. In item No. X, under the heading 'Family Law', the Commission proposed the following studies :

(a) Matrimonial law : a further examination of the matrimonial law having regard to the variety of views expressed in and following the Report of the last Royal Commission on Marriage and Divorce (1956 Cmd 9678), the Morton Commission.

(b) Family inheritance and property law. . . .

(c) Jurisdiction in family matters. . . .[34]

They also included, as a separate item, the recognition of foreign divorces, nullity, decrees and adoptions.

Before the publication of *Putting Asunder* in 1966, the Law Commission described its attitude in its *First Annual Report 1965–66,* paragraph 78, as follows :

> We have decided to make no attempt to formulate views on such topics as the grounds for divorce and the bars to relief until after the publication of the Report of the Commission set up by the Archbishop of Canterbury which is examining these questions under the Chairmanship of the Bishop of Exeter. This Report will be of great value as an indication of the present state of an important and responsible section of public opinion. In the meantime we are collecting and studying the available legal, sociological, and comparative material. In this connection we have received invaluable assistance from many quarters. . . . As regards financial rights and obligations arising out of marriage and its termination, we have made a detailed and critical study of the present law, as found not only in the provisions of the Matrimonial Causes Act 1965 and the Magistrates' Courts (Matrimonial Proceedings) Act 1960, but also in a number of other statutes. Wider consultations will take place before we formulate our proposals.

When the Report of the Archbishop's group on divorce, *Putting Asunder,* was published, the Lord Chancellor immediately referred it to the Law Commission for their advice under section 3(1)(e) of the Law Commissions Act on the legal practicability of its proposals. In pursuance of this request the Law Commission, in October 1966, submitted its most important report on divorce : *Reform of the Grounds of Divorce : The Field of Choice,* which the Lord Chancellor presented to Parliament (1966 Cmnd 3123 : Law Com. No. 6).

The Field of Choice consisted of 124 paragraphs and 5 appendices in 62 pages. At the outset of the Report and in its conclusion, the Law Commissioners carefully described the purpose, method and scope of the document and their own duty under the Law Commissions Act. It ran :

> *Putting Asunder,* the Report of a Group appointed by the Archbishop of Canterbury in January 1965, was published on 19th July 1966. You immediately referred this important document to us, in accordance with section 3(1)(e) of the Law Commissions Act 1965, for our advice and asked that we should submit a Report to you as early as possible. 2. Item X (a) of our First Programme required us to furnish you with an examination of the

Matrimonial Law having regard to the variety of views expressed in and following the report of the last Royal Commission on Marriage and Divorce. Our Report may be regarded as the first step towards carrying out that examination and its scope will be wide enough to include the study not only of *Putting Asunder* but also of the other proposals for reform of the existing grounds of divorce which have received support. It is not, of course, for us but for Parliament to settle such controversial social issues as the advisability of extending the present grounds of divorce. Our function in advising you must be to assist the Legislature and the general public in considering these questions by pointing out the implications of various possible courses of action. Perhaps the most useful service that we can perform at this stage is to mark out the boundaries of the field of choice.[35]

They made it clear that they had tried to keep the Report as short and non-technical as possible, and to restrict it to a consideration of what appeared from a lawyer's point of view to be practicable. After a brief description of the background of the divorce problem, it confirmed that 'marriage as an institution in present-day England is in a fairly healthy state as compared with the past', and defined the objectives of a good divorce law as follows:[36]

(i)   To buttress, rather than to undermine, the stability of marriage; and

(ii) When, regrettably, a marriage has irretrievably broken down, to enable the empty legal shell to be destroyed with the maximum fairness, and the minimum bitterness, distress and humiliation.

In the latter part of the Report, they pointed out the arguments for and against divorce by consent, and in paragraph 120 they summarized the Report and their conclusions as follows:

(1) The objective of a good divorce law should include (a) the support of marriages which have a chance of survival, and (b) the decent burial with the minimum of embarrassment, humiliation and bitterness of those that are indubitably dead (paragraphs 13–18).

(2) The provision of the present law whereby a divorce cannot normally be obtained within three years of the celebration of marriage may help to achieve the first objective (paragraph 19). But the principle of matrimonial offence on which the present law is based does not wholly achieve either objective (paragraphs 25–8).

(3) Four of the major problems requiring solution are:—
     (a)   The need to encourage reconciliation. . . .

(b) The prevalence of stable illicit unions. . . .

(c) Injustice to the economically weaker partner—normally the wife. . . .

(d) The need adequately to protect the children of failed marriages. . . .

The Report pointed out that a thorough inquest is procedurally impracticable, although it accepted the proposal made by the Archbishop's group in *Putting Asunder* and welcomed the rejection by that group of exclusive reliance on the concept of 'matrimonial offence'. The following alternative proposals, which the Commission thought could be implemented without insuperable legal difficulty, were made in the Report.[37]

(a) Breakdown without Inquest—a modification of the breakdown principle advocated in *Putting Asunder,* but dispensing in most cases with the elaborate inquest there suggested. The court would, on proof of a period of separation and in the absence of evidence to the contrary, assume that the marriage had broken down. . . .

(b) Divorce by Consent—This would be practicable only as an additional, and not a sole comprehensive, ground. It would not be more than a palliative and would probably be unacceptable except in the case of marriages in which there are no dependent children. Even in the case of childless marriages, if consent were the sole criterion, it might lead to the dissolution of marriages that had not broken irretrievably. . . .

(c) The Separation Ground—This would involve introducing as a ground for divorce a period of separation irrespective of which party was at fault, thereby affording a place in the law for the application of the breakdown principle. But since the period would be substantially longer than six months, it would be practicable only as an addition to the existing grounds based on matrimonial offence. . . .

The Report also proposed the following safeguards as necessary, if any of the above proposals were adopted :

(a) The three year waiting period . . . should be retained. . . .

(b) The court should have power to adjourn for a limited period to enable the possibilities of reconciliation to be explored. . . .

(c) The court should have a discretion to refuse a decree if attempts had been made by the petitioner wilfully to deceive it; but the present absolute and discretionary bars would be impracticable to petitions on these new grounds. . . .

(d) Additional safeguards would be needed to protect the respondent spouse and the children. These should include :—

(i) A procedure to ensure that the respondent's decision to consent to or not oppose a divorce, had been taken freely and with a full appreciation of the consequences. . . .

(ii) Retention, and possible improvement, of the provisions of the present law designed to ensure that satisfactory arrangements are made for the future of the children. . . .

(iii) Provisions protecting an innocent party from being divorced against his or her will unless equitable financial arrangements are made for him or her. . . .

The Report further stated that 'if the Separation Ground were added on the lines suggested and divorce became obtainable after two years' separation if the other party acquiesced, it would appear to be logical and sensible to reduce the presently prescribed period of desertion from three years to two'.

On 23rd November, 1966, the Report was actually debated by the House of Lords.

In the course of the debate it was suggested that the Archbishop's Group and the Law Commission should start discussions to see if the gap between their approach and ours could be bridged. This suggestion was taken up. The discussions have now been completed and we are satisfied that the gap can be bridged. As we said in our Report, it is for Parliament, not the Law Commission, to decide whether divorce law reform is desired and the nature of any such reform. . . . We are satisfied that, if Parliament were to accept the principle of breakdown as the basis of divorce, practical and feasible proposals, making use of the 'separation ground', could be prepared for the consideration of Parliament.[38]

The outcome of these discussions and the terms of their understanding with the Archbishop's group were published in July 1967, and it was also recorded in Appendix III to their *Third Annual Report*.[39] Eight proposals with eight notes were then put forward. They were supported by all the group with the exception of one member who abstained.[40] They maintained the principle (affirmed by the Church Assembly on 16th February) that the concept of breakdown of marriage should replace that of matrimonial offence and that it should become the sole and comprehensive ground for divorce. But in place of the proposed inquest, the Court was directed to infer breakdown in the absence of evidence to the contrary and on proof of the existence of certain matrimonial situations. 'The Law Commission is satisfied that these amended proposals would be practicable and could form the basis of a really worthwhile reform of the Divorce Law.'[41]

It will be noticed that section 5(1) in the proposals contained crucial clauses: (c) and (d).[42] These provided the reformers with further controversial grounds which later became the basis for the Clause 2(1) of the Divorce Reform Act 1969. This agreement between the Law Commission and the Archbishop's group formed the substantial basis of Mr Wilson's Bill—the one which was later reintroduced by Mr Alec Jones in 1968.

Neither Lord Gardiner, nor indeed any of the Law Commissioners, admit that they played any significant political or social role in divorce reform legislation other than by pursuing their statutory duties, by making reports, giving advice and supplying the necessary information. In other words, they describe their part of the work as purely legal and technical in character.[43] But even if they never emerged from their legal shell they effectively played a far greater role than any other single group involved in achieving a reform of the divorce law. And that role both in framing the Divorce Reform Bill itself and in creating a consensus of public opinion cannot be underestimated. One may perhaps call the Law Commission the hidden prompter in the drama of the Divorce Reform Act, while the sponsors of the Bill were the Official Directors and the main actors on the parliamentary stage.

Although the Lord Chancellor maintained in his speech at the Annual Conference of the National Marriage Guidance Council[44] that 'The Field of Choice recommends nothing', the Report did function as a practical and catalytic document. The Field of Choice and Consensus—the result of discussions between the Archbishop's group and the Law Commission—prepared the ground for reform. It clarified several vague points and indicated which of the available lines of approach were practicable; it sifted and narrowed down controversial views to debatable points and presented them to the public and the legislature. This was its major contribution to the legislation. It was also an immense help to the reformers in obtaining public support. Public opinion accepted Consensus as a reasonable and practicable proposal, and several newspapers assessed The Field of Choice as the most brilliantly written document on divorce ever published in England.

After November 1967 when Mr Wilson's Bill, which was drafted by the Law Commission,[45] was introduced in the Commons, the role of the Law Commission in divorce reform legislation became more significant, as will be seen in the succeeding chapters. When Mr Leo Abse had introduced his Bill six years before, he lacked[46] the advantages of its expert assistance because of course the Law Commission was not yet in existence. Messrs Wilson's and Jones's Bills, however, received a great deal of assistance from the Commission, and part of the success of their proposals must surely be attributed to the solid foundation of knowledge on which they rested.

In concluding this chapter, it may be fair to say that by establishing the Law Commissions, Lord Gardiner personally made an important contribution not only to the divorce law reform but also to the future prospects of keeping the law of England and Wales (and Scotland) in step with contemporary society.

NOTES

1 The Law Commissions Act 1965, § 1.

2 Scarman, Chairman of the Law Commission, 'The Law', *The Times* (3rd Oct., 1970).

3 The Law Commission for England and Wales, and the Scottish Law Commission. They were set up by § 1 and 2 respectively of the Law Commissions Act 1965.

4 See 'Factors in Political Socialisation', *Studies in British Politics*, ed. by R. Rose, p. 49.

5 *Law Reform Now* (1963), ed. Gardiner and Martin, describes their designs and claims on the law reform.

6 Matrimonial Causes Act 1967.

7 The Scottish Law Commission is also active in doing the same kind of job in Scotland.

8 The Law Commission, *First Annual Report, 1965–66*, p. 1

9 'A Programme was submitted on 17th November, received your Lordship's approval, on 14th January 1966 and was laid before Parliament on 26th January'. (Ibid.)

10 The Commissioners were prominent lawyers: Sir Leslie Scarman, O.B.E., Chairman; Mr L. C. B. Gower; Mr Neil Lawson, Q.C.; Mr N. S. Marsh, Q.C.; Mr Andrew Martin, Q.C.; Mr Arthur Stapleton Cotten, a special consultant to the Commission, was also appointed by the Lord Chancellor. The Secretary of the Commission is Mr J. M. Cartwright Sharp; its present offices are at Conquest House, 37/38 John Street, Theobalds Road, London WC1. As under the Law Commissions Act 1965, a Law Commissioner's term of

appointment cannot exceed five years, all five Commissioners had to be re-appointed, but Mr Andrew Martin, who returned to practice at the Bar, was replaced by Mr Claud Bicknell, O.B.E., a solicitor in active practice until appointed. Mr Arthur Stapleton Cotten also became a part-time consultant. Mr Lawson is now a justice of the High Court assigned to the Queen's Bench Division. Mr Gower has since retired from the Law Commission to take up an appointment as Vice-Chancellor of Southampton University. Professor Aubrey Diamond has been appointed in his place. Mr Derek Hodgson, Q.C., has been appointed in Mr Lawson's place.

11 At least three well-known reformers were appointed: Mr Martin was a co-editor with Lord Gardiner of the book *Law Reform Now*; Mr Gower was a prominent advocate of family law reform and a member of the Divorce Law Reform Union to which Lord Gardiner also belonged; and Mr Justice Scarman was also a specialist in family law and has been a judge in the Divorce Court. In fact these two lawyers—Mr Gower and Sir Leslie Scarman—played a decisive part in the Law Commission for divorce law reform.

12 Scarman, *Law Reform: The New Pattern* (1968), p. 7.

13 'Of course, we all regard the Law Commission with the very highest respect and admire the work which it does,' said Sir Lionel Heald in the Commons. See Official Report, Standing Committee B, col. 131.

14 Law Commission, *First Annual Report 1965–66*, p. 27.

15 Ibid., and Scarman, op. cit., p. 11.

16 Sir Leslie was referring to both the Commission of England and Wales and that of Scotland.

17 Scarman, in *The Times*, (3rd Oct., 1970); see also *Law Reform: The New Pattern*, pp. 10 *et seq.*

18 Scarman, 'Family Law and Law Reform'.

19 p. 25.

20 Ibid., p. 28.

21 *Law Reform: The New Pattern*, pp. 8 *et seq.*

22 See Scarman in *The Times* (3rd Oct., 1970).

23 There is no veto on what the Commission does outside its approved programme, but the Lord Chancellor is under no obligation to present to Parliament proposals made outside the ambit of the approved programme. Nevertheless, he normally does publish—*The Field of Choice* is an example (see p. 69, above).

24 *The Times* (3rd Oct., 1970).

25 The Law Commission (Law Com. No. 36), *Fifth Annual Report 1969–70*, pp. 19 *et seq.* A further nine bills influenced by Law Commission proposals are at present before Parliament.

26 Scarman, *Family Law and Law Reform*, p. 1. He made it clear that his views expressed in the lecture were purely personal, and were not to be regarded as those of the Law Commission.

27 Ibid., p. 2.

28 See Appendix IV.

29 A year later, on 21st July, 1967, this fiction was removed by the Matrimonial Causes Act 1967, which gave the Lord Chancellor power to designate any County Court as a Divorce Court to have jurisdiction over any un-

D

defended matrimonial causes, thus giving formal recognition to existing practice.

30 Four years after his speech at Bristol, the 1970 Administration of Justice Act guaranteed the rearrangement of the High Court to include a Family Division in place of the present one covering a job lot: Divorce, Probate and Admiralty, although no vesting date for this part of the Act has been fixed.

31 Scarman, *Family Law and Law Reform*, pp. 20–1.

32 In fact some of his ideas reached the Statute Book through these reports.

33 Hansard (House of Lords), Vol. 303, col. 317.

34 *Law Commissions Act 1965, First Programme of the Law Commission,* p. 11.

35 Cmnd 3123, p. 5.

36 Ibid., p. 10.

37 Ibid., pp. 53 *et seq.*

38 Law Commission, *Second Annual Report 1966–67,* p. 15.

39 Law Commission, *Third Annual Report 1967–68,* p. 11.

40 The one member who abstained did so because he took the view that once the group had reported it was *functus officio.*

41 Law Commission, *Third Annual Report 1967–68,* p. 30.

42 '. . . the parties had ceased to cohabit for a continuous period of at least two years and the respondent either
  (i)   had deserted the petitioner, or
  (ii) did not object to the grant of a divorce; or
  (iii) the parties had ceased to cohabit for a continuous period of not less than five years.'

In giving evidence to the Royal Commission on Marriage and Divorce, Professor Gower (now a Law Commissioner) had argued powerfully for the reform. He doubted whether there was any remedy other than abolishing divorce altogether or introducing divorce by consent and divorce based on a period of separation in the absence of consent. See the Morton Commission, *Evidence,* 1st Day, p. 15; and McGregor, op. cit., pp. 134 *et seq.*

43 Although Sir Leslie Scarman was technically head of the Family Law team, most of the actual work was done by Mr Gower and other staff members of the Law Commission.

44 5th May, 1967.

45 Contrary to Mr Ronald Butt's article in *The Times* (20th June, 1969), which blamed the Government for not having provided parliamentary draftsmen, the Government did provide the draftsmen. The parliamentary draftsmen attached to the Law Commission drafted Mr Wilson's Bill and the Law Commission helped the reformers throughout. See the Law Commission, *Third Annual Report 1967–68,* p. 11; and Hansard (House of Lords), Vol. 303, col. 315. See also p. 168, below.

46 After the committee stage, the aid of the Government's parliamentary draftsmen was given to him.

Chapter 5

THE DIVORCE LAW REFORM UNION

As already mentioned, the Divorce Law Reform Union was founded in 1906[1] by Mrs M. L. Seaton-Tiedemann. Sir Alan Herbert gives this description of Mrs Seaton-Tiedemann : 'This brave fighter had been at it for I don't know how many years, speaking in Hyde Park on Sundays, lobbying the House of Commons, writing letters and answering letters, and all the time keeping her little Union alive with hardly any resources.'[2] The Union supplied Mr A. P. Herbert with the Matrimonial Causes Bill and actively supported it, although they had earlier criticized Mr Herbert for not being successful in the ballot.[3] This criticism merely reflected a sad ignorance of parliamentary practice.

Unlike the CBI, the TUC or other strong pressure groups, the Divorce Law Reform Union was a small lobbyists' group 'with hardly any resources'. It lacked certain characteristics of a pressure group or even of an interest group. As S. E. Finer points out, it is fair to call the CBI or the TUC 'interest' groups : but the promotional and propaganda bodies, such as the CND (Campaign for Nuclear Disarmament) or the Abortion Law Reform Association do not represent 'interests' in the same sense at all. They represent a cause, not a social or economic stake in society. The DLRU is too weak to be a pressure group if 'pressure group' 'implies that some kind of sanction will be applied if a demand is refused'; nor is it accurate to call the DLRU an 'interest group'. Although we are not concerned with the definition of the term 'pressure' or 'interest' group or the 'lobby', it is convenient to see the characteristics of the DLRU through the definitions of these terms, as some people use the terms almost synonymously while others distinguish them.[4]

For example, for Finer, the 'lobby' is : 'The sum of organisations in so far as they are occupied at any point of time in trying to influence the policy of public bodies in their own chosen direction; though (unlike political parties) never themselves prepared to undertake the direct government of the country.' Stewart modifies Mackenzie's definition of a pressure group, '. . . the field of organised groups possessing both formal structure and real common interests, in so far as they influence the decisions of public bodies', into 'the field of organised groups possessing both formal structure

77

and real common interests, *in so far as they seek to influence the process of government'*. In the United States, lobbying is the process of 'addressing or soliciting members of a legislative body, in the lobby or elsewhere, with intent to influence legislation'.[5] If these definitions are more or less representative,[6] the DLRU may fall into the category of a lobbyist group, although we have already used the term pressure group as it is a more common expression, and will continue to do so when necessary.

The DLRU is a small group in comparison with the Church of England or other Church groups which have a national network. In terms of financial resources, strength or organization, membership, motive, or indeed from any other point of view, the DLRU is a much smaller and weaker lobbyist group than that giant religious organization, the Church of England, although both of them have been prominent figures in divorce law reform legislation. Yet this small lobbyist group, with only a little money, by writing letters and lobbying Parliament, struggled for divorce law reform. Admittedly, social change, together with the enthusiasm of a group of M.P.s for this kind of social reform, particularly divorce law reform, helped them greatly, as did the aid of the press and other media of communication. It is, rather, true to say that the members of the DLRU were outsiders who succeeded with the help of a few lawmakers in Parliament.

Past Presidents of the Union have been Sir Arthur Conan Doyle, and the First Earl of Birkenhead, former Attorney-General and Lord Chancellor. Past Vice-Presidents include[7] Sir Hall Caine, Professor Gilbert Murray and Bertrand Russell.[8]

The DLRU has nearly 300 active members and has for some time published pamphlets and bulletins advocating divorce reform legislation. It should be noted that the Union is a voluntary organization and is financed by funds donated mostly by its members and the receipts obtained from their publications. Consequently, there was no permanent independent office for the DLRU; there were two different addresses for mailing purposes.[9] They did not even have a proper meeting-place and often depended upon the goodwill of Miss Arnold[10] who generously offered her flat for the DLRU meetings and entertained its members there.

After three years of service for the Union as a member of the Committee, Mr Banks[11] became the Chairman of the Union in 1965. Mr Banks described the activities of the Union by saying that they had tried to educate the public by holding public meetings, the average cost for a meeting being about £40. He also mentioned Mr Stephen Keleney, a solicitor and one-time secretary of the Union, who contacted the Hopkins Donations Fund of Santa

Barbara, California, from which the Divorce Law Reform Union received £300 for its campaign fund. Mr Banks gave full credit for obtaining the £300 to this unfortunate lawyer who later committed suicide,[12] and said that it was the largest amount of money the Union had ever received. Much of this money later became an important part of the fund for their parliamentary campaign.

Indeed there was a time when the business of the Union did not run smoothly and there were difficulties in administration, although they tried to have regular meetings every month. Until 1967 the DLRU's main activities consisted in having public meetings and advertising their beliefs. It was at the time when the abortion law reform campaign had reached its climax that the DLRU also launched its active campaign. It was this campaign that brought an interesting meeting between Mr Banks and Mr Service, an energetic and articulate young man who was then thirty-five years old. His profession was described[13] as writer, publisher and lobbyist, working for ALRA (Abortion Law Reform Association) as its Parliamentary Officer. On Thursday, 16th March, 1967, after attending a public meeting at Livingstone House, where Mr Leo Abse delivered a speech to an audience of about a hundred people, Mr Service made himself known to the Chairman and other officials of the Union. He also proffered his help if the DLRU needed it and volunteered for service when his own campaign for Abortion Law Reform was completed. Mr Service also invited Mr Banks to luncheon. Mr Banks brought the case of Mr Service before the Committee[14] of the DLRU and the Committee decided to offer Mr Service a suitable position[15] in the Union, because they needed someone who could handle their campaign effectively. Mr Banks agreed with Mr Service that the latter should join the DLRU as soon as the ALRA campaign was over.

Upon the successful passage through both Houses of Parliament of the controversial Medical Termination of Pregnancy Bill (13th July, 1967), Mr Service formally joined the DLRU and became one of the most formidable men in the divorce law reform campaign. If accidents affect politics, Mr Service's joining ALRA, which eventually led him to the DLRU, represents a case in point, although on Mr Banks's part it may have been the result of an intentional campaign. Mr Banks certainly found the man he had been looking for. *The Times* commented (30th Oct., 1967): 'The Divorce Law Reform Union has also had a significant recruit. Mr Alastair Service, the Abortion Law Reform Association's Parliamentary Liaison Officer. Service, publisher and writer, naturally worked closely with David Steel's whip, Peter Jackson.'

Mr Service had read History at Queen's College, Oxford. He

recalls his student life as ordinary but he was already slightly interested in some kinds of social reform. His grandparents belonged to the Church of Scotland, although Mr Service himself is a nominal member of the Church of England. He became an agnostic when he was at Oxford but was 'not an atheist'. He did not believe in the doctrine of Christian marriage—indissolubility. In describing himself to the present writer he used three words: 'intelligent', 'arrogant' and 'ambitious'. To the question 'Why did you work so hard, spending your own money and time?' he replied : 'I suppose I have always worried about the futility of my life. I wanted to do something useful to justify my own existence.' Although an avowed agnostic, Mr Service explained that his motive was rooted in his 'puritanical conscience' and that he wanted to do something for those who were less fortunate. He claimed that he had no desire for power nor had any plan to run in politics. He simply thought that he had found something which was worth doing as well as being challenging.

His career as an amateur lobbyist had begun with ALRA. He had learned how to organize, how to promote, and how to lobby in Parliament during the campaign for abortion law reform.[16] He was already fairly well known and confident in the corridors of Westminster by the time he joined the DLRU. Since 1967, Mr Service organized campaigns to support the two Divorce Reform Bills and played a most important role in these campaigns.[17]

In any so-called modern free democratic country, the success of political campaigns largely depends upon available funds. However, when Mr Service joined the DLRU, there was only about £500[18] and nothing more. There was neither a paid secretary for the Union, nor a comfortable office to work in. There was only a list of about 300[19] members of the Union; among them appear the names of Lord Gardiner and Professor Gower (now a Law Commissioner), although Lord Gardiner resigned from the movement before he became Lord Chancellor.

Nevertheless, this small group of people had made a considerable impact on the movement for divorce reform legislation. The *Scottish Daily Express* (20th Dec., 1967) described the group for divorce law reform as follows : 'Mainly a group of Labour M.P.s including Leo Abse, Peter Jackson, William Hamling and Lena Jeger, plus the man who created what *The Times* called "the most sophisticated pressure group of recent times"—Alastair Service, Parliamentary Liaison Officer for abortion law reform.'

What was the attitude of the DLRU toward divorce? They believed that when a marriage has completely broken down, it should be dissolved as quickly as possible with the minimum of bitterness and suffering. Before that last stage is reached every effort can be made to reconcile the parties to the marriage . . . when, however, it is clear that a marriage has failed, a just divorce law should free the two partners. Such a law will not increase the number of men and women who are free to marry more suitable partners. . . . The DLRU can find no better words to sum up its attitude to the problem than those used in the Law Commissioner's 1966 Report. . . .[20] We believe that this attitude will have the support of humane people of all creeds.[21]

Proposals made by the DLRU for the reform of the divorce laws were : '. . . in addition to the existing grounds for divorce there should be added grounds' that :

1. the marriage can be dissolved with the consent or acquiescence of both partners after a separation of two years.

2. the marriage may be dissolved after a couple have been separated for five years and there is no prospect of reconciliation, even though one of the partners does not wish for divorce. In the latter case, the granting of a divorce should be subject to safeguards for the protection of the financial position of the partner not wanting divorce. . . . When new divorce legislation is introduced, a thorough revision should be made of the present system regarding financial provisions after divorce and the security of divorced partners and children. The law of domicile should also be revised.[22]

There was nothing new in the DLRU's campaign techniques; they mainly involved : holding public meetings, writing and answering letters and lobbying Parliament. They made a list of likely supporters and used all available tactics to approach and persuade Members of Parliament. They also published a number of bulletins and reports as well as contributing articles to magazines and daily newspapers. Their influential sympathizers included the highest law officer of the land, the Lord Chancellor, and a Law Commissioner.

The next stage in the long struggle to alter the Divorce Law of England was opened by Mr William Wilson's Bill.

NOTES

1 Incorporated 1914.

2 *The Ayes Have It*, p. 73.

3 The report of the Union said: 'We believed, like many thousands of others throughout the country, who had followed his great Press publicity, that Mr Herbert would be a great fighter for this cause, but he appears to have faltered. . . .' See Herbert, op. cit., pp. 41 and 73.

4 See S. E. Finer, *Anonymous Empire* (1966), pp. 1 *et seq.*; J. D. Stewart, *British Pressure Groups* (1958), pp. 1 *et seq.*; and W. J. M. Mackenzie, 'Pressure Groups in British Government', *British Journal of Sociology* (July 1955), p. 137.

5 *Webster's New International Dictionary.* Finer's term 'lobby' covers 'both classes of organisation, since it embraces all groups but only in so far as they seek to influence public policy'. (*Anonymous Empire*, p. 4.)

6 Obviously, the point is arguable but it is not essential to our discussion here.

7 Past Vice-Presidents: Lord Aberconway, Lady Camrose, Sir John Cockburn, the Hon. John Collier, G. S. P. Haynes, Admiral Sir W. H. Henderson, Sir Henry Norman, Eden Phillpotts, Sir Frederick Pollock, Mrs Bernard Shaw, Lord Snell, Lord Sydenham, and Dr Alic Drysdale Vickery.

8 The present officers are: President, Lord Meston; Chairman, Mr R. V. Banks; Joint Vice-Chairmen, the Marquess of Donegall and Mrs Margaret Munsey; Secretary, Mrs E. Ramsden; and Treasurer, Mr Charles Skilton. See also p. 79, above.

9 The addresses of the Union: 39 Clabon Mews, London, SW1, which is the official address; and the Marquess of Donegall's business office, 50 Alexandra Road, London SW19, was also used for mailing purposes. However, later Mr Service used 47 Boundary Road, London NW8 as mailing address.

10 See p. 79, above.

11 Mr Banks, an agnostic although a baptized member of the Church of England, was not happily married and had been through a series of divorce suits. He volunteered to join the DLRU by writing a letter to the Union after he saw its address in a newspaper. His motive for the reform of the divorce law was based on personal experience.

12 Reportedly because of his own matrimonial trouble.

13 *The Times* (30th Oct., 1967).

14 Five members of the Committee: Mr R. V. Banks, Chairman; Charles Skilton, Joint Vice-Chairman; Mrs Margaret Munsey, Hon. Secretary; Capt. R. L. P. Sergeant, Hon. Treasurer; and Miss Roxanne Arnold, Barrister and one-time Treasurer.

15 That of Parliamentary Officer on a voluntary and unpaid basis.

16 See K. Hindell and M. Simms, *Abortion Law Reformed* (1971), pp. 122 *et seq.*

17 The *Sunday Times*, 21st April, 1968, reported the description made by Mrs M. Simms, Vice-Chairman of ALRA, of Mr Service's activities as 'invaluable'.

18 Mostly from the donation made by the American Hopkins Donations Fund, and their subscription fees and other small donations.

19 According to my count, there were 293 members in the list, but 42 had either resigned, were deceased, or their addresses were unknown. Therefore, the official number of the DLRU members must have been around 293—42 = 251. There were 83 females, 5 peers, 5 clergymen, 11 doctors, 10 service officers and one knight. The rest of them represented various professions, including several professors.

20 See p. 100, above, and *The Field of Choice*, p. 53.

21 See the DLRU's *Divorce in a Modern Society* (1968).

22 Ibid., p. 2.

PART THREE

Chapter 6

DEVELOPMENTS IN 1967

I. *Preparation*

On 18th June, 1967, the *Sunday Times* reported its poll conducted by the Opinion Research Centre. According to the *Sunday Times*, 'there is widespread support in Britain for making the breakdown of a marriage the sole ground for divorce. The proposal was first put forward in 1966 by the Archbishop of Canterbury's Commission. This year it has been supported by the Church Assembly and, in a personal capacity, by Lord Gardiner, the Lord Chancellor.' The result indicated that 72 per cent of the population agreed with the reform plan, while one person in ten claimed to be adamantly opposed to divorce in any circumstance. The details are:

Divorce is always wrong and should not be allowed:

Agree	11%
Disagree	85%
Don't know	3%

Any couple should be able to get a divorce when they both want it:

Agree	48%
Disagree	48%
Don't know	3%

Divorce should be allowed where a marriage has clearly broken down and in no other circumstances:

Agree	72%
Disagree	24%
Don't know	4%

The poll revealed several striking differences in attitudes when the responses were analysed into different categories. Labour voters, those over 65 and members of the lower working class all took a sterner view. While 10 per cent, or less, of all other age groups said that divorce is wrong in all circumstances, 23 per cent—almost one in four—of those over 65 took this line. Whereas only 6 per cent of upper- and middle-class voters said divorce should not be allowed, 17 per cent of the unskilled working class took this stance.

On the other hand, the young were more liberal : 91 per cent—the highest percentage—of those aged 21–34 disagreed with the statement that divorce is always wrong and should not be allowed. A considerably higher percentage of this category than of any other believed that any couple should be able to get a divorce when both want it. The *Sunday Times* pointed out that, for this reason, perhaps, fewer people in this age group than in others support the idea that breakdown of marriage should be the only ground for divorce; it also emphasized that 'it would, of course, be wrong to expect most people to have clearly thought out any logical views on a subject of this kind. The poll should be thought of as measuring not rational and detailed opinions, but reactions to different propositions', as some people apparently gave contradictory answers.

Nevertheless, it indicated the general attitude of the public towards divorce and later polls confirmed the trends. It was pleasant news for the reformers during the summer of 1967, and they thought that time would turn the tide more clearly in their favour.

As a matter of fact, during this summer, another important event was taking place in the history of divorce law reform in England. Following the publication of *Putting Asunder*, and, in November 1966, the appearance of *The Field of Choice*, discussions had been going on between the Archbishop's group and the Law Commission in an attempt to bridge the gap between the views which each body had put forward. The outcome was reported in a statement issued by the Law Commission in late July.[1] Eight proposals with eight notes[2] were widely reported in the lay press, although, as a result of condensation and selection, they were, in some instances, mis-stated, or at any rate presented in a misleading form, as the *New Law Journal* stated in its issue of 3rd August, 1967.

Nevertheless, the agreement received favourable comment from the press. The Law Commission's statement that it was satisfied that those amended proposals would be practicable and could form the basis of a really worth-while reform of the divorce law became a decisive punch-line for the reformers. The proposals were supported by the Archbishop's group, which was therefore also responsible[3] for them, and this provided the reformers with a sound basis on which to work. Agreement had finally been reached on the issue, bringing a fairly clear line into the controversial arguments. It removed a great deal of ambiguity and prepared the ground for the reform of the law.

Towards the end of this eventful July, Mr Abse called a meeting of twenty interested Labour M.P.s in the House of Commons, to tell them about his discussions with the Bishop of Exeter, hoping that the Government would move the Bill. Mr Abse was also ready to build a parliamentary group in the hope of getting the Bill through. In his turn, the Chairman of the DLRU, Mr R. V. Banks, made an announcement[4] on behalf of the DLRU supporting the proposals accepted by the Law Commission and the Archbishop's group. However, the leaders of the Roman Catholic Church made no comment on the proposals and it later became clear that they had not changed their attitude. It was obvious that there were divisions of opinion on divorce amongst Roman Catholics, but on the whole they still held to their traditional view—indissolubility of marriage, which was, in principle, the most rigid barrier to divorce reform legislation.

Another important event was that on 3rd September the Lord Chancellor, Lord Gardiner, wrote to Mr Abse urging his group to get the Bill before Parliament in the coming session, even without the financial provisions which were under consideration by the Law Commission. This assured the reformers that they would have Lord Gardiner's advice and help during the session. Accordingly, Mr Leo Abse was busy working out his strategy before the new session started.

With these events the summer was over, and on 30th October, 1967, *The Times* described the legislative situation in Parliament and the prospect of divorce reform as follows :

Hanging was abolished, the law on homosexuality had been liberalised, and then the Abortion Act has been safely passed. What next? Divorce law reform, most likely. A group of Labour M.P.s—Leo Abse, Peter Jackson, Lena Jeger, William Hamling and others—had already been set up to press the Government to give time for legislation. In their view the Law Commission's recommendations had been widely accepted and reform should not therefore be left to the luck of the Private Members' draw. . . .

On the same day Mr Heath said on television[5] that 'divorce is next on the reformer's list'. Then, on 1st November, the day after the Queen's Speech, the Leader of the House, Mr Richard Crossman, in a briefing to journalists, said that the Government was smoothing the way for divorce reform on the lines of *Putting Asunder*— without disclosing how far things had progressed since the 'impracticable' document was published. None the less, by this time it became clear that the Government was in favour of a new divorce reform bill, although, as Mr Murray Sayle[6] put it, they still regarded it as a 'hot potato'.

On 8th November in the Commons, Mrs McKay begged to give

notice that on Friday, 24th November, she would call attention to the subject of divorce law reform, and move a resolution.[7]

In practice, however, the only hope for the reformers was to win a number in the first five or six in the ballot for private members' bills,[8] and they knew the odds against that were very high. But if someone were lucky enough to draw a number within the first ten, they could try and wait for other earlier numbers to be withdrawn. Many of them eagerly wrote down their names, but there was no luck for the divorce law reformers.

Indeed, the ballot is an unsatisfactory method of deciding what legislative proposals shall be discussed in Parliament, but there is perhaps no better alternative, as every member thinks that his bill is as important as another's if not more so; and the limited time has to be distributed somehow. The ballot may, however, play a very crucial part in the modern legislative process. One may argue that the point is different, but late in 1970 there was a case ruled by a branch of the Government that selecting a teacher by lot was invalid even though the candidates have equal qualifications. If selection by lot is denied in the administrative process, why should it be permitted in the legislative process? Which is more important is debatable, but certainly the effects of an Act could be more far-reaching than the influence of a teacher over a limited number of students.

II. *Mr Wilson's Bill*

In any case, on Thursday, 9th November, 1967, Mr William Wilson (Labour, Coventry, S.) was successful in the ballot. He learned through his local Coventry newspaper the next day that he had drawn number four and decided to go back to London. On his way to Parliament, Mr Wilson recalled his Law Society's final examination and the first case which he handled as a solicitor in 1938 at Coventry under the Herbert Act 1937. Although he was not one of those who were closely associated with Mr Leo Abse, he was interested in social reform and thought of presenting a bill which would bring about a meaningful change in English social life. When he arrived in London, however, he found that the *Evening Standard* was already reporting his intention of introducing a divorce bill, despite the fact that he had not yet said a word about the matter. It ran : '. . . one of these men[9] will sponsor the Bill to change our laws . . . the name of the M.P. who will sponsor a Bill to reform the divorce law is expected to be known by Monday'. The paper also mentioned that efforts were being made by Mr Leo Abse and his divorce law reform group of Labour M.P.s to interest Mr Wilson in sponsoring the Bill. There was also another member, Mr William Hamling (Labour, Woolwich) who drew number nine, mentioned in the same column as a man likely to introduce a divorce reform bill. Thus politics by parliamentary lobby correspondents was in action.

One may wonder whether the press report influenced Mr Wilson's intentions, but it seems that his motives were in fact fairly simple and well grounded. As a solicitor, he had handled many divorce cases and felt that something ought to be done to reform an irrational law and to redress the prevailing injustice.[10] Nevertheless, he had not been successful in drawing a lucky number until that moment, when he decided to dedicate his time to the cause of divorce law reform.

Another important factor which must be mentioned here is that on 10th November, 1967, before Mr Wilson announced his intention to introduce a divorce reform bill, the *Daily Telegraph* also[11] reported : '. . . the Government seeks a Divorce Reform Bill sponsor . . . if the Government can find an M.P. who came high in the ballot, prepared to introduce the Bill, it would give him drafting and other assistance'. The following event also speaks for the Lord Chancellor's concern over the issue. Mr Wilson's statement of his willingness to introduce a divorce reform bill was made on Friday, 10th November, 1967, and the following Monday, 13th November, the Lord Chancellor wrote a letter to him expressing his concern over the Bill and inviting him to lunch to discuss it.

Thus, in addition to his genuine motive, events and comments inside and outside of Parliament clearly indicated which bill would be most likely to have a good chance of success, and this might have encouraged Mr Wilson to take his chance.

On 11th November, 1967, *The Times* prematurely reported :

Mr Wilson will take over a Bill which has already been prepared by the Lord Chancellor on the basis of the recommendations of the Law Commission.[12] The most important clause is one which would include the concept of 'breakdown of marriage' as a ground for divorce in addition to the present matrimonial offences of adultery, desertion and cruelty.

Then the *Evening Standard* contributed an article (15th Nov., 1967) about Mr Wilson, and said that he had been identified with a number of social reforms; the previous week he had supported Mr Quintin Hogg's private bill to give more aid to unmarried mothers. In the same paper, Mr Wilson's own words also appeared as follows: 'I wasn't really a part of the Leo Abse group but when I came fourth on the Private Members' Ballot Box I decided this was my chance.'

Mr Leo Abse[13] immediately started selecting the sponsors of the Bill, since a bill must be backed by at least twelve members. Mr Abse also arranged a meeting with the Lord Chancellor who was due to leave for Holland. Upon Mr Abse's request, Lord Gardiner agreed to see them and the meeting was arranged for 4.30 p.m., Monday, 20th November, 1967.

On the other hand, on 14th November, following a letter from Mr Banks congratulating Mr Wilson on his decision to introduce a bill to reform the divorce law, Mr Alastair Service wrote to Mr Wilson, introducing himself and offering the DLRU's support. Mr Service also met Sir George Sinclair (Conservative, Dorking) who willingly agreed to support the Bill and to meet Mr Wilson. Mr Service sent out copies of a new leaflet to over 250 M.P.s known to be particularly interested in social reform, and was ready to send out others when the right moment came.

Public reaction was immediate; letters, for and against, were continually arriving. Mr Gerald Sanctuary, a solicitor and the National Secretary of the National Marriage Guidance Council[14], wrote a letter expressing concern over the Bill, while the BBC, Granada Television and the *Birmingham Post* expressed their interest in Mr Wilson's Bill. On 18th November, 1967, an article appeared in *The Economist* indicating the climate of the time :

> There seems a good chance that reform of the divorce law will be accomplished this Session. An M.P. with a high place in the ballot for private members' bills has agreed to sponsor a measure, and he has been promised Government support for it—although this may, of course, not be forthcoming if considerable opposition to the bill is apparent among Labour back-benchers on its second reading.

On 21st November, Lord Gardiner wrote to Mr Wilson and confirmed their luncheon meeting on 1st December to discuss the matter.

On 23rd November, Mr Wilson met Mr Service, who suggested that there were a number of Conservative M.P.s who would possibly sponsor the Bill. These included Sir John Foster, Sir George Sinclair and Mr Nicholas Ridley. Mr Service also agreed that he would contact the National Opinion Poll to see if they would do an Opinion Poll (free of charge). On 28th November, 1967, Mrs Eirene White wrote to the National Council of Women of Great Britain expressing her attitude, which was 'strongly in favour of reform in the divorce laws'. The atmosphere, however, was not always so cheerful;[15] for example, on the very same day, 28th November, Lady Summerskill wrote to Mr Wilson informing him of her opposition to the Bill, to which Mr Wilson immediately replied.[16]

On the same day, Mr Leo Abse was ready to write to Mr Wilson suggesting the names of the following sponsors:[17]

Conservative:	Labour:
Mr Ian Gilmour	Mr Leo Abse
Mr Nicholas Ridley	Mr Peter Jackson
Mr Anthony Royle	Mrs Lena Jeger
Sir George Sinclair	Mr David Kerr
Dame Joan Vickers	Mr John Parker

Liberal: Emlyn Hooson

The sponsors, therefore, were made up of five Conservative and five Labour M.P.s and one Liberal. Thus they were considered by many to represent a well-balanced cross-section of the House.

Upon receiving Mr Abse's letter, Mr Wilson met the potential sponsors and on 29th November formally presented the Bill 18 to the House.[18] On the same day, *The Guardian* had reported a list of the sponsors and the date of the second reading as 9th February, 1968. Subsequently, Mr Wilson sent a letter of thanks to the sponsors; but some of them were worried by the date of the second reading. They had hoped to have it as soon as possible, so that the Bill would have sufficient time for the remaining stages.

By this time, the campaign for the Bill was making steady progress. On 29th November, on behalf of the DLRU, Mr Service sent a copy of the draft questions for Opinion Polls to Mr Wilson, and Mr Banks invited Mr Wilson to the House of Lords cocktail party on the 11th to speak 'a few words' about the Bill, to which Mr Wilson agreed. On 12th December, he also accepted an invitation from the National Council of Women of Great Britain to attend their conference on 1st February, 1968, at which the Bill would be discussed. By the time Mr Wilson's article on the Divorce Reform Bill appeared in the *New Law Journal* on 14th December, Mr Leo Abse had an assurance from the Leader of the House, Mr Richard Crossman, who promised to do his best to help the Bill go through. The Attorney-General also confirmed the intention of the Government to give the House an opportunity to make up its mind on the issue.

Then, on 18th December, from the Conservative front bench, Sir Edward Boyle wrote back to Mr Service:

... Yes, I am strongly in favour of legislation on these lines, but one point which does cause concern—even to those of us who have no social or religious objections to the widening of the divorce laws—is, what is to happen to the widow's pension for women divorced under the circumstances set out in the Bill? ... While I am strongly opposed to the notion that a matrimonial offence should be a *sine qua non* for a divorce, I should consider it unjust that a woman, who is deserted by her husband and has herself committed no offence, should be deprived of the right to a widow's pension when the time comes. I should be very interested to hear the views of the Divorce Law Reform Union on this point.

Sir Edward Boyle's letter was representative of many which expressed concern over this issue, and it led the reformers to consider the Bill's financial provisions more carefully.

On 20th December, 1967, the drafting of the Bill was completed, the short title given it by the Lord Chancellor's Office being the Divorce Reform Bill 1968. In a letter to Mr Wilson from the Lord Chancellor's Office, the formal attitude of the Government was clearly stated: '. . . although the Government have arranged for the drafting of a Bill to give effect to the proposals agreed between the Law Commission and the Archbishop's Group, they are not committed to any view on the policy of the Bill as a whole or any of its provisions in particular'.

On the same day, an article from Lady Lothian, warning the British public that the Bill 'may give England and Wales the most liberal divorce laws in the world', appeared in the *Scottish Daily Express*. The Earl of Balfour, Vice-President of the DLRU, was surprised by the article and immediately wrote to Mr Banks suggesting that he should look for someone, if possible a Catholic, who could write in reply to it, since in any event Lady Lothian had not seen the Bill. Lord Balfour also offered his support to Mr Wilson in a personal letter which he sent with a copy of his letter to Mr Banks.

From 22nd December, many national newspapers, magazines and other small papers, such as *The People* and *Tribune*, asked Mr Wilson to contribute articles or discuss the matter with them so that they could use it in an issue early in the new year. Thus the Bill received wide publicity and in general the press and public appeared to favour it.

In late December 1967 Mr Service was preparing to send out another 370 letters, after receiving replies from about 200 M.P.s promising their support for the Bill. In a letter to Mr Wilson written on 28th December, 1967, Mr Service stated that he would expect about 170 members to be present on 9th February for the second reading, although he mentioned that the DLRU was hoping to get a vote of at least 200 for the Bill so that they could get a strong Standing Committee and show the Government that there was real interest in the subject. Mr Wilson privately (i.e. before it was disclosed to the public) sent a copy of the draft of the Bill to Mr Service, and he studied it with the DLRU's legal secretary, Mr Michael Cohen, so that he could send their joint comments to Mr Wilson.

On the other hand, the opponents of the Bill, including a former Attorney-General, Sir Lionel Heald (Conservative, Chertsey), Mr Kenneth Lewis (Conservative, Rutland and Stamford) and Dame Irene Ward, were busy inside and outside Parliament attempting to unite public opposition, which was reflected in such activities as Mr Latey's letters of protest to the newspapers and the resolutions of women's organizations. Although the opponents were not as well organized as the promoters of the Bill, their strength was not to be discounted. On 4th January, 1968, after receiving a letter from the Law Society's secretary for law reform concerning their interest in financial clauses, Mr Wilson received a letter from Mr Service which ran :

> As you say we shall certainly receive substantial opposition and I have had several telephone calls from the Press who have spoken to people opposed to the Bill. Much alarmism is going on about the financial provisions and we are preparing a leaflet for circulation as soon as possible, pointing out the various safeguards already available to divorced women. . . .

Many reformers recall that they felt a kind of chill, although they thought they represented majority sentiment both inside and outside Parliament.

The DLRU Committee meeting on Tuesday, 2nd January, discussed Lord Balfour's letter to the DLRU, mentioned above. On the decision of the Committee, Mr Banks wrote on 5th January to the Editor of the *Scottish Daily Express*, replying to Lady Lothian's article. When the Bill is published, he commented, 'Lady Lothian will find that if the Bill is passed divorce could well be more difficult, not less, for the unscrupulous. . . .' It was a typical letter of protest written by a lobbyist group against what was called 'a very misleading piece of journalism'. On the same day, Mr Service also wrote a campaign letter to the *Spectator*, in which he commented on an article by R. A. Cline entitled 'Divorce English-Style', which had appeared in the paper on 22nd December, 1967. He stressed that the DLRU did not pretend to have any final answer to the question of what the law of divorce should be, but asserted : 'We believe that Mr William Wilson's Bill should be a major step in the long process of improvement.'

On 16th January, 1968, the BBC sent a contract sheet to Mr Wilson for a discussion in the programme *Whicker's World* on 8th February, which Mr Wilson's secretary confirmed, as Mr Wilson was in India at the time.

The reports of the National Opinion Polls and Gallup Poll were published respectively in the *Daily Mail* on 16th January, 1968 (NOP), and in the *Daily Telegraph* on 8th February, 1968 (Gallup). The principal results were :

NOP

Question

Should the divorce laws be changed?	44% Yes 39% No
Should complete breakdown of marriage be the principal ground for divorce?	55% Yes 34% No
Should the fact that the couple have lived apart for two years and both agree to divorce be a reason for divorce?	60% Yes 29% No
Should the fact that the couple have lived apart for five years and only one of them wants it be a reason for divorce?	71% Yes 10% No
Is it better for a child to live with one divorced parent rather than two unhappily married parents?	61% Yes 31% No

GALLUP

Question
Should the divorce laws
be changed?

	1968	*1958*	*Change*
Leave as it is :	39%	51%	− 12
Easier :	34%	28%	+ 6
More difficult :	20% ⎫	10% ⎫	+ 6
	⎬ 27%	⎬ 21%	
Not allowed at all :	7% ⎭	11% ⎭	

Do you approve or disapprove of these provisions in the Divorce
Bill :—

(1) That the complete breakdown of the marriage is to be the
    only ground for divorce?

(2) That no one can petition for divorce within three years of
    marriage except in cases of exceptional hardship?

(3) That a court shall be able to adjourn every divorce case for
    up to three months for attempts at reconciliation?

	Approve	*Disapprove*	*Don't know*
Complete breakdown only ground :	48%	37%	15%
Three years' rule :	62%	26%	12%
Three months' adjournment :	71%	18%	11%
That the husband and wife have lived apart for at least two years and both agree to divorce	70%	17%	*Undecided* 13%
That the husband and wife have lived apart for at least five years even when only one of them wants a divorce :	56%	26%	18%
It is better for a child to live with one divorced parent rather than two unhappily married parents :	83%	10%	7%

The polls speak for themselves : the majority supported the reform.
   On 8th February, 1968, in a leading article headed 'Divorce at
Will', the *Daily Telegraph* commented on the results of the Poll :

> Sponsors of the Divorce Bill, which comes up for the second
> reading in the Commons tomorrow, will derive at least some
> measure of satisfaction from the results of the Gallup Poll which
> we publish this morning. They show substantial majorities for
> the views that two years' separation accompanied by mutual
> willingness for divorce and five years' separation plus a demand
> for divorce from one partner alone both constitute evidence of
> the irretrievable breakdown of marriage. . . .

The article's main objection, however, was to the lack of protection for wives and children. It also carried an article under the
heading 'Tories Will Try to Kill Divorce Bill' : 'A group of Conservative M.P.s, led by Sir Lionel Heald, a former Attorney-General,

will try to kill the Divorce Reform Bill at the end of tomorrow's
debate in the Commons. . . .' The back-benchers published a Commons motion that the House should decline to give a second reading to the Bill. It said that the Bill failed to ensure proper protection
for wives and children, particularly over pensions. The motion was
supported by Sir Lionel Heald, Dame Irene Ward, Mrs Jill Knight
and Mr Norman St John-Stevas. Then, on 10th February, the
Daily Telegraph reported a further movement of opposition by
carrying an article with the heading 'Tories Attack . . . Roman
Catholic[19] Voice' : 'The attack on the Bill is being led by Sir
Lionel Heald . . . Roman Catholics on both sides of the House, particularly Mr Norman St John-Stevas, Conservative M.P. for
Chelmsford, are supporting him. . . .'

During the week, Mr Wilson's draft of the whipping letter was
completed :

> . . . the Divorce Reform Bill is due to have its Second Reading
> on Friday, 9th February, 1968. This Bill has, perhaps, a better
> chance of success than other recent attempts to reform the
> divorce laws. We cannot deal with all aspects of the divorce law
> in the Bill, but I believe it will go a long way to establish in
> statutory form a change in the divorce law acceptable to wide
> sections of the community. The Bill is now published and its
> sponsors are Mr Leo Abse, Dame Joan Vickers, Mr Ian Gilmour,
> Mr Emlyn Hooson, Mr Peter Jackson, Mrs Lena Jeger, Sir
> George Sinclair, Dr David Kerr, Mr John Parker, Mr Nicholas
> Ridley and Mr Anthony Royle.
>
> On Friday, 9th February at 4.00 p.m. we shall require at least
> 100 supporters to vote for the closure. It is, moreover, important
> to obtain as large a majority as possible to demonstrate the
> interest of the House in the Bill. I am seeking your help in
> this. . . .

With only two weeks to go to the second reading stage, Mr Peter
Jackson invited all the sponsors, together with members of the
Steering Committee, to attend a meeting. Mr Jackson particularly
reminded Mr Wilson of the fact that 'some of the sponsors are
somewhat anxious as there appears to have been little consultation.
I very much hope therefore that you will be able to attend. We
can then discuss tactics, etc.' The meeting had been changed from
30th January to 1st February, as Mr Leo Abse could not manage
the earlier times arranged.

In fact, from 6th January to 27th January, while Mr Wilson was
away, the reformers' affairs had been largely taken care of by Mr
Abse and Mr Jackson in the Commons, while the DLRU was

mobilizing its full capacity inside and outside Parliament. Upon returning from India Mr Wilson joined in the campaign and lobbied until the last day, 9th February, when the second reading was given.

On 25th January, the Humanist lobby, a division of the British Humanist Association, circulated a leaflet urging the members to write to their M.P.s in support of the Bill.

As a Private Member's Bill, it is not subject to the party whips, and is therefore threatened by the possibility of being talked out if not enough supporters attend the debate. (M.P.s like to get away to their constituencies on Friday.) The fullest possible attendance is required to avert this danger and if possible to inflict a demoralising defeat on the Bill's opponents. It is urgent, therefore, that *all* humanist lobby correspondents write immediately to their M.P.s urging them to support the Bill on 9th February. If you do nothing else, at least please write to your M.P. today.

It also pointed to the activities of the opponents :

The opposition that is building up to the Bill is from two main sources : the churches (who see a threat to the permanence and holiness of matrimony) and some feminists (who see in the Bill a threat to the status of women and financial dangers for divorced wives). The Bill is the result of a compromise following reports from the Law Commission, the Methodists and the Church of England Committee under the Bishop of Exeter. However, the Church of England is now split on the Bill : the Archbishop of Canterbury has denounced the provision for divorce by consent after two years' separation and the cutting to two years of the period for divorce following desertion; while some of the bishops give the Bill their reluctant support. . . .

These developments did not mean that the reformers had enough support for the Bill. Within a week, on 30th January, the Mothers' Union sent their document setting out the considered opinion of the Union, and emphasizing that they represented 392,170 members in the United Kingdom. Nor did they forget to add in their letter to Mr Wilson, 'many of whom are resident in your Constituency'. However, the Mothers' Union made it clear that they did 'not wish to oppose the introduction of breakdown of marriage as the sole ground for divorce, in place of the matrimonial offence, provided that the evidence adduced to support the petition shows clearly and indisputably that the marriage relationship has broken down totally and irretrievably'. Their attitude towards the Bill was principally

along the lines put forward by *Putting Asunder* and they urged that
'amendment should be made in the Bill to ensure that the children
of the second union are not given security at the expense of the
first'. Unless the Bill was amended on the lines they suggested, not
only would a grave injustice be done to the women of this country,[20]
but the very foundation of the law—that a person should not be
able to benefit by his wrongdoing—would, they concluded, be
destroyed.

The Open Door Council for the Economic Emancipation of the
Woman Worker, the National Union of Townswomen's Guilds, the
National Federation of Business and Professional Women's Clubs of
Great Britain and Northern Ireland, the Fawcett Society and the
Married Women's Association were equally active and they too
expressed their concern. Most of them welcomed various aspects of
the proposed Divorce Bill, but pointed out their misgivings about
the welfare of deserted wives and children.

On 1st February, the National Council of Women of Great
Britain, at its conference, adopted a resolution by a vote of 112 to 6 :

. . . the National Council of Women considers that where a
husband and wife have ceased to cohabit the law governing
divorce should be reformed if, and only if, sufficient financial
safeguards for the spouse and children are simultaneously introduced within the new draft Divorce Law itself. . . . Divorce
should be available upon proof that the marriage has irretrievably broken down and upon no other ground.

The Council also declared that it would 'not support any proposal
which would make divorce *inevitable* after five years separation
regardless of whether the respondent wished for a divorce'.

Within a week, on 5th February, 1968, five M.P.s—Messrs Daniel
Awdry, Ian Gilmour, Nicholas Ridley, Anthony Royle and Sir
George Sinclair—wrote a letter to the Members of the House asking
their support for the Bill and requesting their attendance for the
second reading and later stages. Then a day before the second reading was given, on 8th February, the DLRU made its official announcement in support of Mr Wilson's Bill and distributed a press
release, which stated :

The Chairman of the Divorce Law Reform Union today
announces that, after strict scrutiny by its legal advisers, the
Executive of the Union has unanimously decided to support Mr
William Wilson M.P.'s Divorce Reform Bill. . . . Much anxiety
has been expressed about the financial security of women
divorced against their will if the Bill becomes law. The Union

has given particular attention to this point and is satisfied that the effect of the safeguard clauses in the Bill will be to provide considerably better security than is given by the existing law. . . . The criticism from opponents that it is a 'Casanova's Charter' is irresponsible and demonstrably untrue.

III. *The Press Reports*

Although the Divorce Reform Bill would affect great masses of people, this issue was treated more calmly than abortion law reform. Politically apathetic, many people were not even aware that the Divorce Reform Bill was going through Parliament, although the press coverage was relatively detailed, frequent and, for the most part, favourable; and the Bill also had the support of the Government. Since Mr Wilson's announcement, most of the mass media had shown interest and fairly frequently devoted a whole or half-page to covering the news on divorce.

The following are summaries of the press coverage and comments on the Bill, from 15th January until the second reading date, 9th February, which speak not only for themselves but also for the issue at stake and the climate of the time.

On 15th January the *Evening News* said : 'Now it's Divorce by Consent', 'faces tough opposition', 'but it stands a good chance of becoming law'; on 16th January the *Daily Mail* commented : '. . . it is not often that a Bill to alter the law so accurately reflects a change in public opinion as yesterday's Divorce Reform Bill'. The *Sun*, the *Daily Express*, the *Daily Mirror*, *The Guardian* and *The Times* (all on 16th Jan.) also expressed their approval, although *The Times* was cautious and the *Daily Telegraph* clearly showed its discontent under the headline 'Till Death or Consent', laying emphasis on the fact that 'the Bill gives too little attention to the interest of children'. *The Times*, the *Church Times* and the *New Statesman* (19th Jan.) all carried articles on divorce reform. On the 24th the *Daily Telegraph* reported Lady Summerskill's famous attack on the Bill; it was she who dubbed it a 'Casanova's Charter' in her address to the Married Women's Association at Caxton Hall, Westminster, and this label reappeared many times during the debate in Parliament. The *Observer Review* (28th); the *Evening Standard* and *The Times* (29th); *The Guardian* (30th); the *Evening Standard* (31st); the *Evening Echo* (1st February) and the *Daily Telegraph* (2nd Feb.) again carried articles on divorce and in general their attitude was one of support for the Bill, with the exception of a few letters from opponents.

For example, on 21st January, the *Observer Review* devoted a whole page to the divorce issue and said : '. . . in theory its chances of success should be relatively high. A majority in the House, as in the country, is probably ready to agree that the present divorce laws are sadly out of date in several respects.' The *Sunday Times* also reported the Lord Chancellor's words : 'I do not think that in the history of divorce law reform there has ever been a time when there has been so great a content of agreement.' On 4th February, the *Observer* carried Miss Joan Rubinstein's reply to Mr John Mortimer's article on the Bill (28th Jan.). She maintained that it was not true that the Bill had been hastily drawn. In fact it represented the fruits of several years of labour by the Archbishop's group on divorce, of which she had been a member, and by the Law Commission, 'both of whom separately came to the unanimous conclusion that the present law is totally inept and failed to meet the realities of life today'.

On 6th February, the *Daily Telegraph* carried an article by Sir Alan Herbert which read : 'The Bill, if it passes, will be a revolution. . . . "Divorce by Consent" has always been anathema to the Church, and to most high legal opinion . . . like it or not, the change in the high minds is remarkable. . . . The Bill is Christian and humane in spirit, courageous in design, and highly respectable in origin.' On 8th February, the *Daily Telegraph* reported the result of the Gallup Poll survey undertaken for that paper on the eve of the debate in the Commons on the second reading of the Bill. It said : 'easy divorce wanted by minority'; 'there is no clear majority'. Its unfavourable attitude towards divorce reform was clearly affirmed : 'This change in the law, as the Bill stands, would seriously weaken the institution of marriage as it is now understood in this country.'[21] On 9th February, *The Times* expressed its view, which was one of support for the Bill, saying in its leading article, 'Making a Bad Law Better' : 'This may not be an ideal Bill but it is seeking to improve a law that is very far from perfect.'

The press coverage was by and large favourable to the Bill throughout the session. It encouraged the reformers immensely and guided public opinion gradually towards the reformers' point of view.

During this period the promoters of the Bill did not miss any opportunity to return the attacks of their opponents. For example, Mr Leo Abse, through the columns of *The Times* (19th Jan.) accused the Archbishop of Canterbury of repudiating an agreement on the proposals contained in the Bill about new grounds for divorce, and again on 7th February wrote an article countering Mr G. Crispin, Q.C.'s article of 27th January. On 9th February, in *The*

Times, Sir George Sinclair (Conservative, Dorking) wrote in reply to articles by Lady Summerskill and Mr St John-Stevas.

It was also at this time that the National Council of Women agreed in London to the principle that 'divorce should be available on the proof that the marriage has irretrievably broken down'.[22]

IV. *Second Reading and Afterwards*

At this important stage, Mr Wilson's Bill won by 159 to 63, a majority of 96, which was slightly smaller than the reformers had expected. Eighteen Ministers, two Tory Shadow Ministers and eleven women M.P.s (nine of them Labour) were among those who voted for the Bill. Only one Minister, Mr Ray Gunter, and four women M.P.s (three of them Conservative) voted against it.[23]

On 10th February, 1968, *The Times* expressed its concern over the Bill by saying 'yes' 'with reservation' in its editorial. It devoted three long articles to the subject of divorce as well as editorial comment. The *Daily Telegraph* stated that, as the Government had itself announced earlier, its position would remain neutral. As *The Sun* reported, the Bill was certainly over its first hurdle; but as the *Daily Telegraph* said (10th Feb.), it was soon in jeopardy because of lack of time, despite a 96 majority on the second reading.

Two days after the second reading was given to the Bill, on 11th February, an article by the Archbishop of Canterbury, entitled 'My Doubts about the Divorce Bill', appeared in the *Sunday Times*. He summarized his misgivings thus :

(1) The matrimonial offence is virtually retained and two new grounds are added. . . . It is recognised that under the present law in practice there can virtually be divorce by consent. But the new law would bring into the state of marriage a new element. A marriage could be entered into by parties who agreed that it would be a temporary marriage. . . . One has to ask whether it can be just or good for the State or the closer community in which it exists.

(2) . . . it is difficult to see acceptable reasons for reducing the period for desertion. The clause permitting divorce of inmates of prison and mental hospitals for desertion will also need serious scrutiny. This clause would seem to ignore completely the moral or mental recovery of the prisoner or patient, and that might have very serious effects.

(3) The present Bill does not give 'all the protection needed by

the deserted spouse and children'. And the last phrase of
Clause 5 of this Bill would give our law a stronger bias
towards divorce. . . . Much more thought should be devoted
to the fundamental question whether this Bill will maintain
the stability of marriage as its sponsors claim. It would
seem that it could create more injustice and unhappiness
than it could remove.

In reply to Dr Ramsey's article, Professor Anderson wrote to the
Sunday Times (18th Feb., 1968) as follows :

It was with regret that I read the article by the Archbishop of
Canterbury in your last issue about Mr Wilson's Divorce Bill.
As a member of the Committee which he appointed to advise
him on the civil law of divorce, I am naturally loth to disagree
with the Archbishop. Yet I feel compelled to say that my understanding of the relative roles of his Committee and the Law
Commission, and indeed of the detailed provisions of the Bill,
does not correspond with his. I was myself one of those members
of his Committee who met with members of the Law Commission to see if differences between us could be bridged. In the
event, they accepted from us that breakdown of marriage should
be the sole ground of divorce, while we accepted from them that
it would not be practicable to hold a full inquest in every case,
but that various matrimonial situations must be recognized as
providing *prima facie* evidence of breakdown.

To say, therefore, that the Law Commission put forward certain proposals, as though they were solely responsible for them,
is not accurate; for the proposals represented a mutually agreed
compromise designed to bridge the gulf between theory and
practice. . . . (1) it is scarcely fair to say that the matrimonial
offence has been 'virtually retained'. . . . (2) . . . the Archbishop's
statement that the period of separation might, under Clause 3
(5) 'amount to only eighteen months' represents, with respect, a
misunderstanding. In no circumstances could the required period
of separation (or desertion) be less than two years, and any inter-
vening time of co-habitation would not count.

He raised three further points on which he disagreed with Dr
Ramsey and concluded :

Personally, I should welcome such change. I hope the Bill may
be improved at the Committee Stages; but I am convinced that,
as it stands, it represents a much more honest, satisfactory and
humane approach than does the present law.[24]

In March 1968, the Church Union officially expressed its concern and gave general support to the comment on the Bill circulated by the Mothers' Union. By this time, it was clear that the DLRU could not win over the Mothers' Union or the Married Women's Association, but they had hoped to get the positive support of the National Council of Women,[25] the Townswomen's Guilds, the Housewives' Register and other more 'enlightened' ones. What the DLRU intended was to send each of the more likely organizations some copies of their new pamphlet, *Financial Security of Divorced Women*, ask them to study it and, in the light of what it told them, to put up positive suggestions for further improving the financial safeguards in the Bill.

Within a few days after the second reading, the DLRU built up the list of supporters to 274, using the voting lists on the second reading division. They also considered who should be on the list of the Standing Committee. On 20th March, the Public Bill Office in Parliament informed Mr Wilson that the Standing Committee would commence consideration of the Bill on Wednesday, 27th March, and confirmed that a marshalled list of amendments would appear on Tuesday the 26th.

At the same time the list of twenty members of the Standing Committee C in respect of the Divorce Reform Bill was distributed to the members. The Committee consisted of the following twenty members : fourteen men and six women :

For the Bill :	Against the Bill :
Mr Leo Abse	Sir Lionel Heald
Dr Hugh Gray	Mrs Anne Kerr
Mr Peter Jackson	Mr Kenneth Lewis
Mrs Lena Jeger	Mr Norman St John-Stevas
Miss Joan Lestor	Dame Irene Ward
Mr Alexander Lyon	Mr Richard Wood
Mr Edward Lyons	
Mr John Parker	
Mr Nicholas Ridley	
Mrs Renée Short	
Sir George Sinclair	
Dame Joan Vickers	
Mr Ben Whitaker	
Mr William Wilson	

Sir Myer Galpern was in the Chair

The Committee met at 10.30 a.m. on Wednesday, 27th March, 1968, and resolved that during the proceedings on the Divorce Reform Bill it would meet at the same time every Wednesday. They had thirteen sittings lasting until 29th May. The Solicitor-General, Sir Arthur Irvine, attended throughout the committee stage with the exception of the seventh and ninth sittings.

During this period the reformers had gained considerable experience and support from various groups and sections of the country. It was also significant that the Lord Chancellor's Office worked so closely with the promoters of the Bill and offered all possible legitimate service. The Lord Chancellor's Office wrote to Mr Wilson asking him whether he had a peer to sponsor the Bill in the House of Lords, and the Lord Chancellor suggested an Opposition front-bench spokesman, Lord Colville, who had been a member of the Archbishop's group. Their concern was to have someone who had considerable experience of handling difficult legislation in the Lords and hopefully someone with a legal background. However, soon afterwards, in fact in early June, Lord Stow Hill's name was brought forward by Mr Leo Abse, who knew him very well since they had once worked together in the Commons before Lord Stow Hill[26] received his peerage. Lord Stow Hill (formerly Sir Frank Soskice) had also been a close friend of the Lord Chancellor for over forty years and both of them belonged to the Inner Temple. A former Solicitor-General, Attorney-General and Home Secretary, Lord Stow Hill was the promoters' choice for the Bill in the Lords. The Attorney-General, Sir Elwyn Jones, was also sympathetic, while the Solicitor-General, Sir Arthur Irvine, opposed the Bill. In addition, Mr Abse approached Lady Gaitskell and Lady Wootton to enlist their aid for the later stages of the Bill.

During the committee stage, the Medical Women's Federation, the Law Society, the National Council of Women of Great Britain, the Royal Medico-Psychological Association and the Co-operative Women's Guild brought forward their views to call attention to the committee stage amendment. For the reformers, the most difficult task was to find a way to adjust all these conflicting views and yet make the Bill practicable. Fortunately, the Lord Chancellor's Office and the Law Commission provided valuable suggestions as well as the necessary information. Consequently, after various amendments were made in the committee stage, the Bill finally got through its committee stage upstairs, but it eventually lapsed for lack of parliamentary time. The Leader of the House, Mr Peart, who had once thought of introducing an 'enabling motion' so that the Bill could be carried forward to the next session, informed the reformers that the Government could not afford to donate time for the final stages.[27]

The House devoted more than thirty-eight hours to the discussion[28] of the Bill in this session. Yet, after all, the opponents won the contest once again. Sir Lionel Heald, Q.C. (Conservative, Chertsey), a former Attorney-General, led the debate for the opponents against Wilson and Abse's team. Although the reformers won the battles both in the second reading and the committee stage, they had lost the race against time. The only noticeable gain for them was that they could count over 350 M.P.s as probable supporters for their next attempt, and that public sentiment in favour of reform had crystallized during the parliamentary struggle. In particular the attitudes voiced by the press during the campaign encouraged them to try again as soon as possible.

On a rough estimate the financial balance of profit and loss for the DLRU was: £500 − £300 = £200. £200 was their whole campaign fund for the next battle.

To sum up : Mr Wilson's Bill went no further and died when the session came to an end. However, in spite of the failure to reform the law and the existence of antithetic views,[29] Mr Wilson's Bill achieved three important points. First, it proved that majority opinion of the lawmakers, at least in the Commons, was in favour of the reform; by and large the Bill represented not only public opinion but legislative opinion as well. Secondly, it narrowed down the controversial issues into debatable points and made Parliament the arena for the battle. In other words, it transformed public opinion into legislative opinion and established a *fait accompli* by providing a ready-made Bill for the next round. Thirdly, it gave the reformers a good training and an opportunity to strengthen their bridges to the general public as well as to the Government, although they were beaten by the bell.

NOTES

1 The result of the discussions were recorded in the *New Law Journal* (3rd Aug., 1967), and in the Law Commission's *Third Annual Report, 1967–68* (Law Com. No. 15). See Appendix 3 below for the statement in full.

2 See pp. 72–3, above.

3 See p. 104, above.

4 *Daily Telegraph* (18th Aug., 1967).

5 See *The Times* (30th Oct., 1967).

6 *Sunday Times* (12th Nov., 1967).

7 See Hansard, Vol. 753, col. 1035.

8 For the role which private members' bills play in the British Parliament, see P. A. Bromhead, *Private Members' Bills in the British Parliament* (1956).

E

9 William Wilson and William Hamling. The article also carried their photographs.

10 He mentioned his motive and reason in the *Sunday Times* (3rd Dec., 1967) as follows: 'Because I understand the technicalities of the legal procedures and have an abiding interest in human beings and problems.'

11 *The Evening Standard* said: 'The Government is willing to give time for a Second Reading; and the general climate in the House is favourable to reform. . . .' Mr Wilson was subsequently told by a Cabinet minister: 'When I saw your place in the private members' ballot, I let it be known that you had to be drafted for the job.'

12 It was true that Mr Wilson's Bill was based on the recommendations of both the Law Commission and the Archbishop of Canterbury's group.

13 Although the Divorce Reform Bills were presented by Mr Wilson in 1967 and by Mr Jones in 1968, Mr Abse was the principal promoter of the proposed legislation, and he had long been trying to change the law. Mr Murray Sayle's description of Mr Abse was: Abse 'is a Disraeli-ish figure who describes himself as a Jewish humanist, and goes in for floral shirts, rat-catcher trousers, and chunky seal rings and watch fobs. He is a social reformer of some note (the Homosexual Act, and a previous Divorce Bill were his) and he is a very busy divorce lawyer.' See the *Sunday Times*, 12th November, 1967.

14 The National Marriage Guidance Council is a voluntary organization receiving a Government grant of £42,000 a year. Mr Sanctuary's letter to Mr Wilson fairly described the Council's role in England and its position on divorce law reform. It ran: 'It seems generally agreed that, whatever reform of our Divorce Law takes place, there will be an ever increasing need for matrimonial conciliation work. This Council does not take up a position on Divorce Law Reform, preferring to concentrate its energies on helping people to resolve their marriage problems, and to prevent divorce becoming necessary. We also have a large national programme of Family Life Education, and last year saw over 85,000 young people in schools and youth clubs. In the same period we helped over 18,000 marriages. . . .'

15 One London woman, Mrs M. Wilkins, had already started advertising in the newspapers for deserted wives to join her in a campaign of opposition.

16 'Dear Baroness Summerskill, I am grateful to you for sending me the Hansard of the 8th November. I had in fact already read what you had said, and I have read your article in the *Birmingham Post*. I am thus in no doubt as to your attitude. From my mail I am quite satisfied that there are many women who do not agree with you. Yours sincerely.'

17 All five Labour M.P.s are, incidentally, members of the Humanist Parliamentary Group.

18 Hansard, Vol. 755, cols 446–7.

19 However, on 13th January, 1968, the *Illustrated London News* reported: 'As for the Roman Catholic viewpoint, Kevin Mayhew writing in the *Catholic Herald*, says that the Church is "unlikely to oppose it outright . . ? the new Bill not only tidies up the existing law, it also makes it a better Law".'

20 For an interesting discussion on women's social status and divorce, see D. Morris, *The End of Marriage* (1971), pp. 40–1, 177–8, 178–9.

21 See p. 51, above.

22 *Daily Telegraph* (2nd Feb., 1968).

23 In favour: Mrs J. Butler, Mrs B. Castle, Mrs F. Corbet, Mrs G. Dunwoody, Mrs L. Jeger, Miss J. Lester, Mrs M. McKay, Miss J. Quennell, Mrs R. Short, Mrs E. White, and Dame Joan Vickers. Against: Mrs A. Kerr, Miss M. Pike, Mrs M. Thatcher, and Dame Irene Ward.

24 With regard to the argument between these two prominent members of the Church of England, I have ascertained that Dr Ramsey and Professor Anderson still hold their views in this respect, and Dr Ramsey has confirmed the above-quoted article as his own, although it was rumoured that he did not write the article and was ill-advised in this matter.

25 The Council, later in March, confirmed their earlier statement that 'in future divorce should be available on the petition of either party and where there is proof that the marriage has broken down irretrievably'.

26 He held the neighbouring constituency to Mr Abse's in Wales and they had worked together on constituency matters.

27 The Bill did not take too long in committee; it was out of committee ahead of schedule. It was not the parliamentary business in the House of Commons which caused the difficulty but the clogging of business in the House of Lords, and the Lords could not give sufficient time to get the Bill through. In fact, the sponsors of Mr Wilson's Bill were offered time in the Commons, but it would have meant one or two all-night sittings. It was apparent that even if the Bill went through the Commons, it could not get through the House of Lords. There would, therefore, be a danger that the reformers would not have been able to keep 100 members present in the Commons all night for the Bill. This would have meant that the opponents could have said that the Bill had been defeated. The promoters were not prepared to risk that situation arising, and it was for this reason that any efforts to take the Bill through the Commons, without assurance of its safe passage through the Lords as well, was not attractive to them.

28 On 23rd May, 1968, the *Daily Telegraph* reported that the Bill was threatened by slowness.

29 A leaflet (1969 ed.) published by an anonymous opponent or opponents best describes the opposition's view: 'Yet despite its short life the Wilson Bill established two things:— 1. Only a minority outside Parliament supported the Bill. 2. Despite this, the Commons Standing Committee failed to pass any amendments to the provisions which informed opinion had condemned.'

Chapter 7

MR JONES'S BILL

I. *The Eve of the Second Reading*

During the summer recess the DLRU[1] and the sponsors of Mr Wilson's Bill were occupied in working out their strategy, as they had no wish to repeat the same moves which had led them to an impasse in the last session. If a bill was to be introduced again, it would have to be done by one of their supporters or at least by someone sympathetic to the cause of reform; not many M.P.s were anxious to introduce this kind of measure even though Mr Wilson's Bill had been assured of the support of some 200 members. Moreover, there was the additional problem that the Bill would have to be carried quickly through the Commons to allow sufficient time for it to complete its stages in the House of Lords. With support in the Commons guaranteed it seemed that this might be accomplished if they could find a suitable peer to pilot the Bill through the Upper Chamber in the next session.

The sponsors' first choice was still Lord Stow Hill and he was duly approached : Lord Stow Hill agreed but stipulated certain conditions. He would be glad to sponsor a bill in the Lords if it had been reintroduced and passed in all its stages in the Commons, provided he did not have to do so before the end of the year, since his duties as Treasurer of the Inner Temple would fully occupy his time until then.

This gave the reformers little hope of introducing a bill through the House of Lords, although they had considered it as an alternative course because they knew that ALRA had been successful after a preliminary bill had been passed through the Lords; and furthermore, they did not wish to get bogged down again in the Commons. Lord Stow Hill, however, thought that to introduce it in the Lords would be a mistake, and it was by no means certain that the Bill would pass; a lot more opposition could be expected in the Upper House, for example from judges, than in the Commons. He expressed the view that the peers in favour of the Bill would be in a much stronger position if they were able to say that it had twice been passed in the Commons. Lord Stow Hill also suggested that there were some points which could be altered without damaging the Bill, and might well go far to disarm opposition, especially if these alterations removed points to which the judges took exception.

The Earl of Balfour, Lord Goodman, Messrs Banks, Peter Jackson, Service and Wilson kept each other closely informed of every development. They also reached the conclusion that if they introduced a bill in the Lords it would have to face major opposition from bishops, diehard moralists and feminists. The Bill, therefore, would undoubtedly have a greater chance of success if it arrived at the Lords with the democratic seal of Commons approval, as Lords Stow Hill and Goodman suggested. This being the case there were now two possible courses open to the reformers: a private member might do well in the ballot and utilize his place to introduce the Bill; or it could be introduced under the Ten-Minute Rule when the new session started. In September it became clear that Lord Stow Hill would take over the Bill if it reached the Lords in due course through the Commons.

Towards the end of the summer recess, more letters began to arrive, but this time almost all of them were for the Bill—some gave encouragement to the sponsors, while others made inquiries about the progress of the Bill.[2] The reformers told them that they did not intend to give up the struggle for divorce reform, and like many others hoped that during the next session they would be successful. Some indeed asked why the Bill had to repeat all the stages in the Commons, to which the reformers replied: '. . . it is one of the ridiculous features of Parliamentary procedure that we have to go through all the preliminary stages all over again in the new session'.[3] The reformers also suggested to those people who wrote to them that they should write not only to their own M.P.s in support of the Bill but also to the Leader of the House, Mr Fred Peart, and the Prime Minister, Mr Harold Wilson, suggesting that the Government should allow adequate time for the Bill in the next session. In fact some wrote back to the reformers with the replies which they had received from the Leader of the House and the Prime Minister.

The DLRU was busy at that time making sure that the last failure did not pass unnoticed. They arranged letters of protest to the press and to the Government from many M.P.s with a view to preventing the same thing from happening again in the next session.[4] They circulated all likely supporters in Parliament and received encouraging promises from over 200 of them. Other factors were involved, but it was obvious that the DLRU's campaign was having its effect. During the following months, they were able steadily to increase this list of supporters as they discovered the views of more M.P.s, and the result was that by the time the private members' ballot was drawn in the session, they knew of about 360 supporters in the House of Commons—a clear majority. This knowledge was very valuable later when it came to asking the Government for time to complete the Bill's passage through the Commons.[5] Thus for a while writing and answering letters, making statements, and planning tactics was the main business of the reformers. No positive action could be taken until the result of the private members' ballot was known in November 1968.

After the long summer, another battle for the reform of the divorce law of England was opened with an article, on 22nd October, 1968, by Mrs Lena Jeger in *The Sun*. It seemed that everything was ready for the reformers and the time was ripe to complete the belated reform of the law. Some felt impatient, as all the opinion polls had already demonstrated that the reformers were representing public opinion in general, and they also had the explicit support of the press. Furthermore, they already knew that the majority of M.P.s would vote for the reform bill. The climate of opinion in the country was ready to alter the law; public and legislative opinion were in harmony. The Church of England, the Law Commission and even the most adamant pressure groups such as the Mothers' Union and the Church Union agreed to reform the law along the lines proposed by the Archbishop's group in 1966. For the reformers, therefore, the task that still remained was to decide how to adjust conflicting views and maintain their position, with the support of the Law Commission. They also had a tacit understanding with the Government, despite its wish to remain neutral. The Lord Chancellor, speaking in his personal capacity, openly supported the idea of reforming the law. Above all, there was no one who would argue that the divorce law was satisfactory in its existing form.

However, it became clear that, in practice, there was no alternative to repeating the procedure required for a private member's bill, however thorny or tiresome it might be, as British governments notoriously dislike making themselves responsible for controversial social legislation of this kind, unlike governments in other countries which are prepared to sponsor this kind of legislation.

In any event, Mr Wilson's Bill proved that the reformers had a sufficient majority in Parliament to win the battle against those intransigent opponents who clung to the traditional doctrine of matrimonial offence for divorce. This ground had existed unchanged for over 110 years, with the exception of two dents made by the Herbert Act 1937 and Mr Leo Abse's so-called 'Kiss-and-Make-up' Act in 1963. Indeed by 1968 the reformers had a clear majority both inside and outside Parliament, although some were still concerned about the House of Lords where there were many bishops and moralists as well as well-known feminists who vigorously opposed Mr Wilson's Bill.

To reform the law, all that was needed was an early number in the private members' ballot which would enable the reformers to fight another round against the opponents whom they had met in the same ring only a few months ago. However, even if the Government was not only willing to provide time but ready to facilitate the passage of the Bill, success still depended upon the haphazard method of lottery. Although the business of legislation requires rational planning, in England, like in many other countries, a large part of politics is often dependent upon luck, if not sheer accident.

This ballot, to newly elected M.P.s, is one of the strangest of parliamentary procedures. About 300 members put down their names in the book; about thirty attend the 'draw'. Not many more than twenty are anxious to 'win a turkey' for themselves, being eager for a particular reform. The rest go in to give a friend another chance, or as a Party duty, for the Whips have always a few bills ready for a Friday. As a rule there are about ten private Fridays available for second readings. In theory three bills can be disposed of in a day; but in practice, if the first bill on the paper is substantial and controversial, there is no hope for the others. The later in the year the Friday, the less chance the bill has of thrusting through the congested traffic in the final stages. So the only hope for a prickly measure such as divorce was to win a number in the first five or six, and the odds against that were very long.

Again in the following session (1968-9) all the known reformers were unlucky in the queue for private members' bills at the Commons on Thursday, 7th November, 1968. The next best thing was to look for a foster-father or even a foster-mother. The DLRU and Mr Abse were discouraged, but found, by great fortune, the former schoolteacher, Mr T. Alec Jones (Labour, Rhondda, West), who had won ninth place in the ballot.

In this, as in other fields, truth is indeed a many-sided thing and naturally it is necessary to look at things from Mr Jones's angle too. Like many other M.P.s who went to draw the ballot, Mr Jones did not have any definite idea of what he might do with his place. He seemed to think that planning was useless before he knew what number he had drawn. Mr Jones learned the result of the ballot during the lunch-hour, and as soon as he found that he had won number nine in the ballot, he looked for Messrs Abse and Wilson. An active member of the Church of Wales, Anglican Communion, Mr Jones was a freshman M.P. and naturally looked to Mr Abse who was also from Wales. On the other hand Mr Abse, like A. P. Herbert in 1936, was looking for someone who could take over their Bill; he learned of Mr Jones's position in the ballot and went to see him. It was while discussing the question with his fellow-country-man and Mr Wilson, that Mr Jones determined to use his place to introduce a divorce reform bill. Accordingly, these three M.P.s im-mediately called a press interview to announce Mr Jones's decision. Mr Alec Jones made clear his intention to introduce the Bill, with the support of two lawyers, Messrs Abse and Wilson, the original sponsors. Although his draw was not regarded as an extremely favourable position, the backers of the Bill maintained there had been a Government pledge of parliamentary time if it ran into dif-ficulties in view of its failure last session.

To a question put to him by the present writer, 'Why did you select that particular Bill?' Mr Jones gave three reasons : firstly, the importance of the Bill—he did not wish to waste time on a minor bill; secondly, a good chance of success; and thirdly, personal interest.

After the announcement of his intention to introduce the Bill, he soon realized that Mr Peart and Mr J. Silkin, the Chief Whip, were also sympathetic. They, Jones and Abse immediately went to see the Lord Chancellor who also encouraged them and promised his support.

Thus the Divorce Reform Bill again became an object of national news and reappeared in almost every newspaper in the country from that day onwards.

The Times (8th Nov., 1968) reported the event :

> The Divorce Reform Bill, making the irretrievable breakdown of marriage a ground for divorce, is to be reintroduced in the Com-mons this session by Mr Alec Jones. . . . Mr Jones will have the assistance of Mr William Wilson (Coventry, South) who mar-shalled a similar Bill through second reading and committee stages in the Commons last session. By taking account of the changes made last session, Mr Jones hopes that the Bill will have a speedier passage this year. Ministers take the line that most M.P.s favour this reform and that the Bill deserves to make progress.

Mr Jones's Bill was substantially the same as Mr Wilson's which proposed to give power to the court to permit divorce by consent after two years' separation, and divorce without consent of the 'innocent' party after five years' separation, subject to financial and other safeguards for wives. The Bill merely had a new backer; it maintained all the crucial provisions of Mr Wilson's Bill. If the Bill should become law, irretrievable breakdown of marriage would be the only ground for divorce although an old matrimonial offence could be used as evidence of breakdown.

As the Government promised earlier, the Cabinet, 'while remaining determinedly neutral', immediately decided it would not allow 'the will of the House to be frustrated through lack of time', although there were several ministers who did not support the decision. None the less it was the strongest promise of support the reformers could obtain within a few days, and they had already worked out their tactics for the coming session. As no Whips operate on a private member's bill, Messrs Jones, Abse and Wilson needed to persuade enough members to be present at least for one evening and morning session to get the Bill through. As the opponents of the Bill might well try to talk it out by the parliamentary rules, the sponsors needed at least 100 members to defeat filibusters by carrying the motion that 'the Question be now put'. Another advance for the reformers was that Lord Stow Hill was ready earlier than at first expected to pilot the legislation through the House of Lords; thus, the omens were favourable. The reformers had wasted no time at all; within a week after the ballot they had cleared many obstacles, and press reports also indicated that the Bill now had a good chance of becoming law. Indeed the campaign was building up a momentum of its own.

On the other hand, the opponents felt uneasy, for the Government was lending support behind the scenes and they knew that the tide was turning against them. Nevertheless, Sir Lionel Heald with others, including a non-M.P., Mr William Latey, Q.C.,[6] opened their press campaign and wrote articles against the Bill, criticizing the attitude of the Government even before the second reading started. Sir Lionel Heald's letter appeared in *The Times* on 30th November, 1968, under the headline 'Heeding Public Opinion on Divorce'. He admitted that the criterion of 'irretrievable breakdown' was generally acceptable in principle, but vigorously criticized the Clause 2(1)(e), which allowed unilateral divorce after five years' separation, and the financial protection Clause 6(2)(b) as wholly inadequate provisions. He continued : 'It is well known that, had the previous Bill returned to the floor of the House for the Report Stage, the "five year" provision would have met with strong opposition, and there is clear evidence that it is even stronger today.' He also pointed out that the sponsors should pay attention to public opinion, particularly to the views of the women's organizations which had been virtually ignored when the previous bill was in committee.

Within a week, two days before the second reading, a letter from

Mr William Latey to the editor appeared in the *Daily Telegraph* (4th Dec., 1968) supporting a leading article in that paper on 28th November, which stated that divorce reform merited weightier discussion than it had yet enjoyed. He rejected the two clauses which Sir Lionel criticized and said :

> The Bill is now to be reintroduced practically unaltered, except for the deletion of an important safeguarding clause against abuse. Surely an important measure like this, going to the root of our social structure and threatening the foundation of the marriage institution, would have merited a Government Bill as was pointed out by Sir Lionel Heald and others in committee . . . succeeding Royal Commissions composed of the wisest heads in the judiciary and the Church, have rejected the principle of divorce by consent. . . .

In fact, the *Daily Telegraph*'s leading article appeared on the very day that Mr Jones presented his Bill to be read the first time. On 27th November, 1968, the Bill to amend the grounds for divorce and judicial separation, to facilitate reconciliation in matrimonial causes, and for purposes connected with the matters aforesaid, was officially presented by Mr Alec Jones, supported by the following sponsors, arranged by Mr Abse :

Labour :	Conservative :
Mr Leo Abse	Mr Daniel Awdry
Mr Peter Jackson	Mr Ian Gilmour
Mrs Lena Jeger	Mr Nicholas Ridley
Mr John Parker	Mr Anthony Royle
Mr William Wilson	Dame Joan Vickers

Liberal : Mr Emlyn Hooson

As the chief Conservative supporter of the Bill, Mr Daniel Awdry (Chippenham) replaced Sir George Sinclair,[7] who had been sponsor for Mr Wilson's Bill, and this time Mr Wilson became a sponsor instead of Dr David Kerr. By putting the Bill through its first reading, the sponsors made sure that the second reading would be held on Friday, 6th December, 1968, and the Bill 17 was sent to be printed.[8]

Thus the time-table and the stage were set for Mr Jones's Bill, and its next most critical step, the second reading, took place on Friday, 6th December, 1968. The opponents, although they had buried or watered down all those previous divorce reform bills which contained far less controversial grounds than this one, were now conscious of a new fact, a shadow of fear. Their main apprehension this time was the attitude of the Government and the consequence of their failure in the last two rounds in the Commons. However, this time they had a formidable new recruit, who would lead the debate and fight against the Bill. Mr Bruce Campbell, Q.C. (Conservative, Oldham West), who joined the Commons following a by-election in June 1968, was born in New Zealand and grew up there until he was eighteen. A Baptist, he did not believe in the principle of indissolubility; however, he respected it and firmly upheld the institution of marriage as providing the basis for a strong and happy family structure. Two major reasons determined his stand : he believed that it best served the interest of the community when seen from a national point of view, and he preferred gradual changes to revolutionary ones. Happily married with six children, this experienced lawyer later became the toughest opponent at every step of the passage, and continued his opposition even after the Bill had been passed.[9]

Nevertheless, ever since the Church of England had accepted the principles laid down by *Putting Asunder*, a systematic opposition movement against the Bill had been lacking. In order to stop the Bill, the most effective tactics had to be employed at each step. The opponents' first intention was to attempt to destroy the Bill entirely, but soon they realized that the tide was against them and changed their strategy into watering down several controversial clauses, notably Clause 2(1) (d) and (e).

Against those experienced opponents, namely Sir Lionel Heald, Mr Bruce Campbell and Mr Ian Percival, the most critical test for the reformers took place just before the Christmas recess of 1968. Many of them who had previously tried to put through other bills, realized that the task was not going to be an easy one, for although they had received assurances of support from more than 300 M.P.s, it was uncertain how many would turn up. With the bitter memories of the failure of previous attempts, the advocates of divorce reform legislation worked with renewed determination while their opponents were making light of the strength of the reformers.

As a final effort, Mr Jones made a statement through the BBC and ITV, and sent out soliciting letters to all members except those already known as opponents. Then, two days before the second reading the reformers sent out warning letters saying that all the opponents would be coming to the House to stop the Bill.

They had to mobilize a sufficient number of M.P.s for the passage of the Bill, while the anti-reformers were quickly sharpening their traditional swords of logic and strategy. The reformers hoped that all those who had promised to turn out would be there on time, regardless of their skill, creed and political belief, for they knew that a simple majority could accomplish many things in that conventional arithmetical democracy. Let us now turn to the debates in Parliament. There all the currents in the controversy were exhibited, and the logic of the Bill's opponents, their conviction about the value of the traditional Christian doctrine of marriage and divorce, as well as the attitude of ostensibly neutral parties such as the Government, are faithfully reflected in the pages of Hansard.

II. *Second Reading*[10]

On 6th December, 1968, the crucial test, the second reading, was due to commence in the afternoon, following the most intensive campaign ever launched by the DLRU. Mr Service had been lobbying Parliament almost every day and night while Messrs Jones, Abse, Awdry, Jackson and Wilson were approaching their colleagues in order to obtain a sufficient number for the second reading, although nobody seemed to think that there was the smallest danger of their not getting it. Some, however, worried a little, as there could be so great a press of speakers against them that at 4 o'clock the Speaker would be unable to grant the 'closure'—that is, permit a division—and the Bill would be 'talked out'. In the British Parliament, the member in charge of a Bill may move 'that the Question be now put' and a division taken.[11]

Meanwhile, Mr Jones was busily at work with his supporters, and the sponsors called a meeting and sent out a 'Whip' to every likely supporter. Although he had the assistance of three[12] lawyers with considerable parliamentary experience, Mr Jones was not himself a professional lawyer and this disadvantage combined with relatively short experience of the House made his task an onerous one. Moreover, once again there was some anxiety lest the number of 'Ayes' should be depleted by the absence from the House of a number of supporters who might be engaged with extra-parliamentary affairs—always a hazard to the passage of private business on Friday.

At this important stage, time for the debate was provided from 2.40 p.m., when a mere eighty minutes remained for discussion. It was obvious that the Speaker would not accept a closure motion after so short a discussion on the issue.

However, Mr Jones had no choice but to move the second reading of the Divorce Reform Bill. He said : 'My co-sponsors and I are asking the House to give a Second Reading to a Bill which is substantially the same as the Bill which emerged from the Standing Committee during last Session.'[13] The basis of divorce, which the Bill sought to recast, had endured for 110 years, and centred on the requirement that matrimonial offence had been committed by one of the spouses. Mr Jones pointed out that not only was this doctrine, which necessitated the commission of some matrimonial crime such as adultery or cruelty, unsound, but also that the granting of a divorce on the grounds of the incurable insanity of the respondent hardly can or ought to be regarded as a matrimonial offence.

Growing dissatisfaction with the law had led to the bills which were introduced by Mr Abse in 1963 and Mr Wilson in the last session. Mr Jones emphasized that his Bill took the line laid down by *Putting Asunder* and *The Field of Choice* (Cmnd 3123) and read the Law Commissioners' main conclusions as to the objectives of his Bill.[14] By quoting a more objective view from paragraph 70(v) of the Report of the Royal Commission on Marriage and Divorce, Mr Jones condemned the existing divorce law. It read :

> . . . for whatever reason marriage breaks down, the prevailing law of divorce provides an easy escape from the bond of matrimony for those who are minded to take it. Desertion for three years, or, for those who wish a speedier release, the commission of adultery, is all that is needed. . . . We think it may be said that the law of divorce as it at present exists is indeed weighted in favour of the least scrupulous, the least honourable and the least sensitive.

He spoke for thirty minutes to explain his motive and the content of the Bill. There were several important points put forward by Mr Jones. First, the Bill had been framed to carry out as effectively as possible the proposals for the reform of the divorce law which emerged from the joint discussions between the Archbishop's group and the Law Commission. The Bill recognized the doctrine of 'irretrievable breakdown' of a marriage which would replace the artificial legal concept of 'matrimonial offence' as the ground for divorce. The underlying principle of this substitution was that the notion of punishment in matrimonial causes should be avoided. No longer would one partner of the marriage be punished for the relief of another. The Bill took the line that if irretrievable breakdown was established the marriage should be dissolved, notwithstanding the objection of one party, but only so long as disproportionate hardship was not caused to that party. To avoid such hardship, safeguards were provided.[15]

The Bill reduced the prescribed period of desertion from three years to two. This was because of the close connection between the time provided for desertion and that provided for separation. Clause 2(1)(d) stated that if one party petitions after two years' separation and the other does not object, it is clear that both parties accept that their marriage has irretrievably broken down; this clause pre-supposes that they are likely to be the best judges. Clause 2(1)(e) provided that after five years' separation a marriage may be dis-solved at the suit of one party despite the objection of the other. The basic philosophy of the Bill was that a marriage ought, in the public interest, to be dissolved if it has irretrievably broken down, and the strongest evidence of breakdown is a long period of separation. One of the strongest arguments in favour of Clause 2(1)(e) was that it would enable many stable illicit unions to be regularized, and the children of these unions to be legitimized.

Secondly, a respondent could oppose the granting of a decree by seeking to satisfy the court that the dissolution of the marriage would result in grave financial or other hardship to him or her. Its main operation was likely to be in cases coming under Clause 2(1) (e) under which a so-named 'innocent wife' might be divorced against her will by a so-named 'guilty partner'.

Thirdly, the Bill included proposals for improving conditions for reconciliation. The Home Office recognizes and makes grants to certain voluntary bodies such as the National Marriage Guidance Council, the newly named Tavistock Institute of Marital Studies and the Catholic Marriage Advisory Council. In addition to those grants, local authorities are authorized to make grants to local councils affiliated to the central organizations mentioned above. He urged that the grants be increased as they were too small to meet present needs: they were inadequate in relation to the amount spent annually in divorce costs coupled with the amount of work done by these organizations.

On the whole, Mr Jones, moving the second reading, made an effective speech covering major Clauses 2–8, despite the fact that he was no lawyer and knew less about the tricky business of piloting a private member's bill than the two previous sponsors. Although he did not claim, as A. P. Herbert had done thirty-two years before, that 'the Bill was designed not merely to relieve the misfortunes of individuals, but to strengthen three institutions—the Church, the Law, Marriage itself', he moved the Bill competently, pointing out all the crucial points, and concluded by saying :

> I can only claim sincerely that I have sought to deal with equal justice and importance both with the Bill and to hon. Members on both sides. It is certainly no hastily conceived Bill, its main

provisions were endorsed by the House last Session. It is un-
ashamedly a consensus Bill, it is supported by Members on both
sides. Its structure and fine balance are the result of long discussions between churchmen, lawyers and politicians. I commend it to the House as a sincere and practical attempt to overcome the deficiencies of the present divorce law without weakening the institution of marriage.[16]

In reply, Mr Bruce Campbell said : members tend to get a distorted view of public opinion on the question of divorce, because
most M.P.s are likely to have in their constituencies one or two very
vocal people living in adultery who continually badger their M.P.
to do something about the divorce laws so that they can regularize
their illicit union. Members were also apt to forget that those vocal
people are a minority—they are all guilty; he did not think that
this represented the opinion of the country as a whole. Most people,
he said, have a high regard for the institution of marriage, and
there are some who regard it as a holy institution. 'I am, perhaps,
in a unique position among M.P.s because I have spent my working
life since the war practising exclusively at the Divorce Bar and I
know a little about the topic. . . . This is a disgraceful Bill, and I
shall fight it at every stage.' He made the following points :

(1) Divorces are now running at the rate of about 50,000 a year
     and if the Bill is passed, it will give another surge forward
     to the steady disintegration of family life that has been go-
     ing on in this country for the past 20 or 25 years. Every
     time one makes divorce easier one makes marriage cheaper,
     and people tend more and more to enter into marriage as
     an experiment, feeling that if it does not work out there is
     always the divorce court.

(2) On the day the Bill reaches the Statute Book—if it ever
     does—everyone who respects English law must hang his
     head, because for the first time in our history it is proposed
     to introduce into the law of England the principle that a
     man may take advantage of his own wrong. For centuries
     we have prided ourselves that it is a basic principle of
     equity in our law that no man shall ever be allowed to take
     advantage of his own wrong. The Bill seeks to give a man
     that right. When he grows tired of his wife, and she ceases
     to be sexually attractive to him, he will be allowed to
     desert his wife and children, go off with a younger woman,
     and after five years, to force his completely innocent wife
     into a divorce so that he can marry the new woman.[17]

(3) Mr Abse talks about the illegitimate children born of illicit
     unions between those who cannot marry. The way to deal

with illegitimate children is to alter the law relating to illegitimacy, not the divorce laws. To try to alter the law of illegitimacy by changing the divorce laws is rather like going to John O'Groats via Lands End. One can deal with illegitimate children by improving their status. I do not see why they should have any poorer status than legitimate children.

(4)   It is said that there will be safeguards for these innocent, deserted and abandoned wives. My reply is to say that it is nonsense. The proposed safeguards will be quite inadequate. In the present state of the law, if a man leaves his wife and lives with another woman, she can go to the court and the court will award her a reasonable slice of the man's income. But once that man is allowed to marry the other woman, he will become legally liable to maintain her as well and that, of course, is impossible. We are not talking about millionaires but the millions of ordinary men and women, who live on a tight budget which simply does not permit maintaining two households.[18]

During Mr Campbell's speech, Miss Joan Lestor (Labour, Eton and Slough) interrupted to ask :

On what does he base his argument that it is only men who leave their wives? I know of no evidence for it. Hon. Members have argued as though it is the man who will leave the woman rather than the woman leave the man, and it must, therefore, be an argument based on economic dependence. Ought we not therefore to be directing our attention to the subject of economic dependence in marriage and not making an assumption about promiscuity among men which is no more valid than the assumption of promiscuity among women.

In the debate that followed, Mrs Lena Jeger (Labour, Holborn and St Pancras, South) also said that the difficulty in legislation covering this area of sensitive and delicate human relationships was that there was no total guilt or total innocence. Replying to Mr Simon Mahon (Labour, Bootle), who had asked whether she was suggesting that there are no such things as wholly innocent people, or completely guilty people in marriage, Mrs Jeger replied :

Yes. I am. Theologically and philosophically I am suggesting that there is no such thing as total guilt or total innocence, and I hope that no one will proudly go to his grave averring that the whole of his life has been spent in total innocence. The provisions that we are discussing today, particularly the five-year

non-consenting Clause, are already the law in Australia. The
relevant period in New Zealand is seven years. There has been
no noticeable collapse of the fabric of the constitution of marriage in either of those Christian countries.[19]

She also said that during the reign of Queen Anne only eight
divorces were legalized in England, but this did not prove that during the reign there had been less guilt, less adultery, less unfaithfulness, or any less marital misbehaviour. She added that although
Mr Campbell had said that towards middle age, 'when women become sexually unattractive [sic] men will go off with younger
women, those of us who are well over fifty like to feel that we are
not totally unattractive.[20] It is middle-aged men who get fat and
bald and unattractive.'

She went on to put the opposite point of view to Mr Campbell,
by quoting a letter from an elderly woman : 'I must write to you
because I am so hoping that the Divorce Bill will go through.' She
was now over sixty; she married for three years over a quarter of a
century ago; then she met a man whom she could love and she
moved in with him, she never took a penny off her husband for
over twenty-two years; the husband refused a divorce; and now the
second man, whom she regards as her husband, had died. She said :
'I went to my solicitor. After all these years, surely I am a widow
now, and he said, no I am not a widow, I am still legally tied to
that my first party. It would break my heart if I went to my grave
without being free.' Mrs Jeger's next points concerned the interests
of the children and the economic status of married women.

After the debate had been enlivened by Mrs Jeger's defence of
older women, Mr Marcus Worsley (Conservative, Chelsea) started
to propound his views against the Bill, but as it was 4 o'clock the
debate stood adjourned.

There were four speeches and fifteen interventions, by twelve
members—two women[21] and ten men, one being the Solicitor-
General. Two opponents, Mr Campbell and Mr Worsley, spoke
against the two sponsors, Mr Jones and Mrs Jeger. The debate was
dominated by two main speakers, Mr Campbell and Mrs Jeger,
who each countered five interventions; the interventions were all
short.

Although it took only one hour and twenty minutes, it had been
a long day for the reformers. The second reading had not yet been
given, but after consultation between Mr Abse and the Government
Chief Whip, Mr Silkin, the decision was taken to allow the debate
to be resumed on Tuesday, 17th December, 1968.[22] The reformers
again had to write[23] to all their likely supporters asking them to

attend the next second reading on the Tuesday morning of the following week. Mr Service, who took over full control of the campaign for the Bill on behalf of the DLRU, put all his energy into lobbying Parliament, working with the sponsors of the Bill. They had another week in which to campaign. With the names[24] and photographs of the Commons members in hand, he virtually spent day and night in Parliament soliciting M.P.s. Among the sponsors of the Bill, Messrs Abse, Awdry, Jackson, Wilson and a supporter, Mrs Short, actively participated in the campaign, while other sponsors and supporters also assisted the effort to obtain sufficient voters for the second reading.[25]

On 17th December, 1968, the promoters of the Bill were busy from early morning in counting how many supporters would turn up, as they had promised, but they were unable to tell until after lunch when the division was taken. During lunchtime, most of the sponsors of the Bill were busy soliciting members to join the division; the members of the DLRU together with a considerable number of opponents were sitting in the visitors' galleries, while Mr Service was still busy canvassing support in the central lobby.

The second reading for the Divorce Reform Bill resumed on Tuesday, 17th December. Mr Marcus Worsley stood up at 10 a.m. and continued his speech from the point which he had reached on Friday, 6th December.

Briefly he made a number of points, the first of which was that the Government should take over the Bill on this occasion and not put it at the end of a day's business when discussion, even if continued overnight as had happened in the last session but one, is necessarily inadequate, just as it must be in 'idiotic and truncated' morning sittings. Secondly, Mr Worsley stressed the fact that the Government was now morally responsible for the well-being of those many thousands of innocent wives who, if the obnoxious Clause 2(1)(e) were left in the Bill, would find their rights reduced because they would be shared with another woman or women. Thirdly, he commented that this was a double bill, with two aspects : the first of which was simply to alter what might be called the law and procedure of divorce. The second, however, quite separately, would make easier grounds for divorce. Mr Worsley finally remarked upon the difference between the Bill and *Putting Asunder*, which he considered a brilliant, stimulating, and well-written report. The difference between them was critical. Under the present law, divorce was granted because of a matrimonial offence. Under the Bill it would be granted because of 'breakdown of marriage', but the difficulty remained as to how that was to be shown. He declared :

I do not believe that this reform is of very great significance . . . the real changes are the introduction of two major new grounds for divorce, the so-called divorce by consent under Clause 2(1)(d) and divorce without consent under Clause 2(1)(e). There is a considerable softening of desertion from three to two years. These are the real issues upon which I suggest the House should concentrate its attention. In my opinion, they add up to a Bill for easier divorce, and therefore I oppose it.[26]

Mr David Weitzman (Labour, Stoke Newington and Hackney North), reminded the House that Mr Campbell drew upon his experience to condemn the Bill. Mr Weitzman, with equal modesty, claimed that he also had some knowledge of divorce work as he had practised at the Bar for over forty-six years—a far longer period of experience than that of Mr Campbell. But his convictions were precisely opposed to those of Mr Campbell. Mr Weitzman, who had supported Mrs White's Bill in 1951, regarded the new Bill as a long overdue measure which would not undermine the sanctity of marriage, but, on the contrary, would help to make it more of a reality. It would bring happiness and relief to thousands of couples, who were living in so-called sin, as well as the blessings, such as they are, of legitimacy, to many children.

He supported his argument by quoting the Report of the Royal Commission on Marriage and Divorce (Morton Commission) and *Putting Asunder*, which ran : 'The law as it stands is unsatisfactory. As a piece of social mechanism the present system has not only cut loose from its moral and judicial foundations, it is quite simply inept.'

On Clause 2(1)(d), the so-called divorce by consent clause, he said that as long ago as 1912, the King's Proctor, in giving evidence before the Royal Commission, said that 75 per cent of divorces were obtained by consent. The provision in the Bill would help to get rid of the hypocrisy and perjury which now undoubtedly attended divorce petitions and would assist in putting them on a true basis. He said that he saw no sense in keeping a party tied by a bond which did not exist in reality, while the other party was condemned to live in sin, often with children who were illegitimate. Since it were difficult to say that one party was wholly guilty and the other wholly innocent, such an arrangement was nonsense, and the Bill provided as ample safeguards for the financial protection of the respondent as could be provided.

After Mr Wilkins's intervention, which was ordered by the Speaker to be brief, Sir Lionel Heald (Conservative, Chertsey) made clear his position with regard to the Bill. He said that his concern was with ground (e) rather than with ground (d). It was that 'uni-lateral' or compulsory ground to which many women objected and which was causing a large number of women grave fears. On the whole, his argument was much the same as that of Mr Campbell, and he gave this brief summary of the three major reasons which he considered vital to his decision to oppose the Bill : 'The first is that no one may take advantage of his own wrong; the second is that hard cases make bad law; and the third is that there must not be one law for the rich and another for the poor.'[27] He also said, like Mr Campbell, that it would be a bad day for Britain if the Bill became law, and pointed out that the phrase in Clause 6(2)(b), 'or the best that can be made in the circumstances', made financial provision unclear.

The Solicitor-General, Sir Arthur Irvine, spoke after Sir Lionel, and said that the attitude of the Government to the Bill was the same as it had been to a similar bill introduced by Mr Wilson in the last session—'that is to say, an attitude of neutrality'. He continued : 'It is right and natural that that should be so. We are considering a matter of the greatest importance, but it is not a party issue.' Mr Simon Mahon asked : 'If that is the case, why have not the Government had the courage to introduce the Bill themselves?' and Sir Cyril Osborne (Conservative, Louth), said that 'The Govern-ment are finding time for this Measure and are thereby giving it priority over everything else. Thus it becomes a Government Bill, except that the Government will not put their name to it.' Sir Arthur replied :

> The question of courage does not arise here. . . . Although no party issue arises, the Government feel that where there are signs of widespread agreement that reform is called for and where the social importance of the issues which we are discussing are so great, it is right that time should be made available for the House to reach a decision on the Bill.

What was wanted was a firm and clear decision by the House on a matter which had long occupied its attention. It did not become a Government bill just because the Government was facilitating the opportunity which the House had to arrive at a conclusion. It was a perfectly proper attitude for the Government to take.

It was an important moment not only for the Solicitor-General personally but for the other people concerned, as he officially and openly made his attitude towards divorce law reform clear in this speech for the first time. He said firmly :

> I do not hesitate to tell the House this—that for a long time I

viewed with great hesitation and doubt the desirability of abandoning the central concept of the matrimonial offence. However, I have now come to the conclusion that the introduction of the concept of irretrievable breakdown is a welcome development in our treatment of this problem. . . . On any showing, however, it makes it a more overt and honest, and a less secretive, process.[28]

His conversion, from an opponent to a constructive critic and, later, to a collaborator, was also an interesting part of the drama.

After several exchanges between the Solicitor-General and Mr Campbell's team—Messrs Worsley, Lewis, Percival, and Sir Myer Galpern[29]—over the extra legal aid which, if the Bill was enacted, would total £400,000 in a full year, Dame Joan Vickers (Conservative, Plymouth, Devonport) said :

> As one of the sponsors of the Bill I regret that the Government appear to have no social conscience. A similar Bill was brought forward in Australia by the Attorney-General there. I thought that the Bill before the House would be debated with the Whips off.

She then replied to Sir Lionel :

> I was also interested in the point made by Sir Lionel about women. I am chairman of a committee which co-ordinates 23 women's organisations. If there had been the sort of outcry from them which has been suggested, they might have removed me from my chairmanship. They have had plenty of time now to take this matter into account and I have not noticed any such strong opposition.

She then exchanged several more rounds with Sir Lionel, Messrs Peter Mahon, Charles Doughty and Simon Mahon. She cited several interesting sets of statistics to the House.[30] Of just over 93 per cent of undefended divorce cases in 1966, the majority were for adultery. A small percentage of wives and a few husbands resisted the dissolution of their marriages and the defended cases were more often those of cruelty or desertion. The vulnerable age for a marriage to break up is twenty-three or twenty-four. Then there is the question of remarriage. Large numbers of divorced women remarry. In 1965, 23,600 divorced women, or 64 per cent of the number divorced in that year, remarried; while 24,300 men, or 66 per cent of the number divorced in that year, remarried. Of 12,200,000 married couples in England and Wales in 1965 only 0.3 per cent were divorced. She upheld the ideal set by Sir Garfield Barwick, the Attorney-General of Australia, of stable and sound marriage which should be a real relationship playing its part in the organic life of the community rather than a dead marriage not performing its proper social function. She argued cogently in favour of the Bill and concluded her speech: 'I am certain that it will create more happiness for many people than do the present conditions and that it will enable them to lead more honest lives than they may now do when separated.' Dame Joan was one of the only two Conservative women M.P.s who voted for the Bill.

Mr Daniel Awdry (Conservative, Chippenham) now argued against Messrs Campbell, Peter Mahon, Charles Doughty, and Kenneth Lewis in support of the Bill. Mr Awdry, a solicitor and an active member of the Church of England, was a strong sponsor of the Bill and his points were:

(1) Mr Campbell's view is too narrow. It ignores the fact that many distinguished lawyers and leaders of the Church also want to see a major reform made in the divorce law. It ignores *Putting Asunder* and *The Field of Choice*. The people who helped to write those reports were not guilty people; they were sensible, humane people who realised that the present divorce laws are neither fair nor just.

(2) I have had several meetings in my constituency with the clergy in my area about the Bill, and found almost universal support for the ideas in the Bill. Practically all the clergymen agreed that the concept of the matrimonial offence was out of date.

(3) Mr Campbell said that 'if the Bill is passed, it will give another surge forward to the steady disintegration of family life . . .', but I regard that as a cynical view and a great exaggeration. The divorce rate has increased, but so has the marriage rate. The average number of petitions (number of divorces per 1,000 married women between the ages of 20 and 49) filed annually from 1950 to 1954 was 4.42 per 1,000 married women. In 1959 it was 3.52 per 1,000 married women. In 1965 it was 5.77 per 1,000 married women.

He summed up his reasons for supporting the Bill: 'I believe that it is humane, fair and realistic. As I have said, I do not think that it will weaken marriage. I believe that it will strengthen it. . . . This Bill removes the sham and hypocrisy from the law and a great deal of bitterness.'

Dr Hugh Gray (Labour, Yarmouth) rose and said that the Bill was an interim measure which did not go far enough, although as far as it went he supported it, since it would remove some hypocrisy. However, he felt that:

. . . the sponsors of the Bill have missed a great opportunity. One can rally behind reform only a certain political and social dynamic. I regret very much that the Bill is such an interim Measure and that in 10–20 years' time somebody else will have to come before the House and introduce a new one. . . . Indeed, I look forward to the time when divorces will be dealt with not by the courts, but by the registrar of births, deaths and marriages, in cases in which agreement is reached on the division of property between the two partners and there are no children. . . .

In reply to this extreme view expressed by Dr Gray, Mr Ian Percival, Q.C., the most formidable Opposition spokesman, joined the debate from the Tory front bench :

Sooner or later, this House will have to face the question of whether Private Members' business is to remain Private Members' business. . . . What has happened is that, with the assistance of the Government's authority, a procedural device has been used to continue the Second Reading debate on a Tuesday morning. . . . Can the Government really claim to be neutral in this matter any longer? Has not the position been reached when they should take over responsibility for the Bill?

Before Mr Percival finished his speech, Sir Cyril Osborne cut in to repeat a point he had made earlier : '. . . the Government are, therefore, making a choice, and the Bill therefore becomes a Government Bill'. Mr Percival stated that he was prepared to go as far with the promoters of the Bill as saying that dishonesties had crept in under the present practice, and that these could be remedied only by a change of this kind. He was not opposed to that and thought it should at least be tried. What he was sceptical about was the two-year period—Clause 3(3) and (5), and the five-year unilateral divorce, Clause 2(1)(e).

At 12.53 p.m. Mr Richard Wood (Conservative, Bridlington), attacked not only the Bill but the Government for allowing time for the Bill. He said that it was likely to be a marriage-breaking measure. A large number of women were frightened.

This proposal—the one substantial change in the Bill—would do two things : first, it would bring relief, but it would bring pain to many more; secondly, it would relieve hardship, but it would do so at a very heavy price, and the price would be the threat to the security of a large number of marriages.

At last, the promoter's anchor, Mr Leo Abse, who had been waiting for this moment without a word, from 10 a.m. to 1.15 p.m.,

rose to speak. As *The Times* said : 'If the Bill's defenders were not
so vocal today, in Mr Leo Abse they had a champion who made
up for all their reticence.' Abse delivered his carefully prepared
speech with force, dealing tactfully with persistent heckling from the
opponents.[31] It was a long speech but it deserves quotation here :

> It is right that the Government should decide that every member
> of every party should have the opportunity freely to vote accord-
> ing to his conscience on an issue of this kind. That is what the
> Government have decided. I believe that in the country even
> people who oppose the Bill will be glad that there has not been
> a party dog-fight over the Bill but that it is entirely free from
> party partisanship. . . . As the Archbishop of Canterbury's Com-
> mittee, in its Report entitled *Putting Asunder*, says, all the
> judges and lawyers who gave evidence before it agreed that the
> law as it stands is unsatisfactory, however much they differed
> concerning the remedies which should be applied. . . . It em-
> bodies faithfully proposals for divorce reform put forward by the
> Archbishop of Canterbury's Committee which were regarded as
> practicable by the Law Commissioners. . . . The Law Com-
> missioners assisted in drafting this Bill which was believed to be
> not only practicable but which faithfully embodied the agree-
> ment reached with the Archbishop of Canterbury's Committee. . . .
> Because of the doctrine of the matrimonial offence, judges and
> lawyers are reduced to the role of scavengers, having to scrape
> round for the worst obscenities they can find within a married
> life and, within the present accusatorial system, hurling all their
> wretched findings across the court room . . . the Bill seeks, I
> admit, falteringly, but with a clear general sense of direction—
> to hack our way out of the jungle of lies, half-truths, miserable
> stratagems and ugly publicising that the grounds of the matri-
> monial offence has proliferated. The declared situation in the
> Bill of the doctrine of matrimonial breakdown means that
> attention can at last be given—I do not claim any more—to be
> riveted, not upon punishment, not upon the public branding of
> alleged sinners, but on the question of whether the marriage can
> be healed; and if lamentably it cannot be healed then at least it
> can be ended by the parties, who, after being apart for two
> years, could almost privately, with dignity and without public
> recrimination, see the end of their lamentably dead marriage. . . .
> At the risk of appearing to lack chivalry, I am bound to point
> out that divorce statistics do not confirm the claim of the inno-
> cence of womankind. Last year, in the provinces more husbands
> divorced wives on grounds of adultery than wives divorced hus-
> bands. Infidelity is, alas, or perhaps inevitably, no male mon-
> opoly. What is more, marriage statistics certainly do not reflect
> a picture of unmarriageable middle-aged women. Between 1941

and 1945, the largest concentration of divorced women remarrying was in the 30 to 44 age group. Now, the greatest concentration of divorced women remarrying is in the over 45 age group.
This is part of the general trend which is reflected in the fact
that the average age of remarriage of widows has increased
from 45 in 1931 to 52 in 1961, and I understand that the trend
is continuing. The fact is that in three out of four marriages
ended by divorce, the women fortunately remarry. Middle-aged
women today are certainly not prepared to accept the assumption either of shrewish members of their own sex or the conceit
of some male Members of this House who would write off a
woman at 45. Moreover, the myth—and it is a myth—that
middle-aged husbands are manoeuvring to discard their wives
and children finds no substantiation in the Registrar-General's
figures. Apart from the fact that divorce rates are higher for
childless couples—in two-thirds of divorces there are either no
children or only one child—the most vulnerable point in marriage appears to be in those between five and nine years' duration. Long duration marriages of the middle-aged are remark-
ably stable. As a middle-aged husband with children, that is
what I would expect. Middle-aged couples are bound together
not by law, but by love. Fortunately for most, it grows through
the years as the couples share together the memories of family
crisis, travail, joys, struggles, and concern for the little ones,
their defeats and their successes. . . . In the meantime, the Bill
affirms its intention not to have an easier divorce law, but to
have a more rational one, one that is more humane, more compassionate, and, in my view, more in keeping with the civilised
feelings of our people.[32]

As soon as Mr Abse had wound up the debate, Mr Peter Jackson
moved 'That the Question be now put'. The House divided : Ayes
188, Noes 103, and then voted on the Question. The results were :[33]

Ayes : 183
Noes : 106

Majority : 77

After 25 M.P.s[34] had exchanged vehement argument, 268[35] silent
members joined the division with the above 25 and a silent majority
of 173 out of 268 said 'yes' for the Bill, while 92 said 'no'. It was
at 2 p.m. on Tuesday, 17th December, 1968, when the long and
bitter debate ended with the sound of cheers during the luncheon
hour. Some members had gone out for an hour; others were having lunch with the intention of arriving (and some did arrive) after
lunch, to hear the end of the debate and vote.

In four hours, 13 speeches and 77 interventions by 24 members

—two women[36] and 22 men—were exchanged. The 13 speeches were equally shared between the reformers and the opponents, one being the Solicitor-General who spoke for the Government. Forty-four out of 77 interventions were made by 13 opponents[37] and three were by Mr Kenneth Lewis (Conservative, Rutland and Stamford) who did not join the division, while 30 were shared by 12 supporters.[38] No woman had protested against the Bill although 4 women voted against it. As some newspapers commented, the debate was an excellent one; but some sponsors were worried at the length of the speeches from their side; what they needed were short but good stirring speeches, as they had to worry about time. As a rule, when there are enough supporters, it is expected to carry through the debate as quickly as possible, allowing the maximum time for the opponents. The supporters tend to refrain from speaking unless it is inevitable, for if the opponents do not get plenty of time to talk, they may not 'get the closure', although in this case the Government had promised that it would provide sufficient time for adequate debate. In fact, as has already been seen, there was ample opportunity for the expression of a rich variety of views ranging from the extreme traditionalist to the iconoclast.

TABLE 1

The following 25 M.P.s spoke during the second reading:

For the Bill:*	Against the Bill: †
1. Mr Leo Abse (Lab.)	1. Mr Bruce Campbell (Con.)
2. Mr Daniel Awdry (Con.)	2. Mr Charles Doughty (Con.)
3. Mr Donald Dewar (Lab.)	3. Mr James Dunn (Lab.)
4. Dr Hugh Gray (Lab.)	4. Sir Myer Galpern (Lab.)
5. Mrs Lena Jeger (Lab.)	5. Sir Lionel Heald (Con.)
6. Mr Alec Jones (Lab.)	6. Mr Kenneth Lewis (Con.)**
7. Miss Joan Lestor (Lab.)	7. Mr Peter Mahon (Lab.)
8. Mr Nicholas Ridley (Con.)	8. Mr Simon Mahon (Lab.)**
9. Dame Joan Vickers (Con.)	9. Sir Cyril Osborne (Con.)
10. Mr David Weitzman (Lab.)	10. Mr Ian Percival (Con.)
	11. Mr Raphael Tuck (Lab.)
	12. Mr. W. A. Wilkins (Lab.)
	13. Mr Richard Wood (Con.)
	14. Mr Marcus Worsley (Con.)

The Solicitor-General (Sir Arthur Irvine) attended the debate and spoke for the Government.

* Seven Labour and three Conservative M.P.s stood for the Bill.
† Eight Conservative and six Labour M.P.s (the majority of whom were Catholics) stood against the Bill.
** Messrs Kenneth Lewis and Simon Mahon did not vote, while the Solicitor-General voted for the Bill.

The actual debate[39] for the second reading thus lasted for five hours and twenty minutes, over two days—one hour and twenty minutes on the 6th December and four hours on the 17th December, 1968. Seventeen speeches and 92 interventions were made by 25 speakers[40]—3 women[41] and 22 men—one being the Solicitor-General who spoke for the Government. In all, 293 M.P.s out of 625 joined the division, Ayes and Noes. 332 M.P.s did not vote, chiefly because they were absent from the Chamber: 153 of them were Labour, while 140 were Conservatives.[42]

TABLE 2

The following table shows the actual division which took place on the second reading:

	Total	For	Percentage**	Against	Percentage**	Absent
M.P.s	625*	185	30%	108	17%	332
Labour	326	154†	47%	19†	6%	153
Conservative	251	23†	9%	88†	35%	140
Liberal	13	6	46%	1	8%	6
Independent	2	1	50%	0	0%	1
Welsh Nationalist	1	1	100%	0	0%	0
Others	32	0	0%	0	0%	32
Women M.P.s	26	9	35%	4	15%	13

* Five vacancies.
† Including the four tellers – two Labour and two Conservative members respectively.
** Numbers in this and all following tables are given to two significant figures.

Table 2 clearly demonstrates that more Labour M.P.s voted for the Bill while more Conservatives were hostile. 111 Tories (23 for; 88 against) out of 251 joined the division, while 173 Labour M.P.s (154 for; 19 against) out of 326 joined. As Table 1 shows, less than 10 per cent of Tory M.P.s voted for the Bill while 35 per cent voted against. Six Liberals out of 13 voted for the Bill. Little generalization can be made about the results, but one thing is clear: Labour and Liberal M.P.s were predominantly in favour of the reform and consequently nearly 50 per cent of each party voted for the Bill, or at least demonstrated their interest in the subject. Another point which may be significant is that there appears to be a strong correlation between the backgrounds of M.P.s and their attitudes towards the issue, although it is a little difficult to explain in these terms the existence of non-Roman Catholic Labour M.P.s who voted against the Bill.

Many factors are, of course, involved in the formation of political, social and religious belief,[43] and therefore it is difficult to generalize, but the voting result revealed that the number of legislators for the reform had been increasing.[44] It was also true that the opposition had increased its strength this time from 63 to 106, while the promoters increased their supporters from 159 to 183. Therefore the actual majority for reform went down from 96 to 77, which demonstrated how hard the opponents had worked behind the scenes, to rally traditional moralists and feminists. Catholics and other Church members who saw a threat to the permanence and holiness of matrimony and those who saw in the Bill a threat to the status of women and financial dangers for divorced wives joined the opponents.

Thirteen women attended and divided into 9 Ayes and 4 Noes.[45] All the ministers who voted, except one, were for the second reading. The exception was the Minister of Public Building and Works, Mr Robert Mellish, a Catholic, who voted against the Bill. The Cabinet ministers who voted for were: Mr Benn, Mr Crossman, Mr Diamond, Mr Healey, Mr Mason, Mr Stewart and Mr Thomson. Sir Arthur Irvine, the Solicitor-General, who had abstained on the second reading of Mr Wilson's Bill, voted for the Bill. Later he said he changed his mind after listening to the debates; a move which *The Guardian* (18th Dec., 1968) described as an 'acrobatic feat', saying it looked more remarkable to many when he suggested that he may have been 'walking a tightrope'.[46] Mr George Brown also voted for the Ayes. The Liberals who voted for the Bill were: Mr Bessell, Mr Grimond, Mr Hooson, Mr Lubbock, Mr Steel and Dr Winstanley.

The principal Conservatives who opposed the Bill were: Mr Boyd-Carpenter, Mr Gordon Campbell, Mr Gibson-Watt, Mr Godber, Sir Lionel Heald, Mr Selwyn Lloyd, Mr Noble, Mr Enoch Powell, Mrs Thatcher, Mr Whitelaw (Opposition Chief Whip) and Mr Richard Wood. While a number of Catholics, regardless of their party, voted against the Bill, one Labour family was divided on the issue; Mr Russell Kerr supported the Bill, when his wife Mrs Anne Kerr voted against it. All three party leaders, Mr Wilson (Labour), Mr Heath (Conservative), and Mr Thorpe (Liberal), abstained from voting.

Thus, in spite of powerful opposition, Mr Alec Jones's Bill successfully received its second reading within the time allotted by the Government. It was the reformers' greatest feat, for the Bill represented a new departure in that it embodied the controversial 'mutual consent' clause.[47] All those humorous but serious debates and struggles finally brought about long awaited Christmas presents for those who had worked hard alongside the sponsors of the Bill and the DLRU.

On the other hand, it was a great disappointment and shock for those opponents who stood firmly against the Bill. Indeed there was a protest from Conservative and Labour members against the decision to provide Government time for the second reading. Two Conservatives—Mr Raymond Gower (Barry) and Mr John Biggs-Davison (Chigwell)—and one Labour member, Mr Peter Mahon, had signed a motion (tabled after the second reading of the Bill had been carried) protesting against the Government's action. All three members voted against the Bill. They said that it would be more appropriate and fair if the Government either allowed the fate of all private members' bills to take a normal course, or had the courage to take full responsibility for social measures. It was actually what Messrs Percival and Wood had said during the second reading.

Certainly the success of the efforts of the DLRU can be measured by the fact that Mr Alec Jones[48] had drawn only ninth place in the private members' ballot, in November 1968. But in fact it owed much of its success to the Government which provided enough time for its early second reading before Christmas, although the reformers had had to prove themselves able to obtain enough support in the Commons. It was an excitement as well as an exhaustion.

However, the Bill had to face yet further tests if it were to reach the Statute Book, and the reformers, recalling their earlier failure, refrained from anticipating an early victory. Indeed, after the success of the second reading they lost several battles because of lack of time in the later stages. As a matter of fact, following this serious struggle, there came another long committee stage : starting on 29th January, it lasted until 26th March, 1969. Before the drama reached its climax in the third reading of the Bill, the politics of divorce reform legislation in Britain was to witness further problematic stages.

Sir Lionel Heald had already begun to encourage female resistance to the Bill through the *Sunday Post* (22nd December, 1968) :

> Women should fight this to the last ditch . . . the Bill is a bad one for the women of this country. It's not too late to kill it. It still has to go through the committee stage, third reading and report in the Commons before going to the Lords. The womenfolk, however, can kill it if enough of them make their views known.

III. *The Voting Analysed*

The following tables give an analysis of the voting.[49] The second reading has been selected because the total number voting upon the Bill was substantially higher than for any other division. Perhaps because of a free vote members expressed their views on the issue without reserve.

1. *Voting by Party*[50]

2. *Voting by Age Groups*

TABLE 3[51]

Age	For	Percentage	Against	Percentage	Not voting
Under 35	13	48%	3	11%	40%
35–44	55	34%	19	12%	44%
45–54	57	30%	45	24%	46%
55–64	44	24%	27	15%	60%
65+	16	23%	14	20%	57%

As the above table shows, age is an important factor in predicting the attitudes of M.P.s to the Bill. As Table 2 and Table 3 demonstrate, party and age are the two general predictors of opinion on the issue. Younger members tended to be far more heavily in favour of reform, while older members tended to oppose it. The high non-voting among older members is also well demonstrated.

3. *Voting by Sex*

TABLE 4

Sex	For	Percentage	Against	Percentage
Male	176	29%	104	17%
Female	9	35%	4	15%

There were 26 women M.P.s in 1969 and 13 of them attended the division. Seven out of 17 Labour women and 2 out of 7 Conservative women M.P.s voted for the Bill, while 3 out of 17 Labour and one out of 7 Conservative women M.P.s voted against the Bill. Their attendance was 50 per cent compared to the men's 44 per cent. The party line cannot be applied to the women's case on this issue although a considerable percentage of women M.P.s from the Labour Party voted for the Bill.

4. *Voting by Religion*

TABLE 5

Religion	For	Percentage	Against	Percentage
No information	88	29%	45	15%
Anglican*	32	21%	39	25%
Roman Catholic	3	9%	13	41%
Free Church	20	32%	7	11%
Jewish	13	42%	4	13%
Atheist and agnostic	29	66%	0	0%

* Includes Church of England, Church in Scotland and in Wales.

Another important influence on opinion is religion, although it is impossible to estimate the intensity of individual conviction and the religion of 133 members was unknown. Sixty-six per cent of known atheist and agnostic members voted for the Bill, while over 40 per cent of Roman Catholics voted against. It appears that no atheist or agnostic member in the Commons voted against the Bill, unless there were atheists among the 45 opponents on whose religious opinions no information was available. However, the division of opinion amongst atheists is reflected by the fact that Mrs Short voted for the Bill in the Commons, while Lady Summerskill, an avowed atheist, voted against it in the Lords. Nevertheless, one may say that atheist and agnostic members are likely to favour reform while Roman Catholics are likely to vote against this kind of measure. According to Professor Richards, Roman Catholics strongly opposed the Abortion Bill and, to a lesser extent, the Divorce Reform Bill.[52]

5. *Voting by Schooling*

TABLE 6

Schools	For	Percentage	Against	Percentage
Elementary School Leavers	15	36%	7	17%
State Secondary	115	37%	32	10%
Public	54	20%	69	25%

Education seems always to have an important influence on opinion. More elementary school leavers were for the reform and belonged to the Labour Party, while more public school pupils were Conservative and voted against the reform. The next table shows patterns of voting by higher education.

6. Voting by Higher Education

TABLE 7

Universities	For	Percentage	Against	Percentage
Oxbridge	53	22%	44	19%
Other Universities	51	36%	19	14%
Other Higher Education	19	61%	2	7%
None	58	29%	39	19%
Forces	4	25%	4	25%

Non-Oxbridge graduates tended to be more favourable to reform than Oxbridge graduates; there were more non-Oxbridge graduate members in the Labour Party and more Oxbridge graduates in the Conservative Party.

7. Voting by Region

TABLE 8

Region	For	Percentage	Against	Percentage	Total members by region
N.W.	28	33%	17	20%	82
N.E.	20	24%	7	8%	75
Midland	27	28%	17	18%	96
S.W.	14	33%	8	19%	50
S.E.	65	32%	36	18%	203
Scotland	18	25%	17	24%	71
Wales	13	37%	1	3%	36
Northern Ireland	0	0%	5	46%	12

Although this table invites a variety of comment, few conclusions can be drawn. Members for Wales represented the highest percentage of those in favour, while more Scottish members than any others were hostile to the Bill. As the table shows, Northern Ireland, Scotland and N.W. regions showed the top three anti-Bill voting-rates, while the N.W., S.W. and S.E. came after Wales in favouring reform. Nevertheless, this table shows a more well-balanced voting trend than any previous table.

Other factors may have been involved but it is interesting to note that three M.P.s—namely Mrs White, Mr Abse and Mr Jones who brought in the measures, were from Wales, although Mr Wilson was from Coventry South.

IV. *After the Second Reading*

During this period, almost all groups concerned, ranging from the Humanist lobby to a group of Catholics, were in action. Their efforts were directed to one of two different ends : some worked for the promoters in supporting the Bill, while others worked against it. Their main activities were holding public meetings and sending their resolutions and signatures as well as personal letters to the sponsors, other members and leading public figures. The following statement in an anonymous leaflet describes the activities of pressure groups outside Parliament : 'The minority who favour the Bill will write to M.P.s, to the Press, to the BBC and ITV, to public figures, urging support. Those who oppose the Bill must be equally active. Otherwise a minority will be allowed to assume the appearance and influence of a majority.'[53]

Indeed after the Bill had received its second reading, many more protesting letters arrived daily for the sponsors of the Bill. While the DLRU was directing its attention to the sponsors in Parliament, opposing pressure groups not only concentrated their pressure upon these sponsors but also actively supported the opponents and supplied them with resolutions which were later used in the House by the parliamentary opposition. At a meeting held on the 15th January, 1969, the representatives of the following organizations unanimously resolved to inform the sponsors of the Bill that they were gravely concerned about its implications : the Central President of the Mothers' Union, Mrs Joanne M. Hallifax; the past President of the National Board of Catholic Women, Mrs Evelyn White; the Medical Women's Federation, Mrs Jean Lawrie; and the Council of Married Women, Mrs Helen Nutting. They wrote :

> We the undersigned affirm, that we do not wish to dispute in principle the main purpose of the Divorce Bill as set out in Clause 1, but we believe that fundamental reforms in family law should precede any change in the law of divorce. Mr Edward Bishop's Matrimonial Property Bill is a step in this direction but it by no means meets all the problems of matrimonial property and social insurance. . . .
>
> *Clause 2(1)c and d.* We consider that the period of two years desertion by the petitioner . . . is not sufficiently long. . . . In our view these Clauses would seriously undermine the institution of marriage and encourage irresponsible entry into marriage. . . .
>
> *Clause 2(1)e.* We believe that this Clause, which introduces

F

divorce by compulsion after five years' desertion by the petitioner, weights the scales heavily against those who have done no more than maintain their marriage rights and, for the first time in English law, it allows a defaulter to benefit from wrong-doing. In addition it could over-ride the respondent's religious and conscientious objections.

The provision against hardship is unsatisfactory. *Clause 6(2)b* requires that the financial provision shall be 'fair and reasonable', or 'the best that can be made in the circumstances'. This is a paradox and means that the financial provision need not be 'fair and reasonable'. . . . The Bill is intended to legitimate some 200,000 children of second families. . . . The number of illegitimate children could be assured to balance fairly equally the children of the first marriage who are deprived of a father. Clearly the second family already has the advantage in having a father in the home. We would wish for more consideration to be given to the children of the first marriage.

We therefore urge that most serious account should be taken of these views during the Bill's further Parliamentary stages. The Organisations in which we serve represent a broad spectrum of societies which, in spite of many diversities in outlook, may justly be considered as representative of hundreds of thousands of responsible women in this country.

The above statement best describes the anxieties expressed by many other groups and individuals during this period. On 6th February, Mrs John Tilney, the President of the National Council of Women of Great Britain, also sent a constructive memorandum carefully prepared by the Council to the sponsors. Their memorandum, as they themselves recognized, followed the lines laid down by *Putting Asunder* and *The Field of Choice*. It said that 'the Council would not support any proposal which would make divorce inevitable after five years' separation regardless of whether the respondent wished for a divorce, and urges that a divorce should not be granted unless satisfactory arrangements have been made for the children of the family. . . .'

Thus most of the criticism was concentrated on Clauses 2, 4, and 6. On 8th February, the Catholic Parents and Electors Association also sent their views to the sponsors and requested amendments in Clauses 2 and 6.

For the opposition, Mr William Latey again appealed to the public by writing a letter to *The Times*,[54] and articles by Sir Lionel Heald also appeared later.[55] Their main targets were still the 'five years unilateral' clause and the financial protection clause, although Mr Latey criticized the so-called 'divorce by consent' Clause 2(1)(d) by saying that 'it was turned down by the Archbishop's Committee in its report *Putting Asunder* and by the Primate himself'.

On 21st February, 1969, on behalf of the Coventry Free Church Federal Council, Mrs E. Hawthorn, Secretary, Women's Section, had written to Mr Crossman who, on 26th February, forwarded her letter with his own to Mr Wilson. Mrs Hawthorn's letter was concerned with the financial provisions of the Bill; upon receiving Mr Crossman's request, Mr Wilson immediately wrote to Mrs Hawthorn and informed her that he had received her letter and would consider the matter and offered to talk to the members of her council. The sponsors also received a letter from Mrs Hart, Paymaster-General, who enclosed a letter of protest which she had received, asking her to stop the Clause 2(1)(e) being passed. Thus the opponents of the Bill were slowly but steadily building up their campaign and consequently the sponsors were busy in replying to those letters on behalf of their colleagues and themselves.

THE PRESS REPORTS

Most national newspapers and magazines carried articles on divorce, and indeed some devoted many columns to the issue. In July, and every month after that except August, *The Times* carried fairly frequent articles and news on divorce. On 7th December, 1968, *The Times* devoted 4,000 words to reporting the debate on the second reading of the Divorce Reform Bill and confirmed that the Government was to provide time for it. On 14th December, *The Economist* commented that the Bill was an admitted compromise between the views of the Church and the Law, more specifically between the Archbishop's group and the Law Commissioners. Because it was a compromise, its supporters in committee were not disposed to accept amendments readily in the proposals that had aroused most controversy. It also pointed out that most of the criticism was concerned with the possible financial hardship that a woman divorced against her will may well suffer, especially if she loses her pension rights on her ex-husband's death.

On 15th December, the *Sunday Times'* leading article said: 'Divorce Reform is the hardiest of private members' causes. . . . During the centuries of discussion no time has seemed riper and no bill so widely backed. Compromise it may be. But the measure deserves to get another second reading despite the feminist hostility aroused by its earlier success.' On 16th December, *The Times* again reported that there would be strong opposition, but on 18th December it gave an optimistic account of the result of the second reading, and its leading article ran :

There can be little doubt that the House of Commons was wise to give a second reading yesterday to the Divorce Reform Bill. It is by now widely accepted that the basis for divorce should be the breakdown of the marriage not a matrimonial offence. . . . Most of the sound and fury has concentrated mistakenly on the two new grounds for divorce by separation. . . .

Thus, *The Times* made its attitude of support for the Bill clearer than it had been towards Mr Wilson's Bill and suggested that Clause 2(1)(d) and (e) was essential if the principle of marriage breakdown were to be retained. It also pointed out improvements to be made during the committee stage, but it considered that : 'The valid criticism of the Bill, of which too little has been heard, is that it would still permit divorce for one isolated act of adultery and would make it even easier to obtain a decree for cruelty. These causes are no more than the matrimonial offence in modern dress. . . . Those who are rightly determined that the marriage bond should not be weakened in the effort to make the divorce laws more humane and more realistic should concentrate upon tightening these clauses.'

On the same day, 18th December, *The Guardian*[56] also treated the second reading as important news and devoted more than 3,000 words to it, in addition to its leading article which ran under the heading 'An Improved Divorce Law' :

The Divorce Reform Bill promises improvement, by substituting a realistic test of irretrievable breakdown for the obsolete and obnoxious notion of the marital offence, by introducing economic safeguards for the family of the first marriage, and by making flexible, generous, and positive provisions for reconciliation. The Bill *deserves to go forward.* . . .

Then it urged :

We cannot expect everyone to agree about marriage in a society where some hold that it should be indissoluble while others regard it as obsolescent and even unnecessary. In such circumstances the majority consensus should prevail. . . . So long as there is a majority for the Bill, and it was a large one yesterday even though only half the House voted, the *Government must keep open the channels to enable the Bill to proceed.*

On 18th December, the *Daily Telegraph*'s leading article criticized both the attitude of the Government and the Bill itself, saying that it would merely create two new grounds without adequate financial safeguards for the interests of children. It said also that the measure was one of those many bills which tended, in general, towards the establishment of what was vaguely described as the 'permissive society' in Britain. On 19th December, 1968, the *Daily Mirror* carried a long article by Mr George Gale[57] who wrote that it was a positive joy to be able to congratulate the House of Commons, and the Government, on taking the right decisions in an important matter. 'Charity,' he said, 'prevailed over principle and prejudice.'

On 20th December, the *Spectator* carried a lengthy article on the Bill, in which it was stated that

> while a measure of divorce law reform is plainly desirable, it is far from clear that the present Bill is the right answer, and certain that the financial clauses within it are gravely inadequate. They must now be strengthened in Committee, as best they can, before the Bill becomes law.

The above extracts are more or less representative of the trends of the press reports during this period and they continued in the same vein.

The next view is from a professional body. The *Law Society's Gazette* for January 1969 carried nearly 6,000 words on the Bill. It gave a brief historical survey and examined the Bill from a practical angle by studying its implications. It also commented on the future of the Bill:

> ... the reactions of the House of Lords are as yet unknown, save for public fulminations from a few members of the House, including Lady Summerskill, who is reported to have said that she had some 150 amendments to propose! What will be the results if it does become law? Undoubtedly at first there will be some rise in the divorce rate. ...

Before the committee stage started there was another voice which deserves citation here: the *Justice of the Peace and Local Government Review* carried an article of 1,300 words in its issue of 11th January:

> England is one of the few countries outside those where the Roman Catholic religion is established, where the matrimonial law is so unsatisfactory a compromise between a specious adherence to ecclesiastical principles (now considerably modified by the Archbishop's Committee) and a practical effort to meet the realities of human frailty. Nearly all the arguments in opposition to reform boil down to attempts to put the cart before the horse and to confuse effect with cause. To say that a more

rational divorce law will increase the number of broken homes is like saying that the provision of more hospitals will increase the prevalence of disease. . . . When the opponents of reform attack 'divorce by consent', they forget that 90 per cent of divorces are at present undefended, and petitions are filed frequently on the initiative of the respondent, so that proceedings are in fact taking place by consent in all but a small minority of cases. And complaints by the women's organisations that the Bill constitutes a 'Casanova charter' ignore the fact that 'offending' wives are no more rare than 'guilty' husbands.

Thus, 'for better, for worse' the press comments were favourable to the Bill and the committee stage began on 29th January, 1969.[58]

V. *Committee Stage*

By giving the Bill a second reading the House, as we have seen, approved of it 'in principle' without committing itself to the details. 183 votes to 106—in a House of 625[59]—was not an overwhelming majority, but there it was, an official seal of the House of Commons on the general principle of the Bill.

TABLE 9

The Committee consisted of the following twenty members, with Sir Harry Legge-Bourke (Conservative, Isle of Ely) in the Chair:

For the Bill: (8 Lab. and 3 Con.)	Against the Bill: (6 Con. and 3 Lab.)
1. *Mr Leo Abse (Lab.)	1. Mr John Biggs-Davison (Con.)
2. Mr Daniel Awdry (Con.)	2. †Mr Albert Booth (Lab.)
3. Mr Ian Gilmour (Con.)	3. Mr Bruce Campbell (Con.)
4. *Dr Hugh Gray (Lab.)	4. *Sir Lionel Heald (Con.)
5. *Mr Peter Jackson (Lab.)	5. Mr Ian Percival (Con.)
6. *Mrs Lena Jeger (Lab.)	6. Dr Shirley Summerskill (Lab.)
7. Mr Alec Jones (Lab.)	7. *Dame Irene Ward (Con.)
8. *Mr John Parker (Lab.)	8. Mr W. A. Wilkins (Lab.)
9. *Mrs Renée Short (Lab.)	9. Mr Marcus Worsley (Con.)
10. *Dame Joan Vickers (Con.)	
11. *Mr William Wilson (Lab.)	

* They were also members for the Standing Committee C for Mr Wilson's Bill – eight veteran members for the Bill, and two against, remained.
† As is pointed out on p. 190 n.61, Mr Booth more frequently voted with the promoters of the Bill, and consequently he may also be regarded as a supporter of this measure.

The attention of supporters of divorce law reform had been

focused on Parliament; but as the battle switched from the floor of the House to Committee, the progress of the Bill was followed only by a few anxious people. The members of Standing Committee B were duly chosen by the Chairman of the Committee of Selection, Mr Clifford Kenyon, Labour M.P. for Chorley. Half of the twenty members of the previous year's Standing Committee C[60] were replaced by new members, and the Chairman of that committee, Sir Myer Galpern, was replaced by Sir Harry Legge-Bourke. In accordance with the rules of the House, the balance of the Committee was kept at 11/9.[61]

Both sides consolidated their forces for this stage. Although the promoters of the Bill replaced only three of the members who had sat on the committee of the previous year, the opponents found it necessary to change seven out of nine of their members.[62] (see Table 9.)

In 1937, A. P. Herbert interestingly described the scenes of committee stage in his pioneer works, *The Ayes Have It* and *The Birth of an Act*. In a similar situation the reformers, in 1969, encouraged, but still alarmed, began the long and exhausting business of committee. In the Committee Room, through which the Bill had already once passed, without publicity or glamour, the real work of Parliament is being done; here is the true test of the merits of a measure and the quality of its promoters and opponents. Even the Government, commanding an assured majority, may make slow progress with an unpopular measure, when resisted with resolution and skill by a small minority in committee. Experts know stories about bills, thus opposed, of which not more than a couple of *words* had been passed after days of debate. The reformers were not the Government, but a small group of private members with an extremely vulnerable cargo. It was certain that the promoters would face a determined and skilled opposition, backed by the forces outside which, for decades, had successfully resisted other bills. True, the opponents had not shown much fight yet, but that, some believed, was part of their strategy. They had not wanted it to be said that they had prevented a fair examination of the Bill, and so they had permitted the second reading to go through. Now, having met the promoters in the swamps of committee upstairs, the opponents would tactfully and slowly destroy the Bill as they had nearly succeeded in doing on the previous occasion.

In committee, every clause, every line, every word and comma, may be questioned, amended, deleted and put back. In committee there are not the same restrictions on debate as there are upon a second or third reading, where a member may not speak more than once; in theory, he may speak as often as he will upon any question. Furthermore, he may put down almost any number of amendments, which, if they are called, must be met and discussed.

In committee few members sit and vote without proper study and a member must prepare for the debate and follow the line of argument closely. The Chairman, too, must not merely sit in the chair and preserve order. He must also study long pages of amendments before each day's business, and understand precisely the purpose, meaning and propriety of each of them. His intellect must equal his tact. He must let everybody talk who will, yet seize every opportunity to drive the business along and, above all, he must be fair. The Chairman of the Standing Committee B, Sir Harry Legge-Bourke (Conservative, Isle of Ely), was later praised by a promoter for his fairness during the committee stage, although he voted against the Bill at both the second and third reading.

The full Bill, which was 6 pages long, contained 11 clauses. The committee stage occupied 13 sittings[63] during which 28 divisions were forced. It took 26 hours and 29 minutes from 29th January to 26th March, 1969, and the debate is recorded in 500 columns. As the debate in the second reading had suggested, when the committee stage of the Bill resumed, the major attack was concentrated on the controversial Clause 2. It took nearly 16 hours to consider, as opposed to Clause 1 which was passed within 50 minutes. The remaining nine clauses were debated in short batches, and took less than 10 hours altogether.

The first sitting of the Standing Committee B[64] for the Divorce Reform Bill resumed at 10.30 a.m. on Wednesday, 29th January, 1969, and immediately Clause 1, which made breakdown of marriage the sole ground for divorce, became a target of attack. Sir Lionel Heald and Mr Bruce Campbell represented the two main streams in the opposition. Sir Lionel was for the principle but suggested 'some substantial amendments' because the principle was an abstract proposition, while Mr Campbell, as might have been expected from his earlier statements, made evident his intention to fight the Bill through all its stages, clause by clause. Mr Campbell said that the Bill retained matrimonial offences and relied upon them.

> All that the Bill does, in effect, is to alter the present grounds for divorce by adding some extra grounds and slightly altering those which already exist, and by adding a few words to Clause 2 we could make Clause 1 a mere surplusage. That, I suggest, is what it is. It will have no practical effect upon the administration of the divorce of this country. However, it introduces the new idea that marriages should be dissolved not on the basis of a matrimonial offence but on the basis that the marriage has irretrievably broken down. All it does is to introduce the idea.[65]

He thus strongly opposed Clause 1, claiming that it achieved nothing apart from implanting that idea in people's minds. After his speech, Messrs Awdry, Abse and Dame Irene Ward expressed their views and the Question was put on Clause 1, which had actually passed through the previous year's committee stage unopposed. The Question was, however, agreed to and attention was turned to the far more inflammatory provisions of Clause 2.

Although the debate on Clause 2 took nearly 16 hours and 11 divisions were forced, there were no substantial amendments, except that several superfluous words were deleted. The promoters made no concessions in respect of Clause 2(1)(d) and (e). Indeed these two provisions were the most controversial parts of the Bill, and naturally incurred most of the criticism; objections were also raised to the clauses devoted to financial protection, namely Clauses 4 and 6. Some of them were merely occasioned by a fear of change, but most of them were substantial or at least worthy of debate.

There were eloquent, vigorous and effective speakers for both sides. Three major opponents, namely Sir Lionel Heald, Mr Campbell[66] and Mr Percival had no strong religious objection to divorce, but they were concerned about the interests of the children and wives concerned. These three Q.C.s disliked Clause 2(1)(d) and (e); they foresaw the nation set upon 'the slippery slope' to 'easy divorce'.

However, on the whole, the debate was mainly carried on by lawyers[67] of great experience and their speeches pointed out almost all possible consequences that the Bill might bring about. Apart from the lawyers, four members were active: Mr Jackson and Dr Gray, who proposed the Amendment 41,[68] against Mr Campbell's proposal[69] to leave out paragraph (e), and Messrs Worsley and Wilkins, who supported Mr Campbell's proposal. They represented the two extreme views on the issue.

The Solicitor-General attended throughout the committee stage except for the fourth, fifth, ninth and tenth sittings. During the committee stage, there was a tense occasion when the reformers' members fell below the strength of their opponents. This was mainly because of Mr Leo Abse's absence owing to appendicitis and the illness of Mrs Lena Jeger. From the sixth sitting Mr Abse could not attend;[70] however, Mrs Jeger returned to the proceedings upon her recovery. It seemed that, for some reason or other, the opponents did not realize[71] that the reformers did not have enough numbers to maintain a majority, although even if they had noticed it and tried to put the motion, the promoters could have continued talking for long enough to bring in their members in time to secure a majority. Nevertheless, on many occasions, the promoters were rescued from the defeat only by the absence of their opponents. Dr Shirley Summerskill, for example, attended only the fourth sitting.

There were also a number of attentive spectators in the Upstairs Committee Room; among those who followed the proceedings, a promoter recalled one woman with a pink hat who attended every sitting of the committee stage. During this period one of the spectators, Mr William Latey, also assisted Sir Lionel Heald by providing an amended bill.

The reformers had expected the most bitter antagonism from the Catholic quarter, but in fact they were much more harassed by the Anglican lawyers. Indeed, on every motion at least eight resolute and able speakers could have talked—and talked again. It might have been called 'obstruction'; but it would have been within the rules of the game; and often in the past controversial measures had been met with such manoeuvres. But on this occasion they were not employed; the fair play of the opponents contributed much to the final outcome.[72]

The Lord Chancellor and the members of the Law Commission could not be the reformers' active champions in public, but their tactful explanations of difficult points were always helpful, and outside the Committee Room or the Chamber, they were generous with encouragement and advice. On the other hand there were civil servants behind the scenes who had drafted the Bill and supplied all the necessary information for the reformers. Without this constructive and tireless toil, a promoter said, he doubted if the Bill would have reached the Statute Book.

To sum up : the opponents had rightly pointed out the problems which were or might be involved, as well as their anxieties, while the promoters presented their powerful and persuasive arguments. But the debates were more or less a repetition of discussions which had already taken place during the second reading. Arguments or amendments presented by one side were completely unacceptable to the other; there was no dialogue between the two sides. Their ultimate aim may have been the same,[73] but they saw different aspects of the problem.

The report of the committee stage, which filled no less than 500 columns[74] of Hansard, proved that the provisions of the Bill were controversial, although more than half of the report was devoted to Clause 2. As a matter of fact, the only important discussion other than that on Clause 2 was on financial Clauses 4 and 6.

When the Bill had completed its very lengthy committee stage, there were a number of small amendments made to it. Of these, two were of some significance. First, it made clear that the respondent must be given adequate opportunity of objecting to a divorce petition based on two years' separation, if he or she wished to do so. Secondly, the court was given the power to adjourn the proceedings as many times as it wished if it believed breakdown was not irretrievable and that there was a chance of reconciliation. But the main provisions of the Bill remained unaltered and it was expected that the report stage could be started late in April or in early May.

VI. *Interval: 26th March-24th April*

The committee stage was completed on 26th March, 1969. Next came the report stage, which the reformers had expected to start within a month. But meanwhile, the opposition forces outside Parliament were rallying to the aid of the opponents in the House; they had already begun a massive postal bombardment of members, from which both the reformers and the opponents in the House were able to draw some useful lessons. It was chiefly the work of the women's organizations and of several religious groups. Foremost among them was the Mothers' Union, which claimed that their members throughout the country, a total of over 390,000, were united against the Bill. The Union and other women's organizations did their best to alter Clause 2 and to strengthen the financial clauses for wives and children. They were not happy with the outcome of the committee stage and naturally began to put all the pressure they could bring to bear on the remaining stages to alter the Bill, if not to stop it altogether. In fact, the reformers were a little worried, since such a bombardment might cause a stampede among sensible members, but they remained unimpressed by the substance of the protests. Sir Alan Herbert had said that thirty-two years before that 'the Mothers' Union claimed to speak for the women of England', but some other women's groups wrote to the reformers in support of the Bill, although they had their own proposals and in general most of them were against Clause 2(1)(e).

On the other hand the reformers made slow but steady progress. Firstly, they had established a firm and clear understanding with the Lord Chancellor's Office. Secondly, most of the press reports were still favourable to the progress of the Bill. Thirdly, on 16th April, three main sponsors of the Bill—namely, Messrs Jones, Abse and Wilson—were invited by the Chairman of the Law Commission to discuss certain matters regarding the Bill at Lacon House, then the office of the Law Commission. For the reformers it was a kind of extra rehearsal after the full rehearsal made during the passage of Mr Wilson's Bill and, whatever the reason behind it, their campaign was gaining momentum as it had done during the last session.

On 25th March, Lord Gardiner wrote to the Chairman of the DLRU in reply to Mr Banks's letter of 20th March, which had asked for Lord Gardiner's view on the likely effect of the Divorce Reform Bill on the position of wives. It ran:

I do so gladly, but emphasise at the outset that what follows is strictly a personal view; my opinion that the Bill will not really prejudice their position is not to be taken as indicating that the Government is supporting the Bill. As has been made clear on many occasions, the Government is entirely neutral and its concern is to see that Parliament has an opportunity of reaching a decision on those questions raised by the Bill which have been the subject of public debate ever since the appointment of the Royal Commission in 1951. The first, and, in my view most important point to bear in mind is that any defects that there may be in the existing law relating to the economic position of a married woman or the legal machinery available to enforce maintenance orders in favour of deserted wives do not stem from the current proposals for reforming the divorce law. . . . Those who have expressed the fear that the Bill will cause hardship in these circumstances have directed their criticisms at the proposal in the current Bill whereby after five years' separation an 'innocent' wife could be divorced whether or not she agreed. But it must not be forgotten that, if the spouses have been separated for five years, during that period the wife (unless in possession of adequate resources of her own) will have been in receipt of maintenance from her husband under a Court Order or a voluntary agreement or, if she has not been supported by him, will have been receiving social security payments. The dissolution of the marriage will make no difference to her position. . . .

Lord Gardiner also said that he accepted the proposition that few men can afford to support more than one family. However, once again it makes very little difference whether the second family is a legitimate one or not: in the nature of things, the man is bound to give priority to the family with whom he is actually living and no amount of legislation is going to make any difference to that. The next point was the question of a deserted wife's prospective rights to a widow's pension, which he said was a difficult one. He also included the results of the Opinion Polls on Divorce in Britain (by NOP and Gallup Poll)[75] and the New Zealand Divorce Statistics 1964–7.

On 11th April, the reformers received a letter carrying a list of thirty known and unknown women's organizations which requested an alteration of Clause 2(1)(e), and it affirmed:

At the Joint Conference between the Women's Group on Public
Welfare and the Standing Conference of Women's Organisations
held in October 1968 the following resolution was carried by an
overwhelming majority . . . the resolution reflects the opinion of
a very large number of women throughout the country. It will, I
am sure, be of interest to you.

It was signed by the Secretary of the Women's Group on Public
Welfare. Then came another request for further amendments from
the Men's Committee of St Columbas Roman Catholic Church
which read : 'May we, the Men's Committee of St Columbas
Roman Catholic Church, draw your attention to the convictions
which are shared by most of the four million or so Catholics in
England and Wales.' They also demanded alteration of Clauses 2
and 6.

However, the promoters were ready to uphold the principal
clauses of the Bill and, on 16th April, sent out letters to all likely
supporters reminding them again of the date of the report and
third reading. Four days later, on 20th April, they received another
letter, dated 18th April, from the Mothers' Union, with a resolution
which was actually identical to the one they had received earlier.[76]
The letter, signed by the Central Secretary, said :

I have been asked by the signatories, who represent many thou-
sands of women, to draw your attention to the enclosed copy of
a resolution, addressed to Mr Alec Jones, M.P., on the 19th
January last. Copies were sent at the same time to Members of
Select Committee B, to Leaders of the three Parliamentary
Parties, and to the Press . . . we feel that all Members of the
House of Commons should be informed of our views before the
Bill reaches the Report Stage. . . .

VII. *The Report Stage*

This was a particularly difficult stage. A short time was provided
on three different occasions : on 25th April, on 2nd May, and on
9th May. But still the stage had not been completed and finally an
all-night sitting was provided. Furthermore, during this period there
was an important change : the Government Chief Whip was replaced.

On Friday, 25th April, 1969, Sir Lionel Heald,[77] led the debate
for the opponents with an article in *The Times*. At 11.15 a.m.
the report stage was opened by the Speaker and two amendments were brought : one by Mr Jones and the other by Sir Lionel

Heald. While Mr Jones's new Clause 1 (decree to be refused in certain circumstances) was being discussed, the unofficial whip for the Bill, Mr Peter Jackson, attempted the closure, but on the first occasion the Chair refused to accept the motion. On the second, a little after 1 p.m. he moved the question but failed to secure the attendance of the necessary 100 supporters. When the House divided, the Ayes were only 74 against 24 Noes. Since the question was not decided, the debate resumed. It was obvious that the opponents, by whom the debate was mainly carried on, had decided to talk it out if possible. The reformers had learned that they were going to face page after page of amendments: Sir Lionel Heald put forward his amendment, the new Clause 8, a few minutes before 2 p.m. and discussion of it lasted until 4 p.m.

The Times reported (26th April, 1969) that 'although there are difficulties at this stage of the Parliamentary session, there is a good chance that the Government will find time to allow completion of the Divorce Reform Bill, which became bogged down at report stage in the Commons yesterday'. But its leading article supported Sir Lionel Heald's argument by saying: '. . . it is vital that the Bill should not become law until the Government has at least introduced additional legislation to ensure proper financial protection for the first wife'. Sir Lionel, said *The Times*, had made it clear that he intended to move a reasoned amendment declining to give a third reading to 'a Bill which is unfair and gives inadequate financial protection to innocent spouses and their children in the application of the new grounds for divorce introduced by the Bill'.

On Friday, 2nd May[78] the adjourned debate resumed at 2.08 p.m. whereupon Mr Campbell brought forward an amendment, new Clause 9 (voluntary restriction of divorce). It would have allowed the parties to enter into a voluntary agreement that their marriage was a lifelong union dissoluble only by death. He said that, after all, marriage is a contract. Some people regard it as a very solemn contract. There are still many people who think of marriage as a holy institution. 'The purpose of the Clause is to enable people, if they wish, to enter into a marriage which shall last for their joint lives and shall be indissoluble by the court.' Mr Campbell's clause was still being debated when time ran out at 4 p.m. The opponents, inside and outside Parliament, were all out to attack the Bill itself and the Government for giving time and facilitating its passage. On 4th May another article by Mr Latey appeared in the *Sunday Telegraph*. It read:

It has been officially announced that even if the Bill is passed into law its operation will be postponed to a Government measure for a comprehensive overhaul of the present tangled system of maintenance of wives and children after divorce. Would it not be more in keeping with constitutional precedent for the Government to take responsibility for the Divorce Bill and to hold up further consideration of it in Parliament pending the passing of the proposed maintenance and matrimonial property code? As it stands, the Divorce Reform Bill opens the door wide to still easier divorce. Petitions are already running at nearly 50,000 a year, a ratio of one divorce to eight marriages. . . .

Another lawyer from the Temple, Mr John B. Gardner, wrote an article in support of Mr Latey which appeared in the *Daily Telegraph* on 8th May. Thus the campaign against the Bill was intensified, the opponents concentrating their pressure upon the Government and the report stage.[79]

The third day of the report stage began at 3.05 p.m. on Friday, 9th May,[80] but the adjourned debate on Mr Campbell's amendment took the rest of the time available and for the third time the debate was adjourned at 4 p.m.[81] It became clear that the opponents were doing their best to stop the Bill before it reached the House of Lords. Indeed the Bill was almost lost during this period. The reformers were racing against time. They were not afraid of the strength of their opponents and were ready to argue for as long as was necessary; but they had only a few hours. There was a tense phase when they were given three short periods for the report stage to be debated by the whole House. This time was often provided at short notice and it was extremely difficult to get supporters to attend, since it meant upsetting existing engagements. On one occasion, the Bill came close to failing for lack of a quorum in the Chamber.[82]

At last, however, the Government provided the time[83] for completion as they had promised; but it was an all-night sitting on 12th June which meant that the reformers again faced the difficult task of maintaining enough members for the debate. *The Times* reported the situation (16th May, 1969): 'The Government has decided to provide parliamentary time on 12th June for the Commons to reach a decision on the Divorce Reform Bill, which has run into trouble at its report stage. It has yet to go before the Lords and time is running short if it is to have a chance of completing its parliamentary passage this session.'

There were nearly five weeks to go to the last day of the report stage. These five weeks were the turning-point in the struggle and there was no guarantee that the reformers would not fail again. They had to call up their full strength and carefully plan their tactics. Mr Peter Jackson (Labour, High Peak) was in charge of the unofficial whipping and the DLRU actively assisted him. On 16th May, Mr Jackson wrote a letter calling a meeting in the House for Tuesday, 20th May to discuss whipping arrangements for the Bill. The sponsors also received a letter written on 15th May from Mr Eric S. Heffer (Labour, Walton), who forwarded a petition from his constituency. The petition ran: 'Sir, We, the undersigned, respectfully request that you[84] oppose the DIVORCE REFORM BILL on our behalf', and carried about 500 signatures.

Then on 19th May, Mr Jones wrote a letter[85] on behalf of the sponsors to all known supporters in the Commons. Most of the sponsors also helped with the whipping on the Bill by writing letters to their colleagues.[86] One of their letters ran: 'Dear Comrade . . . Could I, on behalf of the sponsors, urge you to make every effort to attend the sitting especially during the night of the 12th–13th. . . .' Fortunately, within a week the sponsors had received enough replies from colleagues who promised to attend the all-night sitting on 12th June, and on 6th June Mr Jones again wrote to all likely supporters, urging that every supporter's vote would be of great importance as they had received only just over 100 promises of support through the night.[87] He also pointed out that a division would be taken after 10 p.m. on the 12th. Messrs Peter Jackson, Daniel Awdry and Emlyn Hooson were also active with Mr Service in an effort to maintain enough members for the night.

During this period, the reformers did not neglect their press campaign. On 18th May, Lord Goodman's article on divorce appeared in the *Sunday Times*. It read:

> The Government decision to provide Parliamentary time for the further stages of the Divorce Bill in the Commons will be welcome. . . . That the Bill has established a democratic claim to enactment now seems incontrovertible. Passed by highly respectable Friday majorities twice on Second Reading . . . the present Bill has enjoyed very comfortable wins in a number of public opinion polls and, so far as can be reasonably judged, has strong popular support in the country. . . . The benefits of this thoughtful Bill should compensate its supporters and the House for the loss of a night's sleep.

It would appear that Lord Goodman's article was aimed at the House of Lords which was about to receive the Bill from the Commons. A week later, on 25th May, Mr Service wrote in the *Sunday Times* in support of Lord Goodman's article, pointing out that New Zealand's divorce law[88] had been altered by reducing the periods of separation from three and seven to two and four years respectively.

However, in the same column there were two letters opposing Lord Goodman's article.

On 24th May, *The Economist* carried an article which urged:

> . . . But even if it then completes its Commons stages, it still has to be considered in the House of Lords, and their lordships' attitude is uncertain. The bishops are unlikely to oppose the bill in principle, because it is an admitted compromise between the proposals of the Archbishop of Canterbury's so-called group and the views of the Law Commissioners, and after all the bill *and its predecessor* received comfortable second reading majorities in the Commons. But Lady Summerskill at least is bound to oppose the proposal to allow a spouse a divorce, despite the other spouse's objection, if they have been separated for five years, on the grounds that it would be monstrously unfair to women. . . . The point is that the courts, or at least most judges, have realised that the interests of society are not served by the perpetuation of a marriage that has irretrievably broken down; nor are the interests of the children of that marriage. *Since the courts have taken the lead, Parliament should not hold back.*[89]

The *New Statesman*, in its issue of 30th May, 1969, published an article by Alastair Service entitled 'The Real Divorce Problems', and which ended: '. . . if enough M.P.s do not support the Bill through the night of 12 June it could fail, and we may be stuck with the hoary old matrimonial offence for another decade'.

Towards the end of May, letters had been sent by the DLRU to 350 M.P.s on both sides of the House who were believed to want a change in the matrimonial law. The *Daily Telegraph* said that the 'opponents of the Bill, who would have killed the measure if the Government had not come to the rescue with a special allocation of parliamentary time, are also marshalling their supporters for an endurance debate'.[90] It also mentioned that Mr Jones had received over 1,000 letters about the Bill, mainly from people wanting a divorce, and critics of the Bill were led by Sir Lionel Heald, who with at least 100 other M.P.s felt that the Bill was unfair and that it gave inadequate financial protection to innocent spouses and their children.

Thus both sides prepared for their final test which would take place within a fortnight. Since the debates during the committee stage were not very well reported in the press, neither side derived any propaganda from the debate. This reduced the opponents' chances of winning significant concessions. The coming stage was the last opportunity for the parliamentary opponents and pressure groups, mainly the womens' organizations, to present their case.

Finally, the crucial day came: 12th June, 1969. After three un-successful attempts to complete the report stage the reformers had now been given an all-night sitting. It was, moreover, a Thursday night when a number of members make an early getaway for the weekend, and it was not to be expected that many M.P.s, apart from those dedicated antagonists and the protagonists with their sympathizers, would sit all night.

Another disadvantage for the reformers was that Mr Silkin was removed from the position of Government Chief Whip.[91] The sponsors of the Bill thought themselves doubly unfortunate because, in addition to losing a strong supporter in Mr Silkin, the new Chief Whip was a Catholic, Mr Mellish, who had opposed the Bill in its second reading. It was disturbing news for the reformers, especially as the Chief Whip would have great influence in providing time for the Bill.

Indeed, as the reformers had feared, the result of the change was felt immediately. An unnecessary motion by an opponent was ac-cepted and tabled before the report stage. A few reformers felt that Mr Silkin, in the same situation, would have opposed the accept-ance of any such motion before the report stage, which was their fourth attempt to complete this stage, although the motion was not and could not have been accepted by the Chief Whip but only by the Speaker. This feeling was later clearly expressed by Mr Abse during the debate.[92]

As soon as the report stage commenced, at 10.09 p.m. Sir Lionel Heald begged to move a motion, which he claimed was not a wrecking motion. It was:

> That this House, having regard to the stated intention of the Leader of the House to order a Private Member's Bill, namely the Divorce Reform Bill, to be brought before the House for further consideration at 10 o'clock p.m. . . . thereby giving to that Bill preference and priority over all other current Private Members' Bills, despite his profession of Government neutrality towards the contents of the Bill, and his refusal to accept it as Government business or to accept any Government responsibility for it, declares that such action by the Government is in contra-vention of Standing Order No. 15, is *unconstitutional, and con-stitutes a grave abuse of Parliamentary procedure by the Execu-tive.*[93]

Sir Lionel then said that the House was now empowered to con-tinue to discuss the Bill for the next 48 hours, and that it had been given preference over 25 private members' bills which were already down for consideration on the following day. He asked, 'What is the justification for this?' He now came to his next point:

We then come to a small but interesting point which I know has been considered by many authorities in the House. If hon. Members look at the next item on the Order Paper, they will see that, at the side of the heading, '3 Divorce Reform Bill', is a curious thing called an asterisk. That is believed to indicate that it is a Government business. . . . It has been used in the past for such a long time that, like some hon. Members, nobody knows how they ever got here. However . . . one of the purposes of my Motion is to find out what it means.[94]

The ensuing debate on 'Procedure' lasted until 1 a.m. on Friday. It took nearly three hours before the report stage was resumed.

The debate on the motion clarified several important aspects of parliamentary procedure and, despite the protestations of both sides to the contrary, touched on a delicate party issue. First, for nearly 100 years the star had been used to indicate Government business; secondly, Standing Order No. 15 says:

The orders of the day shall be disposed of in the order in which they stand upon the paper, the right being reserved to Her Majesty's Ministers of arranging . . .

[This word 'arranging' gives Ministers a fairly broad discretion.]

. . . government business, whether orders of the day or notices of motions, in such order as they may think fit.

According to this standing order there are only two kinds of business which can be considered by the House : Government business and private members' business. The point made by Sir Lionel was that the present situation, under which the Government can use private members' bills as a convenient way of not opposing ideas and movements of which they may disapprove but which, they think, may affect the voting results at the next election, should be stopped.[95]

By bringing this kind of motion, a member can delay the debate within the rules of the game. Sir Lionel maintained that his move was not a filibustering speech, although Mr Michael Foot (Labour, Ebbw Vale), said : '. . . it must, I think, be regarded as a wrecking Motion. It could hardly be stated in stronger terms . . . if such a Motion were to be carried at this stage of our proceedings, it would be a wrecking Resolution.'

However, the main point of the debate on 'Procedure' was

whether the Government's act in offering time for the Bill over 25
other private members' bills was 'unconstitutional' and a 'grave
abuse of Parliamentary procedure'. Mr Foot said that the action
taken by the Government was a very reasonable conclusion for
governments to have come to and previous governments had done
likewise.[96] He made it clear that the motion was a proposal designed
to wreck the Bill. In supporting Sir Lionel Heald, Mr Enoch Powell
argued that Mr Foot 'is no doubt right in saying that, if the Motion
were carried, the likelihood of the Bill reaching the Statute Book
would be considerably diminished but that does not justify describing the Motion in any ordinary acceptance of the term as a
"wrecking" Motion, for it is a Motion which has a substantive
purpose and importance in its own right'. He also pointed out that
no member of the House 'can deny that the passage has been greatly
facilitated and may well have depended upon the interposition of
the Government's powers . . . therefore that the Government are
here exercising power without responsibility'.[97]

The debates were again largely a rehash of discussions that had
already taken place in earlier stages. There was still no dialogue
between the two sides; the attention of each was focused on the
motion. It was a shrewd move by Sir Lionel Heald and put the
reformers as well as the Government on the defensive. A wide
national consensus in support of a major piece of social legislation
may serve a government, but this Bill did not seem to offer the
Government any political advantage. Nevertheless, it came under
attack, and the opponents, many of them Conservatives, were not
slow to exploit the issue. Finally, at 11.22 p.m., the Lord President
of the Council and Leader of the House of Commons, Mr Fred
Peart, had to stand up. He said :

> Perhaps I should intervene at this stage, although I am not
> seeking to wind up the debate. . . . I suggest that the most com-
> parable and recent case was . . . the Divorce (Scotland) Act 1964.
> Whether or not the debate then was short, the same principle
> applied. The then Leader of the House, the right hon. and
> learned Member for Wirral (Mr Selwyn Lloyd), has signed this
> Motion which is somewhat remarkable. . . . I am not referring
> to isolated cases. I have with me a long list of similar cases. . . .
> During the past 20 years or so, about five Measures a year have,
> in this context, been given special help by the Government of
> the day to get the Royal Assent. . . . It is right that the Govern-
> ment of the day should enable the House to reach a decision and
> that the Government should exercise neutrality, as we have done
> in this case. . . .[98]

Thus the Leader of the House firmly defended the Government's position and its decision to give time for the Bill. He also made it clear that the decision to use an asterisk was made by the authority of the House. 'This has gone back over a long period. . . . It has not happened only to this Bill. Sixty Bills have been treated in this way.'

Mr W. F. Deedes (Conservative, Ashford), spoke against Mr Peart in support of Sir Lionel Heald's motion and said : '. . . the Private Member's Bill is an admirable mechanism, and the Public Bill is a better mechanism than is sometimes supposed, but when the two are mixed there is trouble. That is the short point I make.' Mr Simon Mahon, Mr Percival and Mr Kimball vehemently attacked the Government until 12.33 a.m. on Friday, when Mr Abse rose to conclude the debate on the motion. As previously agreed with the Speaker, Mr Abse was again given the opportunity to wind up the debate. His tone was cynical :

Unlike Mr Foot, I would not say that when the right hon. and learned Member for Chertsey (Sir Lionel Heald) tabled the Motion, he intended it to be a wrecking proposal. I suspect that the right hon. and learned Gentleman's innocence is equalled only by the innocence of the Government Chief Whip who, with great magnanimity, saw to it that this Motion would come up for discussion at this late hour, and before the Bill. I am certain that . . . Gentleman, who is deeply interested in constitutional questions, is genuinely committed to a search for the aetiology of the asterisk. . . . I am equally certain that the Chief Whip wanted to be sure that the equity would be shown in every respect of those who take an opposing view to the sponsors of the Bill. . . .

During his speech, Mr Simon Mahon intervened : 'Will my hon. Friend give way?' Mr Abse firmly replied 'No, I am not giving way', and concluded his speech by saying :

I hope that . . . the Member for Chertsey will believe that we have had a good discussion and had the opportunity through the intervention of the Chief Whip to have such a discussion . . . the Leader of the House . . . gave a hint that he hoped the time would come when he would ask leave to withdraw the Motion. So that the community outside can have respect for this House knowing that it will deal with social problems, I hope that moment has come.

Whereupon the Chief Whip, Mr Mellish, claimed to move 'That the Question be now put' and the House divided as to whether the

Procedure debate should now be ended : Ayes 166, Noes 62. In spite of the late hour, the following members were among the Ayes : Mr Benn, Sir Edward Boyle, Mr Crosland, Mr Crossman, Sir Dingle Foot, Mr Greenwood, Mr Gunter, Mrs Hart, Mr Healey, Mr Houghton, Sir Arthur Irvine, Mr Roy Jenkins, Sir Elwyn Jones, Miss Lee, Mr Peart, Mr John Silkin, Mr George Thomson and Mr Jeremy Thorpe. Mr Mellish also voted with the Ayes. The Noes included : Mr Bigg-Davison, Sir Lionel Heald, Mr Hogg, Mr Powell and Mrs Thatcher. The Kerr family was again divided, the husband voting for the Ayes while the wife voted for the Noes.

Thus the motion was defeated and the Government vindicated, but Sir Stephen McAdden immediately challenged the action of the Government Chief Whip, in moving the closure on a private member's bill, a move which the Deputy Speaker (Mr Harry Gourlay), however, refused to accept. A significant fact was that Mr Abse had openly challenged the Chief Whip and from that moment Mr Mellish never voted against the Bill : he in fact later voted with the reformers against Mr Campbell's amendment. Mr Mellish could not afford to divide back-benchers as he had to have their support for the Industrial Relations Bill, and he abstained on all the remaining divisions.

Finally at 1.05 a.m., after three stormy hours of debate, the remaining report stage was resumed and Mr Hugh Delargy (Labour, Thurrock), who had the floor when the debate was adjourned on 9th May, was given the opportunity to continue his speech. In a few words, Mr Delargy rejected Mr Campbell's amendment. As soon as Mr David Waddington (Conservative, Nelson and Colne) had finished his speech in support of the amendment, Mr Abse again argued forcefully, and wound up the debate, saying : 'After three hours of debate, I trust that the House will now come to a conclusion.'

Mr Peter Jackson moved the Question and the House divided : Ayes 144, Noes 58. All the ministers who had voted against Sir Lionel Heald's motion again voted for the Question. Accordingly the Question was put and the amendment was rejected by 149 Noes to 31 Ayes. However, Mr Campbell brought another amendment, on Clause 1 (breakdown of marriage to be the sole ground for divorce). The rest of the debate consisted of exchanges between Mr Campbell, Dr Gray, Sir Lionel Heald, Mr Percival, Mr Wood, Mr Hogg, Mr Simon Mahon, Dame Irene Ward and Mr Jones.

Throughout the night, a number of amendments were put forward by the opponents, mostly seeking to limit the scope for divorce. There were not more than 50 opponents and their highest vote was 58 for the amendment put forward by Sir Lionel Heald on Clause 6. Altogether seven[99] amendments were put to the vote and all were defeated. The reformers successfully kept the 100 members required throughout the night, but when Mr Abse wound up the debate for the report stage, the results were: 91 for the reformers, 58 for the opponents. It was 11.34 a.m., Friday. They had been debating for more than 13 hours already and yet only the report stage had been completed.

VIII. *Third Reading*

At 11.40 a.m.[100] Mr Jones was moving the third reading; and now for the first time the sponsors did believe that they were almost through, although the opponents still maintained the fight. But it was a winning battle for the reformers; there was resignation in the speeches and generous compliments to the promoters of the Bill from the opposition. There were 17 short speeches and 13 interventions. When the House divided for the third reading it was 2.10 p.m.

In this concluding stage, Mr Jones made his final speech. He said:[101]

> . . . I believe it essential that Parliament come to a decision on divorce reform and although I was the sponsor of the Bill I sincerely believe that I would have preferred it to be rejected rather than fail through lack of Parliamentary time or because of procedural devices. It is important that Parliament, for its own reputation, should make the decision, and it is equally important for the people affected by the Bill. . . . This is a consensus Bill. . . .

He thanked those who had worked for the Bill, and said:

> I want to take this opportunity of paying particular tribute to my hon. Friend the Member for Pontypool for his work on the Bill and for his work for many years in the cause of divorce reform.

He also expressed his gratitude to Mr William Wilson, the DLRU and Mr Alastair Service in particular, and the Law Commission. Mr Jones reminded M.P.s that Parliament had played cat and mouse for many years. 'All the world loves a wedding, because it embodies the love, hopes and aspirations of us all. No one loves a divorce and certainly I do not.'

Then Sir Lionel Heald said that he was sure that the House

would not wish to have a long speech at that stage, but he would put the reasons why he opposed the third reading. He congratulated Mr Jones on the work he had done throughout the passage of the Bill : 'We have always had the most pleasant relations and he must feel very happy that he has today received such remarkable support from his own followers. . . . I must add that those of us who know him know that there is at least one good reason for it—his personality.' He concluded his speech by saying that the Bill with substantially no amendment 'remains unfair and without adequate financial protection to innocent spouses and their children'. By pointing to Clause 2(1)(e), he repeated his argument put forward throughout the year.

After Mr Simon Mahon's bitter attack on the Bill, Mr Awdry said that the Bill would remove from the divorce law a great deal of the hypocrisy which surrounded it and from the divorce courts a great deal of the distress, humiliation and bitterness which surrounded them. Dr Gray also congratulated the sponsors of the Bill on having brought it forward, adding : 'I should make it clear that once again in 10 years' time the hon. Member for Pontypool (Mr Abse) will be bringing forward yet another.' He reminded the House that the Bill had gone through virtually unamended either in Sir Lionel Heald's direction or his own. He rightly pointed out that although the Bill would introduce the irretrievable breakdown of marriage as the basic reason for divorce, at the same time it would retain the doctrine of the matrimonial offence, despite its two principal innovations : namely divorce by consent in a civilized way after two years and divorce after five years against the wish of one party.

At 12.19 p.m. Mr Campbell rose :

On Second Reading I said that I regarded this as a disgraceful Bill which I would fight at every stage. I have fought it at every stage, and I still regard it as a disgraceful Bill. It will bring very little happiness. I am sure—I am sorry to be so sure—that it will bring a great deal of misery. People generally do not realise what the Bill will do. It introduces unilateral divorce. . . .

Following Mr Campbell, Sir Arthur Irvine, the Solicitor-General, said, 'I feel very glad that the prospect is that the House will come to a decision upon this Bill', and reminded the House that the Lord Chancellor would consider the financial protection issues.

Mr Hogg backed Sir Lionel Heald on the issue of the financial clause and said that he could never vote for a bill which retained Clause 6(2)(b)—'the best that can be made in the circumstances'.[102] These nine words were wholly unacceptable. But he made it clear that it had never occurred to him to think that the measure was a disgraceful one. He continued;[103]

> It is a Bill which has been very widely backed by a very considerable section of public opinion, and, quite apart from the section of public opinion in point of size, it is supported, and has been supported, by very highly qualified persons both in the field of morality and in the field of legislation. I therefore do not think it fair to describe it, even if one has reserves about it, as a disgraceful Bill. . . . Whether or not marriage be a sacrament is a matter for the theologians. We are not today legislating about the sacrament, if it be one. . . .

The rest of the debate was mainly carried on by Mr Delargy, Sir Tufton Beamish, the Mahon brothers, Mr D. Mitchell and Mr Tim Fortescue, on one side against the Bill, and by Mr Emery, Mrs Jeger, Mr Peter Jackson, Mr Wilson and Mr Abse, on the other side for the Bill. There was nothing new contributed apart from[104] Mr Fortescue's remark that the Bill, by and large, was a southerners' Bill. He also pointed out that although Mr Abse said that he had received thousands of letters in support of his stand, he did not tell the opponents what his constituents had said to him. To which Mr Abse immediately replied : 'I can assure him that every time I introduce a Divorce Bill, as the election results reveal, my majority goes up.' Then Mr Abse, as arranged with the Speaker, began to wind up the debate. It was 2.03 p.m. when he said 'I shall not keep the House for very long'. After six years of helping to bring the Bill to the Statute Book, 'I should like to participate'. The Bill was neither a Casanova's charter, nor a Jezebel's justification. It would bring out of 'the twilight world perhaps a quarter of a million people who today are denied the right to marry, and will bestow married parents on 200,000 children who are now illegitimate'. Then after making appropriate tributes to Messrs Jones, Wilson, and to the opponents, he called Mr Speaker and said : 'I now make a suggestion of which I am sure you will approve. I hope that the time has come when we can all go home to our marriage beds and to our long-suffering wives.' When he closed the debate, the House divided and the results were :[105]

Ayes : 109
Noes : 55

Majority : 54

There were loud cheers from the supporters when the Bill completed its passage through the Commons by a 2–1 vote. Messrs Peter

Jackson and Christopher Price were the tellers for the Ayes, while Mr Bruce Campbell and Sir Cyril Black were for the Noes.

It had been a long struggle but finally the third reading was obtained. Victory for the divorce law reformers came in the Commons at about 2.15 p.m. on Friday, 13th June. But in parliamentary time, the length of the sitting meant that Friday never happened, for once the debate had continued past 11 a.m. on Friday, Friday's business was automatically cancelled. At that point, barring unforeseen mishaps, there was nothing to stop further progress on the Bill, since the House could have continued debating throughout the weekend if M.P.s had wished. In a sitting lasting 16 hours and 6 minutes,[106] about 13 hours were devoted to the Bill, and 3 hours to a connected procedural motion which held up the resumption of the report stage.

Although numerically never highly impressive, and without any chance of defeating the Bill, the opponents led by Sir Lionel Heald and Mr Bruce Campbell were vigorous and determined until the last minute. There were also several very close shaves during the long proceedings when the vote on closure motions dropped perilously close to the 100 minimum needed to secure progress. It was a hard fight as the opponents, despite their small numbers, and even after all hopes of blocking the Bill had disappeared, continued their vehement opposition against the reformers and managed to show impressive fire-power. Speeches were short and to the point, and arguments worthy of this significant occasion were produced from both sides.[107]

Five minor amendments were agreed to during the long sitting— to Clause 2 (proof of breakdown) and Clause 3 (provisions designed to encourage reconciliation). Clause 3 was made mandatory rather than permissive and the other amendments were drafting.

Most of the national newspapers reported the news in a number of columns. For example *The Times* carried the news of the third reading on three different pages, devoting more than 3,000 words to it. The *Daily Telegraph* devoted a leading article to opposing the Bill, but it also carried a long article on the third reading under the heading 'Divorce Bill Set for Victory after 2–1 Vote'. It reported that ministers in the Lords already predicted that, although there would be opposition in the Upper House, mustered by the formidable Lady Summerskill, with Monday and Friday sittings if necessary, the Bill would go through. The bishops were expected to be divided. Indeed, the opponents hoped that the peers in the Upper Chamber would do something to amend the Bill, even if they were unable to kill it. Thus their attention was thenceforward focused on the business in the Lords.

TABLE 10

The following table shows the actual division which took place on the third reading (including the 4 tellers – 2 Labour and 2 Conservative members):

	Total	For	Percent-tage	Against	Percent-tage	Absent
M.P.s	625*	111	19%	57	9%	457
Labour	326	91†	28%	12	4%	223
Conservative	251	16	6%	45†	18%	190
Liberal	13	4	33%	0	0%	9
Others	35	0	0%	0	0%	35
Women M.P.s	26	7	27%	6	23%	13

* Five vacancies.
† Including the 2 tellers.

Table 10 again clearly demonstrates that many Labour M.P.s and Liberals voted for the Bill while few Tories showed an interest in it. Only 16 out of 251 Conservative members voted for the third reading, while 91 out of 326 Labour and 4 out of 13 Liberal members voted for it. However, this time the division revealed two significant trends. Firstly, the opponents rallied only 45 Conservative M.P.s compared to 88 for the second reading. Secondly, despite the fact that the opponents claimed that the issue was a most controversial and grave one, voting-rates, both for and against, went down considerably. Only 168 M.P.s joined the division whereas 293 had attended the second reading. Consequently, the total 'Noes' fell to below 10 per cent. The main reason was simply that, of the 88 Tory M.P.s who had voted against the second reading, 33 turned their backs on the opponents and only 45 showed up. The all-night sitting also did not help the opponents.[108]

Six members of the Cabinet and 19 other ministers voted for the Bill. The Cabinet ministers were : Mr Benn, Mr Crosland, Mr Diamond, Mr Marsh, Mr Shore and Mr Thomson; the Law Officers : Sir Elwyn Jones, Q.C., the Attorney-General and Sir Arthur Irvine, Q.C., and the Solicitor-General also supported the Bill. Mr John Silkin, former Chief Whip, then Minister of Public Building and Works, was among other ministers supporting the Bill.[109]

Sir Edward Boyle from the Tory front bench was among 16 Conservatives who voted with the reformers. His sympathetic attitude towards the Bill greatly encouraged the promoters.[110]

The principal Conservatives who opposed were : Mr Boyd-Carpenter, Sir Lionel Heald, Mr Powell and Mr Wood. Among the Catholics who had voted against the second reading, Mr Mellish, the Government Chief Whip, abstained in the vote on the third reading and on the amendments, although he stayed through the night for closure motions. On the other hand the Mahon brothers joined the opponents.

In the division, two wives disagreed (see n. 111 below for clarification) with their husbands. The Kerrs were again divided on the issue : the husband for, the wife against. The Dunwoodys also differed : Mrs Dunwoody,[111] Parliamentary Secretary to the Board of Trade, did not vote, while her husband Dr Dunwoody voted for the Bill. The two leaders of the major parties, Mr Harold Wilson and Mr Edward Heath, did not vote, while Mr Jeremy Thorpe, Leader of the Liberal Party, supported the Bill with three other Liberal members.[112]

The 13 women who attended were divided into 7 Ayes and 6 Noes.[113] The 7 Ayes were 4 Labour and 3 Conservative members, while the 6 Noes were equally divided between the two major parties. Fifty per cent of female members attended the division, while only 27 per cent of male members did so.

It may be wondered why the opposition was not more effective. Certainly a large number of women's organizations were deeply concerned over the Bill and their voice was heard in the Commons through the parliamentary opponents led by Sir Lionel Heald. The Mothers' Union, the National Board of Catholic Women, the Medical Women's Federation and the Council of Married Women, including the most influential organization, the National Council of Women, strongly pressed their views on both sides. They were, however, neither well organized nor united in their views.[114] Some accepted the principle of the Bill and demanded to have particular clauses amended, while others rejected it altogether. They protested by sending letters and resolutions to the press and other people concerned, but there was no vigorous and professional lobbying of Parliament. They lacked a systematic link between their forces inside and outside Parliament.

Above all, the results of the opinion polls and the opinion of the House made it clear that there was little hope of building up a sufficient majority against the Bill. Consequently, except for the second reading, the total vote against the Bill never reached 60. The only remaining hope was to try to secure amendments and delay the progress of the Bill. But a blatant filibuster for delay was impossible and they had to rely on the skilful use of the opportunities of protest allowed by parliamentary procedure.

In contrast to the opponents of the Bill, the reformers were a small group, but they were well organized and had a number of active campaigners. Among them, Mr Leo Abse was the dominant figure in the movement. His eagerness, experience, boundless energy, shrewd manipulation of the press, and his close personal relationship with several ministers and other individuals who were holding key positions in various departments of the Government and Parliament, were vital factors in the success. As Sir Lionel Heald said, Mr Jones's personality, though not as colourful as that of Mr Abse, also contributed to the reform in a positive way, and Messrs Jones, Wilson and Awdry with other members campaigned vigorously. Mr Peter Jackson, the unofficial whip, also applied pressure to members.

Outside Parliament, the DLRU, and particularly Mr Service, skilfully worked in support of reform and lobbied successfully. Alastair Service's initiative in soliciting both Gallup and the National Opinion Polls to organize surveys on the divorce issue was an undisputed contribution to the achievement of reform.

Finally, the role of the Government must be mentioned. In the General Election of March 1966, Labour increased its majority to 96 in Parliament.[115] With this comfortable majority, the Labour Government was able to help the reformers, although it was clear that they neither wanted, nor planned to introduce, any of the legislation proposed by the Royal Commission or *Putting Asunder*. The Government desired to see the reform Bill go through the course of a private member's bill.

Within the space of five years, from 21st December, 1964 to 22nd October, 1969, under the Labour Government, a number of controversial private members' bills were allowed[116] to reach the Statute Book : for example, Mr Silverman's Abolition of Capital Punishment Bill, Mr Abse's Homosexuality Bill, Mr Steel's Abortion Bill, and Mr Jones's Divorce Reform Bill. Any of these bills could have been killed if the Government had so wished. A good example was Mrs White's Bill which was withdrawn because of the pressure of the Labour Government.[117] This raises the highly hypothetical question whether these bills could have become law under a Conservative Government, and if one were to risk hazarding a guess, the answer is probably 'No'.[118] Despite the trends of social change, the evidence of the debate and the results of voting on all those so-called 'issues of conscience' in the House speak for themselves. The trends shown in all the divisions on the above-mentioned bills clearly indicate that more Labour members were in favour of change, while more Conservative members supported the *status quo*. The following table gives details of these divisions :

TABLE 11

Voting by Party

Party:		Labour		Conservative		Liberal	
Vote:		For	Against	For	Against	For	Against
Year	Bill						
1964:	Capital Punishment	268	1	81	170	8	1
1966:	Homosexuality*	184	33	51	69	11	0
1967:	Abortion†	130	23	32	62	7	0
1968:	Divorce	154	19	23	88	6	1

* Mr Abse's Homosexuality Bill was a Ten-Minute Rule Bill and received a second reading without a division; therefore the results show the division which took place on the first reading.

† On the Abortion Bill the third reading has been selected as the majority in favour of the Bill was smaller; all others are the second reading divisions.

The most critical division on each of the four issues has been selected for the purpose. All figures include tellers.

POWER WITHOUT RESPONSIBILITY

In a lengthy article carried by *The Times* on 20th June, 1969, Mr Ronald Butt sharply attacked the Labour Government. The article ran under the headline 'Power without Responsibility':

> Future historians may well consider that the existence of a Labour Parliament since 1964 has been of more real significance to the life of the nation than the existence of a Labour Government . . . through the important private members' Bills on social issues that have become law since 1964, the Labour Parliament, for good and ill, has had a significant effect on the life of the nation that was hardly calculable before 1964. . . .

In 1964 and 1966, he continued, the electorate never had any opportunity of registering an opinion on the so-called 'issues of conscience', but the Labour Government enabled the bills to go through by giving a helping hand with parliamentary time. He named the three acts which abolished capital punishment, criminal penalties for homosexual acts, and the Lord Chamberlain's censorship. Except for the abolition of the death penalty, for none of these did Labour have any mandate; for none of these bills can any but the most sophisticated of voters have thought he was opting by supporting Labour in 1964 and 1966. The Government had entirely evaded responsibility, and the Divorce Reform Bill, which had passed through the Commons in the small hours at the end of the previous week, was likely to be another such measure.

'This Bill potentially affects every family in the land and it is vital that it should be a good one. It is not right that it should be hustled through a thinly attended Parliament without proper amendment, by the will of a pressure group, without the Government taking any of the responsibility for what is being done.'[119] The Government was ostensibly standing on the side-line, while conniving at its passage by giving it precedence over other private members' bills and putting it before the Commons after 10 o'clock on Thursday night. It was, in his view, politically wrong and undemocratic that such a measure should not have the benefit of the Government's parliamentary draftsmen. The Bill was badly drafted and therefore he hoped that 'enough peers will prefer the realities of Westminster politics to ceremony, and turn up to send it back whence it came'.

On 23rd June, Mr Sharp, the Secretary of the Law Commission, immediately wrote to *The Times* in reply :

> . . . allow me to correct a serious error of fact in 'Power without Responsibility' in your issue of today. It is incorrect to state that the Divorce Reform Bill did not have the benefit of the Government's Parliamentary draftsmen.[120] . . . Although the Law Commission do not give advice on controversial social issues, they have given technical and legal assistance at all stages and on all amendments tabled; so also the Lord Chancellor's Office, following the usual practice when a Private Member's Bill of legal importance seems likely to reach the statute book. This technical assistance has been publicly recognised on a number of occasions in the House. . . .

On 24th June, Mr Douglas Houghton (Labour, Sowerby) also wrote to *The Times* :

> . . . Private Members do, of course, need all the help Mr Butt says they should have, but the allegation that recent controversial Bills have been badly or 'loosely' drafted or that they would have been better Bills had they been the Government's own work is quite mistaken. That was said merely as a line of attack. Both the Abortion Act and the Divorce Bill received the long and continuous attention of lawyers, doctors, religious leaders and laymen inside and outside both Houses of Parliament. . . .

Mr Houghton added that there was in reality little in Mr Butt's reference to 'hustling' bills through a thinly attended House or in his insistence on the need to have them debated in the middle of the week. 'The House of Commons will nearly always be thinly attended without the discipline of the party whip.' In the same paper, there were two more letters on Mr Butt's article : one from Mr A. Grey in support, the other from Mr G. Causley against.

On 25th June, Mr Abse wrote to *The Times* in reply to Mr Butt :

> . . . It is not surprising that Ronald Butt has proffered bad and presumptuous advice to the Lords to throw out the Divorce Law Reform Bill : his article implying that this is a dishevelled, ill considered and badly drafted Bill reveals he has done little research into the history of the content of this Bill. . . . No private member's Bill passed to the Lords this century has received greater scrutiny. . . .

Mr Abse then described virtually all the occasions on which the divorce issue had been considered since Mrs White's Bill was presented in 1951, and gave several examples of bills, including Mr Quintin Hogg's Bill relating to illegitimate children, which had received assistance from parliamentary draftsmen.

Thus a further and heated controversy preceded the debate in the Lords.

IX. *In the House of Lords*

I. SECOND READING

Although there were 1,061 peers in the Lords[121] in 1969, a large number of peers attended the Chamber only when there was something on the Order Paper of particular concern to them. In fact, the 'working membership' was about 750 and the turn-out on a normal day was just under 300; but peers usually avoid controversial measures, unless they are particularly interested in the subject. Therefore, if the reformers could rally about 150 peers, the Bill could go through without difficulty. Encouraged by this prospect, the reformers began soliciting all likely supporters.

The Bill was piloted by Lord Stow Hill, whose experience made a difficult task appear relatively easy. He was supported by a number of peers who had been fully briefed by the DLRU, notably Lady Gaitskell, Lady Birk, Lady Ruthven, Lord Henley and Lord Platt. Major parts were also played by Lord Goodman and the Bishop of Exeter, but there was no one in the Lords with a personal commitment to reform as strong as that of Mr Abse in the Commons. Although his freedom of action was limited by his office, the Lord Chancellor, Lord Gardiner, was well known as a strong supporter of the Bill and was in fact determined to see it go through the Lords. The DLRU did much work in securing the attendance of supporters of the Bill : the preliminary work that they had done in the House of Lords proved to be very valuable. Above all, a most important recruit to the cause of reform was Mrs Undine Barker,[122] who had been secretary to the Liberal peers for the past four years. She was later to be the voluntary organizer of Lord Gardiner's highly successful campaign to finalize the abolition of capital punishment, and she performed a similar service for Lord Stow Hill in lobbying for the Divorce Reform Bill. This extra duty often kept her at the House until two in the morning, telephoning, compiling lists, addressing appeals, arranging meetings. The following tributes carried by the newspapers on her death describe her activities in the cause of reform. The *Times* article (2nd Oct., 1970) ran :

> Lords' loss. The House of Lords has lost one of its most zealous campaigners : Mrs Undine Barker . . . [who] died early this week. She was 39 . . . she embraced these causes—and others, such as penal reform and race relations—with extraordinary fervour and deep personal commitment. Despite her charm (she was on excellent terms with even some of the most reactionary members of the Upper House) her private life was not happy : her interest in the Divorce Bill was at least partly personal. . . .

On the following day *The Guardian* commented :

> . . . She was also a social campaigner in her own right. She marshalled support for the decisive Lords' vote confirming the abolition of capital punishment, and performed a similar role in the cause of divorce law reform. Earlier this year, she was elected to the committee of the Abortion Law Reform Association. Her strength in all these causes was a mixture of charm, persistence and hard work. . . .

As the newspapers recognized, Mrs Barker's private life was not always of the happiest. She was the daughter (by the first, dissolved marriage) of Sir Mark Turner, the merchant banker and Deputy Chairman of Rio Tinto Zinc; she was divorced and fought a bitter fight in the courts for custody of her four children.[123] It appeared that she committed suicide in her London flat, in late September 1970. Several peers recalled her charm and agreed to the comment in the *Times* article that 'her passionate vitality will certainly be missed'.

On Monday, 16th June, 1969, the Bill was brought from the Commons; first read and sent to be printed.[124] The second reading was to be held on 30th June, which gave the reformers about two weeks in which to campaign for the Bill.[125] Mrs Barker worked with Mr Service and displayed her excellent lobbying powers in her first

G

real campaign for Lord Stow Hill on the Bill. On the other hand, most of the women's organizations which had sent letters of protest to members of the Commons began pressing their demands on the Lords. Lady Summerskill,[126] the leading feminist, led the opponents in the Lords.

At 2.12 p.m. on 30th June, Lord Stow Hill[127] tactfully moved the second reading of the Bill. At the outset, he made two general points. First, he mentioned Mr Butt's article and rejected its allegation by quoting Mr Abse's verdict on the Bill: '. . . the final end thinking of years of consideration by Parliamentarians, Churchmen, academic and practising lawyers'.[128] He also said that the Bill was based on the recommendation of the Archbishop's Group in *Putting Asunder* and the Law Commission's *The Field of Choice*. The Bill was prepared by Parliamentary counsel on the instructions and with the aid of the Law Commission, whose Chairman, Sir Leslie Scarman, was a distinguished and most experienced Judge of the Divorce Division of the High Court. He said, 'I should have thought that if ever there was a Private Member's Bill forged, tempered and fashioned in the white heat of years of intense and anxious Parliamentary and private controversy, it is this Bill.' Nor did he forget to press the advantage which he had brought to the reformers' attention earlier : '. . . the Bill and its prototype have passed, once completely and once most of the way, through all their stages in another place'.

Secondly, he called attention to Lady Summerskill's remark on the Bill : 'This Bill has been described as a "Casanova's charter"— an odd charge to level against the Archbishop's group!' Many burst out laughing and it lightened the atmosphere in the Chamber. He continued : 'Casanovas do not bother with charters. This Bill does not open the door to easy divorce. That door is wide open now, under the existing law, and it would be hard to open it wider.' Nine out of ten of all divorce suits were not contested. The existing system had the vice of playing into the hands of the less scrupulous petitioner to the detriment of the petitioner who respected his oath to tell the truth. It was divorce by consent by means of a legal ceremonial which at times was far from edifying and in which it was not fair to expect the judges, who took such pains in the administration of this difficult branch of the law, to participate. He did not think such a system was conducive to respect either for the law or the institution of marriage.

He emphasized that the Bill was designed to support and strengthen the institution of marriage by ensuring that before divorce was granted the parties had ample time for reflection and reconciliation in all cases where that was possible. It would give the court drastic new power to prevent the weaker party in the proceedings from being overreached, while preserving the existing powers of the Matrimonial Causes Act 1965 to safeguard the interests of the wife and children. Finally, it would bring to many unfortunate and blameless people relief that was denied them by the existing law. The law should not, as it did at present, require a sham combat between the two parties, requiring one to point an accusing finger at the other with all the bitterness that such proceedings engendered. Then he skilfully explained the contents of the Bill from Clause 1 to 9; he spoke until 2.47 p.m.

Lady Summerskill[129] (Labour) immediately attacked the Bill. She began by saying: 'I must confess that I did not know that my mention of "Casanova" would rouse him to such Freudian fury.' She admitted that Lord Stow Hill's plea was very forcible, but maintained that the far-reaching social importance of the Bill had not been recognized. The main purpose of the Bill was to make marriage more easily dissoluble without proper consideration being given to the consequences for the wife and children. As had been said, the Bill was the product of years of talking and reflection. Quite understandably, a tremendous amount of information had been disseminated in another place by the promoters of the Bill, yet after all that propaganda only one-quarter of the members of the Commons voted on the third reading. This could not be regarded as representative of the will of the people and certainly not of the will of inarticulate women and children who might be victimized by the Bill. She asked the Government to pause and reconsider the position, and give the country and Parliament time to do the same. 'How many Members are away in connection with the Investiture? I ask again : why this unseemly haste?'

If the innocent woman was to be divorced against her will the least the House could do was ensure she had financial safeguards. 'Best in the circumstances' in Clause 6(2)(b) meant that provision need not be fair and reasonable. Most men could not afford two wives. That was why she had called the Bill 'a Casanova's charter'.

Lady Summerskill reminded the House that the Royal Commission on Marriage and Divorce voted against both—namely, divorce by consent, and divorce of the innocent spouse by compulsion. After quoting relevant words from the Report of the Royal Commission and *The Field of Choice*, she said : '. . . the institution of marriage may have lost some of its flavour in this permissive society, but it has served us well for so long that, while it needs to be reviewed from time to time, any attempts to modify it should proceed with extreme caution. . . . I would ask your Lordships to vote against the Second Reading.'

The Lord Chancellor, Lord Gardiner, presented a well-argued speech :

> My Lords, this branch of the law falls within my departmental responsibility, and accordingly there are a number of things that I think I ought to say to your Lordships about this Bill. . . . All I want respectfully to point out is that I do not know that we have ever had any Bill to alter the grounds of divorce which has been a Government Bill; they have always been Private Members' Bills . . . we still have one or more Catholics in the Cabinet, and no doubt many in the Government and, of course, in the Party. Obviously, that is one of the reasons why no Government can ever make this particular subject a Government Bill. . . .[130]

He then referred to the financial protection for deserted wives and said that he did not want anyone to think that the Law Commission, Parliament or the Law could, by passing some magic wand, relieve the position of the deserted wives of low wage earners. In 87 per cent of maintenance orders the man was earning less than £16 a week and in 43 per cent less than £10 a week.

He disclosed a letter from the Chairman of the Law Commission concerning the financial protection for deserted partners, which ran : 'It is to these "innocent respondents" that Clause 6 gives the maximum protection possible.' Their recommendations on financial provision would attempt to rationalize the present position by ensuring that the court's powers to award financial provision applied generally, he said. The letter contained seven more items on the issue. The Lord Chancellor pointed out that 'in New Zealand they have now had 14 years' experience of the working of this principle of breakdown and I am told that of those who take advantage of this clause, "the Casanova's charter", over 40 per cent are women'. At this point the debate in the House was adjourned temporarily as the Nigerian problem—relief supplies to Biafra—was brought by Lord Shepherd.

At 4 p.m. the second reading debate was resumed. After Lord Sandford (Conservative) and Lord Henley (Liberal) had made their supporting speeches, the Archbishop of Canterbury, Dr Ramsey, said : 'My Lords, as your Lordships will expect, I approach the subject we are discussing this afternoon from the starting point of the Church's belief that marriage is the lifelong union of a man and woman . . . "those whom God has joined together". . . .' He had known that the existing law of divorce was very unsatisfactory; a law based on the doctrine of matrimonial offences[131] so often led to acrimonious disputes between the parties as to which of them was in the wrong, and encouraged a degree of collusion in such a way that divorce by consent was virtually what happened in the present situation. 'The existing law is bad, and I would gladly see it replaced; and there is evidence that many of my fellow-Churchmen with me would be glad to see it replaced by a law based upon breakdown. . . .'[132] However, he also pointed out three 'blemishes' : first, the so-called two-year clause. Secondly, those nine words—'the best that can be made in the circumstances' in Clause 6(2)(b), which had already been pointed out by Mr Hogg in the Commons and Lady Summerskill in the Lords. The third point was Clause 4 which defined the court's power to refuse a decree. He asked whether the words 'It would be wrong in all the circumstances to dissolve the marriage' corresponded effectively to the safeguard of justice. He appealed to his fellow-peers : '. . . be with me in try-ing to get these specific blemishes corrected. I cannot vote for the Bill as it stands.'

Lady Gaitskell, Jewish by birth but an agnostic, said she did not understand Lady Summerskill's comment that Lord Stow Hill had introduced the Bill with such 'Freudian fury'. Lady Gaitskell thought it was the kind of phrase that can rebound on the person who made it. Lady Summerskill immediately interrupted, but Lady Gaitskell continued :

> . . . views on divorce are based on many primitive and old-fashioned myths and beliefs. Despite the great strides we have made towards sex equality, the idea that men more easily tire of women than women of men is still prevalent . . . I take my figures from the brilliant speech of Dame Joan Vickers in another place : that out of 21,000 divorces for adultery roughly half were for the men and half for the women. . . .

She said that she could not accept Lady Summerskill's expression 'a Casanova's charter' because 'I do not believe that Casanovas are marrying men. . . . Incidentally, I looked up "Casanova" in *Ency-clopaedia Britannica* and found that there is no record of his hav-ing married at all', to which Lady Summerskill replied : 'I think if my noble friend looks again she will find that he did : in Vienna once.' Nevertheless, Lady Gaitskell continued to press her point : 'I should think that the Casanovas, the compulsive womanisers in this world, are rather reluctant marriers.'

The Catholic point of view was put by Lord Longford and Lady Kinloss. Before he became a socialist and a Catholic, Lord Long-ford had been the election agent of Mr Herbert in 1935; indeed, it was he who had persuaded Mr Herbert to stand for Parliament. However, he deeply regretted his part in these events when he contemplated the 'many thousands of divorces' which had resulted. His speech lasted for 17 minutes but the following words of his[133] may serve to describe his whole philosophy on divorce :

> Let me say a few words, briefly about the Catholic point of view. Though I call it 'the Catholic point of view' I realise of course that it is a view which is widely held by many millions of Christians of all denominations. We look upon marriage . . . as a Divine institution. It was instituted by God as a permanent union between one man and one woman. A marriage contract is not a purely secular contract; it is one that is inherently sacred : it is governed by the laws of God which no civil law can change. . . . 'Those whom God hath joined together let no man put asunder.'

Lady Kinloss made two main objections to the Bill. The first one was the problem of the children of the original marriage, and the other was Clause 2(1)(e), which she called 'the wholly immoral provision'. Her philosophy and motive are recorded in Hansard as follows :

> . . . I am speaking to-night because I have been begged to do so by many friends, both Anglican and Roman Catholic. I am myself a Roman Catholic, but I have in common with many of my Anglican friends . . . a belief in the permanence of marriage, in the sacred nature of the marriage bond, and in the Holy Family at Nazareth as the true image and ideal of Christian marriage. . . .

There were 29 speeches and 7 interventions before Lord Stow Hill wound up the second reading. Lady Emmet of Amberley, Lord Hodson, Lady Kinloss, the Bishop of Leicester, Lord Longford, Lady Sempill and Lady Summerskill argued against the Bill, while Lord Denning, Lord Dilhorne, the Bishop of Exeter, Lady Gaitskell, Lord Goodman, Lord Meston, Lord Silkin, Lord Chorley and Lord Stow Hill stood for it. At 9.42 p.m. Lord Stow Hill successfully closed the debate and their lordships divided :

Contents 122

Non-contents 34

Majority 88

It took about seven and a half hours but the second reading speeches in the Lords added nothing to what had already been said, and the victory for the reformers was an easier one than they had expected. As in the Commons, the usual party solidarity fell apart, cleric disagreed with cleric, lawyer with lawyer, and woman with woman. The Lord Chancellor, Lord Stow Hill, the Bishop of Exeter and Lord Denning argued skilfully against the Archbishop of Canterbury, Lord Hodson and Lady Summerskill.

Lord Colville of Culross (a member of the Archbishop's group), Lord Shackleton (Lord Privy Seal), Lord Snow and Lord Stanham were among the Contents, while Lord Ilford, Lord Longford, and Lord Lothian were among the Non-contents. Lord Stow Hill and the Bishop of Exeter were tellers for the Contents, while Lady Summerskill and Lord Hodson were for the Non-contents. Thus Dr Mortimer, Chairman of the Archbishop's group, took a leading role in favour of the Bill, while the Archbishop of Canterbury, who was present, abstained. Five bishops voted for while three were against.[134] Ten peeresses voted for the Bill, while four voted against.[135]

2. COMMITTEE STAGE

On Thursday, 3rd July, 1969, the House of Lords devoted 16 minutes to a discussion of how to proceed with the Divorce Reform Bill. Lord Sandford, who had voted for the second reading of the Bill, raised the question and said that 'it would not be thought right by all of us to have such an important Bill, albeit a Private Member's Bill, discussed on a Friday when, generally speaking, it is not convenient for most Members . . . to be present'. He made clear his concern that the Bill be fully discussed. 'At the moment, I have an open mind about the contents of this Bill and how I shall vote. But I am quite convinced that if we reach the Third Reading of the Bill with any feeling that it has been botched or hurried or rushed, I shall certainly vote against it.'[136]

Lord Beswick pointed out that one of the difficulties in this and other matters was that the opinion of their lordships, when it came to selecting an appropriate day for a particular bill, was not unanimous. 'It is most difficult to find a day which satisfies all noble Lords in all parts of the House . . . it has been found that we shall have time on Thursday of next week.' Lord Carrington stressed that this Bill was far more important than the average private member's bill, and that Thursday was a day on which their lordships normally sat. He said : 'This is a part-time House and an unpaid House, and as a general rule it does not sit on Fridays. There are a large number of noble Lords who do other jobs and who make their plans well ahead and do not get to the House on Fridays.' Furthermore, when the Bill was taken in the Commons and was discussed on a Friday, there was a great deal of criticism, in the press and outside it, about the fact that 'not many people in another place turned up'.

The Lord Privy Seal, Lord Shackleton,[137] said that a number of private members' bills, including the previous Matrimonial Causes Bill, with similar provisions, the Bill dealing with homosexual law reform and others of this kind had in fact been taken on Fridays. Moreover, he said, criticism could occur if Thursdays or Wednesdays, which were normally Government business days, were to be given up, 'on the ground that one would then be favouring this Bill. Friday happens to be more suitable for the Law Lords, because they are not usually sitting then.' However, Lord Shackleton disclosed that the Bill had been put down for the Thursday, and said : 'After all, the Opposition have the majority in this House. We have to conduct our business here in a general spirit of agreement.'

The debate made it clear that a majority of peers would prefer to discuss the Bill on normal working days rather than on Fridays. Lord Dilhorne, former Solicitor-General, Attorney-General and one-time Lord Chancellor, stated that in his opinion 'it would be wise if Government time could be made available' for a measure of this importance.

Lady Summerskill said that the Bill 'must be the most important social measure that is going through Parliament this session. One cannot compare it with the homosexual Bill or Abortion Bill.'[138] Both those bills were related to certain comparatively small sections of the community, while the Divorce Reform Bill was related to the welfare of every family in the country. For this reason she appealed to the House to reconsider the Bill.

After the discussion, the dates of the debate on the Bill were set[139] and on 10th July, the House of Lords went into committee on the Bill. Lord Sandford immediately moved Amendment No. 1, to insert 'in accordance with the provisions of section 11' after 'Act' in Clause 1. There followed a large number of amendments put down for examination at the committee stage. The first day's debate lasted until 9.52 p.m. On the second day, 11th July, the House met at 11 a.m. and adjourned at 3.35 p.m. after Lord Dilhorne's Amendment No. 25 had been accepted by Lord Stow Hill. The reformers lost only one out of five divisions. The debate was businesslike, with no suspicion of a filibuster, or a wrecking motion. On the third day, 15th July, the debate resumed at 3.09 p.m.; there were only two divisions, and the debate adjourned at 8.16 p.m. after Lord Stow Hill had spoken. The House spent about 16 hours debating the Bill in its committee stage.

Consequently, in seven divisions (See Table 12), there was one division won by the opponents; other minor amendments were agreed without division. The first division was on Lord Dilhorne's Amendment No. 3, which proposed to leave out the whole paragraph (a)[140] in Clause 2(1). It would have adopted the Mortimer group's formula, rejected by the Law Commission, and deleted the provision that the traditional matrimonial offences should constitute proof of breakdown of marriage. It was defeated by 106 votes to 54. Five bishops, including the Bishop of Exeter, Dr Mortimer, were among the 54 who supported Lord Dilhorne's amendment, while no bishop voted with the majority. But Lord Longford and Lady Summerskill, who said 'for the sake of the judges we must leave "adultery" in as evidence', voted with the reformers.

The next division was forced on Lady Summerskill's Amendment No. 7, which was to leave out 'two' and insert 'three' in paragraph (c)[141] in Clause 2(1). This would have met the Archbishop of

TABLE 12

The following table shows the results of seven divisions on the main attempts to amend the Bill:

For the Bill:		Against the Bill:
(1)	106	54
(2)	89	34
(3)	61	65
(4)	85	35
(5)	77	55
(6)	95	70
(7)	69	41

Canterbury's demand to extend the period of separation required before divorce by consent is permitted from two years to three. The Amendment was defeated by 89 votes to 34. Again the Lord Chancellor, Lord Shackleton, Lord Goodman and Lord Denning were with Lord Stow Hill, while Lady Summerskill, Lord Hodson, Lord Longford, Lady Kinloss and three bishops supported the amendment. Not one of the bishops had voted with the reformers.

The third division was a difficult one for the reformers. It was on Lord Reid's Amendment No. 9, which was to leave out 'does not object' and insert 'consents' in Clause 2(1)(d).[142] This was the one division that the reformers lost and the Amendment was carried. This made it necessary to obtain the consent of the respondent for divorce, thus rejecting, as inadequate, the mere absence of objection. It was a crucial alteration which would delay divorce in cases where a respondent feels uneasy, if not unable, possibly for religious reasons, to 'consent' to divorce, although willing to abstain from objection. It appeared that the arguments of Lord Reid, Lord Dilhorne and Lady Summerskill that the Bill contained provision 2(1)(e) which allowed divorce without consent and this provision (d) required consent—and it must be a real consent rather than 'does not object'—appealed to some peers who had been voting for the reformers. Lord Reid argued :

> I can understand the case where there is consent, and I can understand the case where there is no consent, but why does the Bill say, 'does not object'? I cannot see the point of that. I have great difficulty in seeing how that distinguishes the two-year condition from the five-year condition.[143]

This Amendment divided the reformers, for Lord Goodman and the Bishop of Exeter[144] supported it while Lord Gardiner, Lord Denning, Lady Birk and Lady Gaitskell were with Lord Stow Hill.

After the first victory was given by 65 votes to 61, Lord Reid again moved Amendment No. 10, to leave out the whole paragraph (e) in Clause 2(1). In support of the Amendment, Lady Summerskill, Lord Hodson and Lord Sandford argued against Lord Denning, Lord Goodman and Lord Stow Hill, just as they had earlier argued for Lord Reid's Amendment No. 9. The aim was to eliminate unilateral divorce after five years' separation, but the Amendment was defeated by 85 votes to 35. For the first time the bishops in the House were divided. The three bishops who supported the Amendment were : the Bishop of Blackburn, the Bishop of Coventry, and the Bishop of Lichfield. The two who voted with the reformers were the Bishop of Exeter and the Bishop of Ripon. Thus for the most crucial part of the Bill, Dr Mortimer supported the reformers, while the Archbishop of Canterbury deliberately abstained from the debate in the committee stage.

The amendment on Clause 4, deletion of the word 'grave' from the condition that a respondent can oppose the grant of a decree and the decree may be refused if divorce 'would result in grave financial or other hardship' was defeated by 95 votes to 70; and the next amendment on Clause 6(2)(b), to leave out the words 'fair or the best that can be made in the circumstances' and insert 'fair' was quickly defeated by 69 votes to 41. All other amendments were minor ones except one amendment on Clause 11. The operation of the Bill was postponed until 1st January, 1971, in order to give time[145] for the completion of new legislation on matrimonial property being prepared by the Law Commission, the aim of which was to guarantee more adequate protection for deserted spouses.

Thus, in the committee stage two notable amendments were made. One was to Clause 2(1)(d), by inserting 'consent' instead of 'does not object', which would make divorce more difficult in some cases, while the other amendment was on the date of operation. In

fact, the most significant change in the Bill was forced through by
the opponents in the Lords. Minor changes in the Bill were made
on the initiative of the sponsors in the Commons although these
were obviously a concession. Nevertheless, in the Commons the
sponsors did not lose any division on the amendments put forward
by the opponents, while the promoters in the Lords did lose one.
The main reason for this was because the reformers in the Lords
were divided and there were more opponents than in the Commons.

3. REPORT STAGE AND THE THIRD READING

After the committee stage was completed, on 18th July, nine peers[146]
wrote a whipping letter[147] to likely supporters of the Bill. It read:

> Report Stage will be on Thursday of this coming week, 24th
> July, starting at 2.30 p.m. and may unfortunately have to con-
> tinue *late that evening*, with many divisions to complete con-
> sideration of the Bill. The Bill has come through Committee
> comparatively unscathed and we are extremely grateful for the
> support it has been given. However, it seems that the critics of
> the Bill will try *again* to remove some of the essential provisions
> at Report and we would be most obliged if you would once more
> be sure to be present to support. In particular, another attempt
> will probably be made to remove the 5-year separation proof of
> breakdown or to alter its effect. . . . Finally, there may be an
> attempt *at the very end of the debate* to make the introduction
> of the new law subject to a resolution by both Houses of Parlia-
> ment. We would urge you most strongly to be present to resist
> this highly undesirable amendment. The possibility of taking
> Third Reading immediately after Report is under consideration.

On Thursday, 24th July, 1969, Lord Stow Hill moved the report
stage. Immediately after the motion was agreed to, Lord Dilhorne
put down four amendments to leave out the superfluous words 'since
the celebration of the marriage' in four different places. The amendments were agreed to without division. Subsequently a number of
amendments were put down, a major one being the Earl of Cork
and Orrery's Amendment No. 6 on Clause 2(5): to insert 'provided
that in the calculation of the period of at least five years for the
purposes of section 2(1)(e) regard shall not be had to any period
during which the parties to the marriage lived apart prior to the
time when one party decided on account of matrimonial difficulties
to live separately from the other'. After an hour of discussion, the
Amendment was rejected by 91 votes to 67.
After another hour and a half of debate on minor amendments

the report stage was completed, but the long summer recess intervened before the third reading on the Bill was moved by Lord Stow
Hill on Monday, 13th October.

Lord Dilhorne immediately moved Amendment No. 3, to leave
out Clause 4 and to insert a completely new clause, which was
accepted by the House. Unlike procedure in the Commons, in the
Lords it is possible for amendments to a Bill to be put forward at
the third reading stage, although by convention, such amendments
should refer to proposals made at an earlier stage of the proceedings
and postponed for further consideration. Under this procedure,
Lord Dilhorne's important amendment was moved and brought a
new element into the Bill. Lord Dilhorne explained why he had
brought Amendment No. 3. It would enable a respondent to a
divorce petition to oppose the petition of an entirely new ground.
No matter how frequently he or she might have committed adultery,
no matter how grave the cruelty proved against the respondent, and
even if there had been desertion and the marriage was really at an
end, the respondent could nevertheless oppose the grant of a decree
nisi on the ground that the dissolution of the marriage would result
in grave or other financial hardship to him or her and that in all
the circumstances it would be wrong to dissolve the marriage. He
said : 'That, as I understand it, is the effect of the Clause as it
stands . . . I doubt whether a respondent who was proved to have
committed adultery on a number of occasions, or to have been
guilty of great cruelty, would be able by invoking this clause to get
the court to dismiss a petition.'[148] He also said that he had felt that
the real need for a clause on the lines of Clause 4 related to petitions
based on a five-years' separation, that is, Clause 2(1)(e).

The Bishop of Exeter also agreed with Lord Dilhorne and said
that 'under Clause 4 as it now stands, it would be possible to oppose
almost any petition for divorce. But the new Clause 4 would be a
very important clause and would give a further necessary protection
to the spouse who might be divorced against his or her will. It is
in the situation covered by Clause 2(1)(e) that this question of grave
financial hardship is really strictly relevant, and the new clause will
be a great improvement to the Bill in protecting such persons to
some extent'.[149] The Amendment, which removed a possible barrier
to divorce, was accepted by the House without a division.

At 4.56 p.m., Lord Stow Hill[150] moved that the Bill now be
passed. Lord Sandford immediately congratulated him and said :

We had a single, thorough, full, seven-hour debate on Second
Reading, while another place had to take it in two bites, one
late on a Friday afternoon and another, nearly a fortnight later,

late on a Tuesday night. We took the whole of our Committee Stage on the Floor of the House in three full days, with never less than 100 Members voting in Divisions and with one Division as high as 160. The other place sent their Bill Upstairs where the total votes cast in the largest Division did not exceed 16; and one day of the Committee had to be adjourned for lack of a quorum. This I find an interesting contrast between a professional paid House and an unpaid part-time one. . . .

Lady Summerskill's final speech against the Bill followed. She concluded it in these words : 'I say that the title, "The Casanova's Charter", remains as appropriate as ever.' Lord Reid and the Earl of Cork and Orrery also opposed the Bill, but Lady Birk, Lord Dilhorne, and Lord Gardiner, the Lord Chancellor, supported it. There was a period when the debate was heated, but with only a few interventions it was given its final reading without division.

After the Lords had finished with the Bill the reformers in the Commons held a brief discussion on whether they should accept the amendments.[151] Because there was no time for further argument as the end of the parliamentary session was a few days away, they resigned themselves to accepting them all. On Friday, 17th October, 1969, Dame Joan Vickers congratulated Mr Jones for getting his Bill to this stage with so few amendments from the Lords, but she also expressed her disappointment at the Amendment on Clause 2(1)(d) made in the Lords by 65 votes to 61—involving only 4 votes which meant only 2 peers. She said that 'does not object' would have been much better than 'consents', because 'if a person holds very strong principles it is difficult to give consent'. She concluded her speech on a note of regret : 'Owing to the lateness of the Bill being brought before the House it was not possible for me to put down an Amendment, other than one which would wreck the whole Bill, and I do not want to do that.'

However, Sir Lionel Heald disagreed with Dame Joan Vickers, adding : 'I cannot resist the opportunity of congratulating and thanking the hon. Member for Rhondda, West (Mr Alec Jones) for having at last, although apparently with slight reluctance, acceded to the arguments that we put forward on such a number of occasions.'

Each amendment was put forward by Mr Jones and, after several speeches were made, Mr Abse quickly wound up the debate. Indeed, apart from Messrs Jones and Abse, the only members who expressed their views during the debate were Dame Joan Vickers, Sir Lionel Heald, Dr Hugh Gray, Mr Eric Lubbock, the Solicitor-General, Mr

Percival, Sir Cyril Black, Mr Worsley and Sir Tufton Beamish. The Commons devoted about an hour and a half to considering the amendments and it was 12.30 p.m. when Mr Abse concluded by saying :

> I trust that within a few minutes tens of thousands of people will find that this Parliament has passed a Bill which will mean that, although there may be many thousands of divorces, after 1st January 1971, there will be tens of thousands of long-overdue marriages helping to stabilise family life.[152]

Accordingly, on Tuesday, 21st October, the Bill returned to the Lords from the Commons with the amendments agreed to, and the Royal Assent was given to the Bill at 2.45 p.m. on Wednesday, 22nd October, 1969.[153]

4. THE ROLE OF THE LORDS

The existence of the House of Lords has been justified by the failings of the Commons and the Government. Errors and omissions in bills can be put right and improved in the Lords. The standard books place the emphasis on the role of the House of Lords in amending bills. In divorce reform legislation, the House of Lords, after the report stage in the Commons, was the last hope for the opponents to amend Mr Jones's Bill. Although the second reading speeches in the Lords brought nothing new to what had already been said, there was a difference in the style, and some authorities stated that their manners were different from those of the Commons : at least less heckling and fewer interruptions. Generally it is claimed that debates in the House of Lords are of a higher standard than those in the Commons, but in this particular instance the quality of debate in the Lords appeared no better than that in the Commons. In fact, it may be fair to say that the debate in the Commons was more comprehensive and penetrating; it was, at the very least, more interesting.[154]

The supporters of the Bill were aware that since there were more Conservatives and aristocrats in the Lords, if the majority of the peers were to turn out then the Bill might not get through. However, past experience indicated that only part of the 'working membership' would be likely to attend. The sponsors were already assured that more than half of those who usually attended could be counted on to support the Bill at the second reading. Even so, the reformers were conscious of the fact that the Bill was likely to be amended in view of the fact that previously other divorce reform bills had been axed in the Lords; there were equally strong, if not stronger, opponents in the Lords. In particular, the attitude of Law Lords appeared to be an influential factor in the debate and it was already known that Lord Hodson[155] whose article opposing the Bill appeared in *The Times* on 2nd February, 1968, was a strong opponent of the Bill. This anxiety was augmented by the fact that peers were neither under the pressure of Government nor of constituents. The reformers' only dependable allies were among life peers and the several bishops, e.g. the Bishop of Exeter and the Bishop of Southwark.

As had been expected, the debate in the Lords was led mostly by life peers (thus proving that life peers have brought a substantial contribution to the Lords) and Law Lords, apart from several bishops and the Archbishop of Canterbury. The debate displayed a wide spectrum of opinion, the views of the Anglicans and Catholics being strongly put forward by bishops and Lord Longford, although they were divided amongst themselves. The House debated not only the causes and possible effects of the reform, but also the procedure of a private member's bill and the technical aspects of the Bill, although it was mostly repetition of discussions held in the Commons.

In the end, critics in the Lords achieved a significant amendment of the Bill, which had been rejected in the Commons. In short, if the main role of the House of Lords is to amend bills, as was achieved in the process of this legislation,[156] the credit for the outcome perhaps should be given to the continuing existence of this Second Chamber.

5. AFTER THE ROYAL ASSENT

Throughout the controversy, the opponents expressed their fears over the Bill, saying that an easy divorce law would produce more divorces and that a higher divorce-rate would destroy the institution of marriage. The second objection was made to the lack of adequate financial protection in the Bill, but in fact it has given the respondent more financial consideration than any other earlier matrimonial causes measure. In addition, the 1970 Matrimonial Proceedings and Property Act and the Law Reform (Miscellaneous Provisions) Act, which in fact came fully into force on 1st January, 1971 with the Divorce Reform Act, together gave far more adequate financial protection than previously to the respondent. It is true, however, that the improvements in the financial provisions were the result of an outcry from the opponents,[157] and the credit for the outcome must be given to them.

Therefore, unreasonable and anomalous as some opponents considered them, the provisions of the Divorce Reform Act 1969 represented a step towards bringing the law into accord with current practice and an attempt to give legal recognition to a consensus of opinion that had emerged as a result of demand and prolonged debate over decades. It should also be noted that the Act made at least four major changes rather than two.

Under the new law, a petition for divorce may be presented to the court by either party and a divorce will be granted if the petitioner satisfies the court of *one* or *more* of the following facts :[158]

(a) that the respondent has *committed adultery* and the petitioner finds it *intolerable to live with* the respondent;

(b) that the respondent has *behaved in such a way* that the petitioner *cannot reasonably be expected to live* with the respondent;

(c) that the respondent has *deserted* the petitioner for a continuous period of at least *two years* immediately preceding the presentation of the petition;

(d) that the parties to the marriage have lived apart for a continuous period of at least *two years* immediately preceding the presentation of the petition and the respondent *consents* to a decree being granted;

(e) that the parties to the marriage have lived apart for a continuous period of at least *five years* immediately preceding the presentation of the petition.

In addition, Clauses 3 (provisions designed to encourage reconciliation), 4 (decree to be refused in certain circumstances) and 6 (financial protection for respondent in certain cases) brought substantial new elements into the law. However, since the breakdown of marriage has to be proved, or the petitioner has to satisfy the court that he or she 'cannot reasonably be expected to live with the respondent', the old matrimonial offence still remains as evidence of the irretrievable breakdown of marriage. But Clause 2(1)(d) and (e) are completely new provisions.

Thus the old ground for divorce, the matrimonial offence, was replaced by the new ground, the breakdown of marriage; certain improvements were made in assuring protection for the respondent, and a new spirit to encourage reconciliation between parties to a marriage was introduced into the law. However, by adding Clause 2(1)(b), (d) and (e) as proof of breakdown, in practice the ground for divorce was widened, although how the court will interpret the term 'intolerable to live with the respondent' remains to be seen.[159]

Upon the successful reform of divorce law, in November most of the major promoters of the Bill became vice-presidents of the DLRU. According to the October 1970 issue of *Just Cause*, the following Members of Parliament accepted the invitation to become vice-presidents: Lady Birk, Lady Gaitskell, Lord Gardiner and Lord Stow Hill, Mr Daniel Awdry, Mrs Lena Jeger, Mr Alec Jones, Mr John Parker, Dame Joan Vickers and Mr William Wilson.

In October 1969, immediately the success for the Bill was assured, the following statement was issued by the DLRU:

> With the passing of Alec Jones' Divorce Reform Bill the principle objective of the Divorce Law Reform Union, after over 60 years campaigning, has been achieved with the substitution of the matrimonial offence by breakdown of marriage as the sole ground for divorce. The Union believes that the new law will make for more logical, more honest and cleaner divorces.
>
> It intends to continue to take an active interest in other outstanding issues associated with the dissolution of marriages such as the division of property, maintenance and the custody of children, many of which problems are to be debated in Parliament during the next Session.

A letter on behalf of the Union was also sent out by the Chairman, Mr Banks, to Mr Alec Jones offering their thanks and congratulations on his success. A similar letter was also sent out to Lord Stow Hill for his sponsoring of the Bill in the House of Lords. Thus, an epoch-making reform movement promoted by the DLRU closed a controversial chapter after an intensive campaign for the cause.

NOTES

1 Messrs Abse, Banks, Peter Jackson, Service.

2 Little publicity had been given to the cause of divorce law reform over the long recess, so that naturally enough people wrote to ascertain the future plans for the Bill and the possibility of advancing its progress.

3 'Unenacted Bills lapse at the end of a Session because if Bills were carried forward from one Session to another, it would result in unmanageable congestion of Parliamentary business.' This reason was given by the Prime Minister's Office (25th Oct., 1968) in reply to one of the many women who had written to him, impatient to see the Bill passed.

4 Bulletin of the DLRU (Oct. 1969).

5 Ibid.

6 Mr Latey, who was eighty-five, had helped to water down A. P. Herbert's Bill in 1937.

7 He was involved in the problems of race relations and could not participate in the campaign actively, although he supported the Bill.

8 Hansard, Vol. 774, col. 508.

9 See p. 194, note 118, below.

10 The debates on the second reading will be quoted extensively, as they were the most comprehensive and embody all the arguments put forward for and against the Bill.

11 But this motion may be challenged, and though it may be supported by a majority in the lobbies, it is not effective unless the total votes are at least 100. So that, although the sponsors of a bill may command a majority of the members present, they may not be able to obtain a division on the main question.

12 Messrs Abse, Wilson and Awdry.

13 Hansard, Vol. 774, col. 2033.

14 See p. 70, above.

15 Notably those in Clauses 4 and 6.

16 Hansard, Vol. 774, col. 2043.

17 Ibid., cols 2043–5.

18 Ibid., cols 2043 et seq. There was also an interesting moment, when Mr Campbell said, 'For my part, it will be a black day when the law of England —'and Mr Dan Jones commented: '. . . Gentleman refers constantly to England. The Bill covers Wales and Scotland as well.' Then Mr Donald Dewar (Aberdeen, South) corrected him: 'Not Scotland.' It was no doubt a slip of the tongue.

19 Ibid., cols 2050 et seq. On 19th December, George Gale wrote in the Daily Mirror: 'It was with relief that I read Mrs Lena Jeger's reply to a Catholic interjection from one Simon Mahon of Bootle, who asked her: "Is my Hon. Friend suggesting that there are no such things as wholly innocent people. . . ." "Yes. I am," said Mrs Jeger. I am not too sure about Lena's theology, but she is dead right otherwise.'

20 To which Mr Abse said: 'May I assure my Hon. Friend that the whole House regards her as one of the most beautiful and attractive women in the land?'

21 Only two women bothered to speak.

22 The Speaker originally announced that the debate would be resumed on Monday, 16th December; but because of the debate on Defence (Army) and the Armed Forces and Reserves on the 16th, the adjourned debate was postponed to the following day.

23 Letters were sent out on 12th December, announcing that a vote would be taken before lunch on 17th December, as the second reading would resume at 12.30 p.m.

24 He also made a list entitled 'M.P.s worth approaching to take a Private Member's Bill.'

25 Meanwhile the opponents were not idle. On 16th December, two Conservative M.P.s, Messrs W. H. K. Baker and John Biggs-Davison, criticized the Government and the Bill in the Daily Telegraph. Their letter ran: 'The

Government's decision to give their Parliamentary time for the Divorce Bill is cowardly and hypocritical. If they favour this private Member's Bill they should have the courage and honesty to take it over as a Government measure, instead of singling it out from a number of private Members' Bills, at least as deserving of Parliamentary time. It appears that our Socialist rulers are furthering the "permissive society" without having the courage of their dubious convictions.'

26 Hansard, Vol. 775, cols 1057 *et seq.*

27 Ibid., col. 1068.

28 Ibid., cols 1073 *et seq.*

29 The Chairman of the Standing Committee C for Mr Wilson's Bill.

30 Divorces were granted in 27,000 cases which were made up in the following way:

adultery over 21,000—10,700 by wives,
                                   10,300 by husbands;
desertion 11,000   — 5,295 by wives,
                                    5,773 by husbands;
cruelty 6,934   —   405 by wives,
                                   6,529 by husbands;
other cases 165   —   62 by wives,
                                   103 by husbands;

31 Campbell, Simon Mahon, Marcus Worsley and Peter Mahon.

32 Hansard, Vol. 775, cols 1124–30.

33 Ibid., cols 1132 *et seq.*; excluding the four tellers.

34 See below: p. 132, Table 1.

35 See below: p. 133, Table 2.

36 Dame Joan Vickers and Mrs Lena Jeger.

37 Mr Percival, nine times; Mr S. Mahon, seven times; Messrs Campbell and Worsley, five times each; Sir Cyril Osborne, five times; Sir Lionel Heald, four times; and others a few times each.

38 Mr Awdry, eight times; Mr Abse, seven times; Mr Dewar, five times; Dame Joan Vickers, four times; and others a few times each.

39 See Hansard, Vols 774 and 775; it is recorded in 51 pages, 101 columns.

40 See p. 132, below.

41 Dame Joan Vickers, Mrs Lena Jeger and Miss Joan Lestor, all spoke for the Bill, although Mrs Jeger did not vote.

42 See below p. 133.

43 See pp. 61 *et seq.*, above.

44 A. P. Herbert's Bill had 72 Ayes and 12 Noes in its second reading.

45 Nine Ayes: Mrs E. M. Braddock, Mrs F. Corbet, Mrs G. Dunwoody, Miss M. Herbison, Miss J. Lester, Miss J. M. Quennell, Mrs R. Short, Dame Joan Vickers and Mrs (now Lady) White. Four Noes: Mrs A. Cullen, Mrs A. Kerr, Dr S. Summerskill and Mrs M. Thatcher.

46 Sir Arthur Irvine, a Scotsman educated at Edinburgh and Oriel College, Oxford, later attended the committee stage as the Solicitor-General.

47 It must be noted, however, that there was little difference between Mr Jones's Bill and Mr Wilson's.

48 On 19th January, Mr Jones wrote to supporters of the Bill in the

Commons as follows: 'I am writing on behalf of the sponsors to thank you for your support at the Second Reading of the Divorce Reform Bill, particularly as we are aware that it was a difficult time for many Members to be present. We hope that the Bill may continue to have your support as it proceeds through its other stages. . . .'

49 For a further discussion, see P. G. Richards, *Parliament and Conscience,* pp. 179 *et seq.*; the detailed numerical analysis presented in this chapter is based largely on Professor Richards' work. I am grateful to Allen & Unwin for permission to use some of the data in Tables 3–8.

50 See Table 2, above.

51 The percentage figures in Tables 3–8 all refer to the percentage within a category of members voting in a particular way.

52 See Richards, op. cit., p. 183.

53 Printed by E. Ainsworth & Son, 15 Little Peter Street, Manchester 15 (1969 edition).

54 On 11th February, and another article of his appeared on 18th April in the *Daily Telegraph.*

55 In *The Times,* on 11th March and 25th April.

56 The italics in the quoted passages are mine.

57 See note 19, p. 188, above.

58 Between the second reading of the Divorce Reform Bill and the committee stage, the Matrimonial Property Bill had its second reading in January 1969.

59 Actually 630, but there were five vacancies during that session.

60 That was for Mr Wilson's Bill.

61 However, as Mr William Latey claimed, there were 12 members for the Bill as Mr Booth often voted with the promoter. See W. Latey, 'Divorce Reform', *The Times* (11th Feb., 1969). Two views are known: (1) the balance of the Committee should reflect the party balance; (2) it should reflect the results of the second reading division. However, both opinions face difficulties depending on whether it is a party issue or an 'issue of conscience'.

62 The six opponents who had sat on the Committee of the previous year were: Mrs Anne Kerr, Mr Kenneth Lewis, Mr Alexander Lyon, Mr Edward Lyons, Mr Norman St John-Stevas and Mr Richard Wood. The four supporters who had sat on the committee were: Miss Joan Lester, Mr Nicholas Ridley, Sir George Sinclair and Mr Ben Whitaker.

63 But the twelfth sitting was adjourned by the Chairman on account of seven members not being present at any one time.

64 A promoter of the Bill recalled that although the reformers had the majority in the committee stage, it was not always a harmonious place because several members of the committee threatened the unofficial whip, Mr Jackson, with their absenteeism from the committee sittings if Mr Abse did not refrain from garrulousness.

65 Standing Committee B, col. 6.

66 Although one promoter recalled that he thought Mr Campbell disliked every comma in the Bill, Mr Campbell later disclosed that he would have supported the Bill if the sponsors had dropped Clause 2(1)(e), even though he was not happy with the Bill as a whole.

67 During the committee stage Dame Irene Ward said: 'It is very difficult for a lay person to intervene among all these distinguished lawyers. I am always conscious that I do not put my case in legal terms. . . . They all use, as all the distinguished people have used in the Committee today, rather legal language.' (Standing Committee B, cols 122 *et seq*.)

68 On Clause 2(1)(e) to leave out 'five' and insert 'three'.

69 Mr Campbell's attempt was defeated by 9 votes to 5, while Dr Gray's was defeated by 12 votes to 2.

70 Upon recovering from his illness Mr Abse left for Japan on a parliamentary mission, and as a result the parliamentary work fell on the remaining main sponsors—namely, Messrs Jones, Wilson and Jackson. For Mr Jones it was a difficult task and he was constantly in need of legal advice and help. Mr W. Wilson, the Lord Chancellor's Office and the Law Commission helped Mr Jones behind the scenes whenever necessary.

71 Indeed, there was one occasion when the reformers lacked a majority.

72 The opponents realized their weakened position: tactics of this nature were arrested since the substance of the Bill had already been fully discussed during the debate on Mr Wilson's Bill and, moreover, the Government was more willing to provide extra time for the Bill than previously. Consequently, the opponents were aware that there was little possibility of killing the Bill.

73 See p. 70, above.

74 The committee stage for Mr Wilson's Bill had occupied 13 sittings and the report filled no less than 634 columns.

75 See p. 96 *et seq*., above.

76 See p. 139, above.

77 His article appeared in *The Times* on 25th April so that every M.P. could read it before he came to Parliament. It ran: 'When the sponsors insisted on retaining sub-clause (e), the Lord Chancellor took the unprecedented step on 5th March of informing Standing Committee 'B', through the Solicitor-General, that should the Bill become law, it was his intention that it should not be brought into force until additional Government legislation had been introduced ensuring better protection for the first wife. . . . With a number of my colleagues, I believe it is wrong and indeed unconstitutional that the Royal Assent should be sought for a Private Member's Bill which is admitted by the highest legal authority to be objectionable as it stands.'

78 On the same day, a letter from Messrs Jones, Abse and Wilson appeared in the *Daily Mail* protesting at that paper's reference to Mr Edward Bishop's Matrimonial Property Bill, which reference they claimed was misleading on the subject of financial provisions for the deserted wife contained in the Divorce Reform Bill.

79 On 6th May, Mr John M. Temple (Conservative, City of Chester) wrote to a sponsor, enclosing a memorandum from the Men's Committee of St Columbas Roman Catholic Church in Chester. Mr Temple, in his letter, said: 'I trust that you will take all these considerations into account and your petitioners have my support.'

80 On 5th May, the sponsors again wrote to their supporters urging them to attend the report stage on 9th May. The letter said, '. . . we urgently request your continued support to complete the passage of this important legislation', and there followed the names of the twelve sponsors.

81 *The Times* said that the Bill failed to complete the report stage.

82 The procedure of the House allows a member to query the presence of a quorum and just after 1 p.m. a count was made. On this occasion, Mr Peter Jackson left the Chamber to round up members and he himself ran back into the Chamber to complete the necessary number just as the time expired.

83 During this period, Messrs Jones, Wilson and Service had organized a private petition to Mr Douglas Houghton, Chairman of the Parliamentary Labour Party, asking him to urge the Government to provide enough time to finish the report stage and the third reading. The above-mentioned three reformers, together with Messrs Jackson, Parker, Humling, Christopher Price and others, collected the signatures of 105 Labour back-benchers, and delivered these to Mr Houghton on 13th May, who in turn passed them on to the Government Chief Whip.

84 Mr Heffer.

85 It ran: 'Dear Colleague, The Government has provided time to allow the House to come to a conclusion on the Divorce Reform Bill. The Bill will come on at 10 p.m. after Government business on the *night of Thursday 12th* June, and will continue through the night and into Friday. This is the final chance to pass the Bill and it will fail unless we have the support of at least 100 Members throughout to ensure the success of closure motions. We ask you urgently to *note this date in your diary* and to attend if you possibly can. We are extremely grateful for your past support, in spite of inconvenience caused by opponents' delaying tactics, and strongly hope that you will now help us to complete the Report and Third Reading. . . .'

86 The names were evenly shared between the sponsors, each writing to the members he knew best.

87 A whipping meeting was organized by Messrs Jackson and Service at which Ten Labour supporters were each allotted twenty names to contact in person and attempt to extract firm promises of attendance for all or given hours of the all-night sitting. This meeting was in the afternoon of 10th June and by the evening of the 12th these amateur whips had reported back over 110 promises of all-night support, with others for part of the night. In the event, only a handful of these verbal promises were not kept, while the written promises (given two or three weeks earlier) had a much higher casualty-rate.

88 Divorce by arrangement after three years' separation and unilateral divorce after seven years.

89 The italics are mine.

90 *Daily Telegraph* (27th May, 1969).

91 This sudden change was made because the Prime Minister, Harold Wilson, preferred Mr Mellish to Mr Silkin as the Chief Whip for the Industrial Relations Bill presented by the Government.

92 See p. 159, below.

93 Hansard, Vol. 784, col. 1797; my italics.

94 Ibid., col. 1798.

95 Ibid., col. 1801.

96 Mrs Lena Jeger reminded Sir Lionel Heald, 'Does the right hon. and learned Gentleman not recollect as I do that in 1938 a Conservative Government set a very respectable precedent by giving Government time to enable

A. P. Herbert's Bill.' Sir Lionel also said '1938', referring to the Herbert Act 1937.

97 Hansard, Vol. 784, cols 1808 *et seq*. His words 'power without responsibility' reappear later in *The Times* in an article by Mr R. Butt. See p. 76 n.45 above.

98 Hansard, Vol. 784, cols 1819 *et seq*.

99 On five occasions the vote was preceded by a successful procedural motion that the Question be put.

100 Incidentally, it was exactly 11.40 a.m. when Mr De la Bère moved the third reading of his Bill in 1936, although that was on 28th May.

101 Hansard, Vol. 784, cols 2027 *et seq*.

102 For a discussion see *The Economist* (14th Dec., 1968).

103 Hansard, Vol. 784, cols 2043 *et seq*.

104 Mr Victor Goodhew said: 'I see it as part of a pattern of gradual erosion of the standards of Christian upbringing which are being forced upon this country by a small minority, the Humanists among them, mentioned by . . . Member for Bootle (Mr Simon Mahon). We know that the next target is the removal of religious education in schools; so the House must be ready for that when it comes.' (Ibid., col. 2067)

105 Herbert's Bill was given a third reading by 190 votes to 37. But there was no all-night sitting.

106 *The Times* described it as the third longest sitting since the war.

107 See 'Divorce Reformers' Victory', *The Times* (14th June, 1969).

108 Another explanation of the low turn-out was the funeral of Mr Jerry Reynolds, Minister of Defence; however, several members recalled that more Labour than Conservative members attended the funeral.

109 Mr Boyden, Under-Secretary of State for Defence for the Army; Mr Ennals, Joint Minister of State, Dept of Health and Social Security; Miss Lee, Minister of State, Dept of Education and Science; Mr Mallalieu, Minister of State, Ministry of Technology; Mr Morris, Minister of Defence for Equipment; Dr Owen, Under-Secretary of State for Defence for the Royal Navy; Mr Prentice, Minister of Overseas Development; Mr Robinson, Minister for Planning and Land; Mr Snow, Parliamentary Secretary, Ministry of Health and Social Security; and Mr Taverne, Q.C., Minister of State, Treasury, were among them.

110 Sir Edward, Shadow Education Secretary, after the third reading warmly congratulated Mr Jones on his success.

111 Although *The Times* (14th June, 1969) reported that Mrs Dunwoody differed from her husband on the issue, the reformers said that she was a keen supporter of the Bill, but had an unavoidable appointment elsewhere at the time of the third reading vote.

112 They were: Messrs Hooson, Johnston and Lubbock, Chief Whip.

113 Those for the Bill were: Mrs Joyce Butler (Labour Co-operative), Mrs Lena Jeger (Labour), Miss Jennie Lee (Labour), Mrs Margaret McKay (Labour), Miss Mervyn Pike (Conservative), Mrs Renée Short (Labour), and Dame Joan Vickers (Conservative). Those against the Bill were: Miss Harvie Anderson (Conservative), Mrs Anne Kerr (Labour), Mrs Jill Knight (Conservative), Dr Shirley Summerskill (Labour), Dame Irene Ward (Conservative), and Mrs Shirley Williams (Labour).

114 The Church of England itself was clearly divided: the Archbishop of Canterbury had denounced the provision for divorce by consent after two years' separation and the cutting to two years of the period for divorce following desertion; while some of the bishops, namely the Bishops of Exeter, Durham and Southwark, gave the Bill their reluctant support.

115 It may be rightly said that the House of Commons elected in March 1966 had differed from its predecessors in devoting more attention to social questions. See P. G. Richards, *Parliament and Conscience* (1970), p. 7.

116 See R. Butt, *The Power of Parliament* (2nd ed. 1969), p. 336.

117 However, the Conservative Government, in 1962–3, gave Government time to Mr Abse's Bill and in 1963–4 to the Divorce (Scotland) Bill.

118 Despite the fact that Mr Campbell won a majority in the debate held by the Hardwicke Society on Thursday, 19th November, 1970, in the Middle Temple, on the Motion 'That this House would repeal the Divorce Reform Act 1969', it seems most unlikely that such a vote would be repeated at Westminster, even under a Conservative Government.

119 R. Butt in *The Times* (20th June, 1969).

120 This was stated in the *Third Annual Report* of the Law Commission. See p. 74 n. 45 above.

121 Peers of the Blood Royal, 4; archbishops, 2; dukes, 25; marquises, 30; earls and countesses, 163; viscounts, 109; bishops, 24; barons and baronesses (of whom 164 were life peers), 704.

122 She was an agnostic, although a baptized member of the Church of England.

123 Her friends felt keenly for her when she was sharply criticized from the bench during proceedings in the court.

124 Hansard (House of Lords), Vol. 302, col. 882.

125 During this period in the Lord Chancellor's Office, Lord Gardiner, Lord Stow Hill, Lord Shackleton, Mr Abse, Mrs Barker, Mr Bourne and Mr Service met to discuss the passage of the Bill in the Lords.

126 Before the second reading, at a Labour Party peers' meeting, she unexpectedly made an effective speech against the Bill. Lady Birk, without proper preparation, had to defend it.

127 Lord Stow Hill, who already had had a meeting with the Chairman of the Law Commission, had lunch with the Bishop of Exeter and exchanged views with Lord Dilhorne. Having agreed in principle, they reached the conclusion that the House should be given sufficient time to discuss the Bill, although Lord Dilhorne remained uncommitted.

128 *The Times* (25th June, 1969).

129 Lady Summerskill and Dr Shirley Summerskill are, incidentally, the first mother and daughter combination in Parliament, being members of the Lords and the Commons respectively, and both are also M.D.s.

130 After describing the general outline of the history of divorce reform legislation, he referred also to Mr Butt's article and repeated what Lord Stow Hill and Mr Abse had said on the subject earlier.

131 In the course of the debate Lord Denning, Master of the Rolls, also said the present divorce law was based on a wrong theory and he would vote for the Bill.

132 Hansard (House of Lords), Vol. 303, cols 338 *et seq.*

133 Hansard (House of Lords), Vol. 303, cols 369 *et seq.*

134 The bishops for the Bill were: Dr Stopford (London), Dr Mortimer (Exeter), Dr Ellison (Chester), Dr Bardsley (Coventry) and Dr Stockwood (Southwark). Those against the Bill: Dr Wilson (Chichester), Dr Williams (Leicester) and Dr Claxton (Blackburn).

135 The peeresses who voted for the Bill were: Ladies Birk, Burton of Coventry, Gaitskell, Hylton-Forster, Llewelyn-Davies of Hastoe, Plummer, Stocks, Strange of Knokin, Swanborough and Wooton of Abinger. The Noncontents were: Ladies Audley, Emmet of Amberley, Kinloss and Summerskill. Although Lady Ruthven of Freeland's name does not appear here, she was a very strong supporter and helped Lord Stow Hill greatly. Indeed, she later acted as a teller for the supporters in many of the divisions.

136 Hansard (House of Lords), Vol. 303, col. 661.

137 He voted in favour of all the divisions of the Bill.

138 Hansard, Vol. 303, col. 667.

139 The committee stage began on 10th July; 11th (Friday), 15th (Tuesday) and 24th (Thursday) July were also devoted to discussion of the Bill.

140 Adultery and the petitioner finds it intolerable to live with the respondent.

141 Desertion—for a continuous period of at least two years.

142 Divorce by consent after two years' separation.

143 Hansard (House of Lords), Vol. 303, col. 1268.

144 Had these two peers voted with the reformers, the results of the division would have been 63–63. Although some reformers mentioned that the provision would affect only a very limited number of people, a considerable number of peers joined the opposition camp during this division. Indeed the reformers' 61 votes in this division was the lowest level they had in all the seven divisions in the committee stage.

145 Another reason given for delaying the introduction of the new Act until 1st January, 1971 was that it would give the judges and the courts sufficient time to work out the new procedures which would be necessary under the Act. Originally, Clause 11(3) of the Bill read as follows: 'This Act shall come into operation on such day as the Lord Chancellor may by order made by statutory instrument appoint.' There was, however, speculation about the date on which the Act should come into force: they were six months, one year, 1st January, 1971, and three years. Lord Stow Hill and the Lord Chancellor agreed that the 1st January, 1971 would be a reasonable date. In fact, there was little consultation between the reformers on the subject. They considered the passage of the Bill through the Lords as their prime objective, and were naturally less concerned about the actual date of enforcement.

146 Lord Stow Hill, Lord Amulree, Lady Birk, the Bishop of Exeter, Lady Gaitskell, Lord Goodman, Lord Platt, Lady Ruthven and Lord Silkin.

147 As they did at all other stages in the House of Lords debates, the letters were drafted and sent out by the DLRU on House of Lords official stationery after seeking the approval of the peers who signed them. Mrs Barker and Mr Service also held a series of unofficial whips' meetings in the Liberal Peers' Office, at which about ten peers each undertook to contact (by letter, telephone or in person) a dozen or more fellow-members, urging their presence. This organization enabled them to keep a comfortable majority of

general supporters at all stages, though the peers were much more liable
take individualistic attitudes to particular amendments than the Commons
had been.

148 Hansard (House of Lords), Vol. 304, col. 1255.

149 Ibid., col. 1259.

150 Messrs Jones and Abse, who attended nearly every single debate in
in the Lords, keeping in touch to ensure that no amendments contrary to the
principle of the Bill were accepted, agreed with Lord Stow Hill not to move
any amendment in the Lords to reverse Lord Reid's Amendment No. 9.

151 Namely, Messrs Jones, Abse, Jackson, Service and Wilson.

152 Hansard, Vol. 788, col. 719.

153 Hansard (House of Lords), Vol. 304, col. 1711.

154 A peer's comment: 'Debates in the Commons have a vitality and
thrust which cannot be reproduced in the Lords; but the Lords has a
maturity and balance and a habit of objectivity which I am convinced make
it a very valuable complement to the Commons. . . . I thought the debates
were very good, on the whole, in my view, better balanced and more reflec-
tive than those in the Commons.'

155 A Lord of Appeal, who practised at the Bar and sat as judge for many
years in the Divorce Court; he was also a witness before the 1951 Royal
Commission on Divorce.

156 Those who opposed the Bill and eagerly fought to amend it should be
given due credit for the amendments, if they were an improvement, which
time will tell.

157 However, I should mention that a promoter took exception to this view
by saying: 'I had always sought as adequate a financial protection as was
possible and in fact helped in the early stages of the 1970 Matrimonial
Proceedings and Property Act introduced by E. Bishop.'

158 Clause 2(1), my italics. It may be useful to indicate more clearly the
difference between sub-clause (a) and sub-clause (b). In sub-clause (a) it is
the *petitioner* who has to find it intolerable to live with the respondent,
whereas in sub-clause (b) the *court* has to be satisfied that the petitioner
cannot reasonably be expected to live with the respondent. It is the difference between a subjective and an objective judgment.

159 For the first defended case, *Goodrich v. Goodrich*, brought on the
ground of Clause 2(1)(a)—see *The Times* (7th Apr., 1971).

Chapter 8

CONCLUSIONS

I. *1857–1969*

One of the recurrent themes of the history of legal thought[1] is the controversy between those who believe that law should essentially follow, not lead (and that it should do so slowly, in response to clearly formulated social sentiments), and those who believe that the law should be a determining agent in the creation of new norms. It was the philosophy of Bentham and the utilitarian school which turned the British Parliament—and similar institutions in other countries—into active legislative instruments, effecting reforms, whether as a result of genuine social pressure or as a consequence of a process of modernization.[2]

Granted these premises, there still remains much room for disagreement. One who believes in the sacramental indissolubility of marriage would almost certainly reject any attempt to widen the grounds of divorce or to depart from the concept of guilt, no matter how overwhelming the evidence of discrepancy between the theory of the Law and the practice of contemporary divorce may be. Equally, arguments expounding the disastrous dangers of over-population would not easily move those who regard birth-control as inherently evil. Nevertheless, many agree that the law has to be constantly reassessed against the changing social framework. It is the more necessary in a society in which the law is an active agent in social change. In the constant and complex battle of social forces on which man's future depends, the law is but one of many moulding elements; it is still a paramount instrument of social order.

In other words, the law, which is a means of social control, bearing the imprint of the forces that shape our social life, is a product of human experience and the needs of society. These two factors in turn virtually determine the nature of law. Given the strong influence of Christianity on English social life for centuries, the whole business of English law and politics has been inextricably bound up with Christian principles and morality.

As already pointed out, the divorce law of England has essentially been governed by the views of the established Church, based in turn upon medieval ecclesiastical law. The core of the notion has always been that people, although they voluntarily enter marriage, cannot voluntarily dissolve it; God or the Church, and later the State, has been held to have an interest in the continuation of a marriage over and above the wishes of the parties involved. Consequently, there was no judicial divorce at all in England until 1857. Before that date the only way of having a marriage dissolved was by a special private Act of Parliament—a very expensive procedure available only to the very rich. And when, in 1857, the courts were for the first time given power to dissolve marriages, the only ground for such a divorce was adultery. Indeed, if it was the wife who was asking for divorce she had to prove something in addition to her husband's adultery, such as desertion or cruelty. It was not until 1923 that the sexes were put on an equal footing so that it was enough for either husband or wife to prove the other's adultery. Adultery remained the one and only ground for divorce in England until 1938 when the Herbert Act came into force. Thus since 1857, although divorce had been available, it could only be granted on proof of a 'matrimonial offence' committed by one spouse against the other innocent party.

The matrimonial offence, as the ground for divorce, remained for over a century, despite the fact that it had often been found an unsatisfactory solution. It was easily faked or exaggerated. However, it stayed unchanged because the alternatives, divorce by consent, divorce by compulsion of an innocent party, or no divorce at all, were considered more injurious to the interests of society. The matrimonial offence was treated as if it were a real crime; the divorce courts became places for accusation, which was hardly conducive to reconciliation or compromise. In practice, many people obtained a divorce when they wanted it although the procedure was a rather devious one. Over 90 per cent of divorces were undefended and perjury was doubtless sometimes involved. To this extent, the law was unrealistic and hypocritical. Inevitably, the whole concept of the matrimonial offence was attacked; critics said that the law forced people into adultery or at least pretence of adultery in order to get a divorce.

The first attempt to break this doctrine of the matrimonial offence was launched by Mr Herbert in 1936, and the result was the 1937 Matrimonial Causes Act[3] which allowed a spouse who was incurably insane, although an 'innocent party', to be divorced after five years. However, the difficulty of defining or recognizing 'incurable insanity' remained as an unwelcome by-product of the Act, and has placed an uncomfortable burden on psychiatrists.

The next attempt was made by Mrs White in 1951, but this failed. In 1963 Mr Abse scored a minor success by securing the passage of the 1963 Matrimonial Causes Act which allowed couples to attempt a reconciliation without losing their grounds for divorce if it did not succeed. Mr Abse, however, failed in his further aim of making seven years' separation a ground for divorce.

Subsequently, the Archbishop of Canterbury's group and the Law Commission attempted to formulate a reasonable approach which would not only meet the Church's own need, but satisfy the general public demand for reform as well as the practical requirements of the court. Their consensus, together with the demands of the reformers, were embodied in Mr Wilson's still-born Bill.

It took nearly a year—from 9th November, 1968 to 22nd October, 1969—for Mr Jones's Bill to reach the Statute Book. Since the principle of English divorce law was laid down by the Matrimonial Causes Act 1857, which embodied the concept of Christian marriage, it has taken 112 years to see a formal departure from the old doctrine. It was again initially led by a few reformers and ultimately Parliament decided to alter it. It may be said that Parliament came to the conclusion that it is necessary to change the law if it is to serve the needs and meet the demands of the people. It had been a long struggle, but the most extensive and important change in the divorce law of England since 1857 was thus made.

II. *Pros and Cons in Retrospect*

Whether marriage should be indissoluble and sacrosanct or a contract and terminable is a matter of opinion, for it has not only been terminated in practice but also recognized by law in many countries. But there are few social questions which touch the individual so nearly and on which such widely divergent views are held, as the problem of divorce. From those who regard marriage as a perpetual and indissoluble bond instituted by God, to those who consider it as a temporary contract between a man and a woman and therefore terminable, every shade of opinion can be found. Personal attitudes towards divorce reflect beliefs about the origin and nature of human life. Between the belief that life occurs by divine gift and is therefore always sacrosanct, and the idea that it is an end-product of biological evolution, there exists a whole spectrum of opinion.

However, almost all the arguments put forward in the course of the debate on divorce law reform, including those of atheists, were ultimately based on one or other of the two main views. Although the proposal for unilateral divorce caused a heated controversy, no one denied the institution of marriage itself, nor did anyone advocate polygamy or promiscuity. We may note the extent to which the arguments of many reformers and their sympathizers were conditioned by the framework of Christian ethics in spite of their rejection of the principle of indissolubility. On the other hand, many who accepted the Church's teaching on divorce came to terms with the need for reform.

Putting Asunder[4] recognized that 'divorce is a perilous theme for churchmen', and assumed that there should be two different laws of divorce : one for the Church and another for society at large.[5] *Putting Asunder* was a notable development of Christian views on marriage and divorce. As has already been seen, until the Ecclesiastical Court was abolished, the law which prevailed was in all essentials the canon law and the Church naturally fought to maintain it. John Keble pointed out before the passage of the Bill in 1857, when the State was preparing to take over the authority which had been exercised by the Church for so long, that if the Bill became law, a State matrimonial law differing from the Church's rule would be established; although he acknowledged the right and competence of Parliament to legislate as it thought fit for those who owed no allegiance to the Church, he insisted that its legislation must not be allowed to override the Church's rule for its own members as expressed in the Book of Common Prayer and the canons.[6]

The Church recognized the State and its law but insisted on having the law of the Church respected in return. It is an interesting aspect of the relationship between Church and State that the Church, while rejecting the State law of divorce for its own members, has traditionally opposed easing the divorce law of the State. Nevertheless, the Church of England was divided in its attitude to the Divorce Reform Bill. The following statement in support of the Bill by Dr Ronald Williams,[7] Bishop of Leicester, best describes the dilemma of reformers :

> The present proposals contain many provisions not easily reconcilable with the Christian ideal of marriage, but are on the whole to be welcomed as civilised changes in a society such as ours. Divorce by consent after two years' separation is very hard to swallow, but whether anything is gained by a compulsory continued marriage in such circumstances is very doubtful.[8]

Dr Ian Ramsey, Bishop of Durham, was able to defend the Bill like this :

> Divorce by consent is a most unfortunate phrase. It implies a casual attitude, whereas under the Bill reconciliation has to be attempted. It does not do justice to other parts of the Bill which uphold the dignity of marriage. The Bill makes divorce procedure more humane, reasonable, sensitive and realistic.[9]

The opinions expressed by the opponents of the Bill varied in origin and emphasis. Some were purely theological objections: for example, this extract from an anonymous leaflet,[10] which voiced a typical Catholic view: 'To Christians divorce is abhorrent; the vast majority throughout the world hold that a valid marriage cannot be dissolved by a civil divorce.' Dr Pat Neville, Chairman of the Union of Catholic Mothers, expressed concern that 'There may be an irresponsible attitude to marriage if this two-year clause is accepted, and a general relaxing of the moral tone of the country.'

Others opposed the Bill on financial and legal-technical grounds. Mrs Juanita Francis, Chairman of the Married Women's Association, said:[11] 'I oppose this Bill completely but I'm not asking for protection, I'm asking for legal rights in hard cash. All you have now is bed and board, afterwards you're dependent on damned maintenance.'

Lady Summerskill also raised financial objections:[12]

Few men can afford to support two wives—so I have called this Bill a Casanova's Charter. . . . If marriage need last for only five, seven or three years, and can be then automatically dissolved, irrespective of the impeccable behaviour of one spouse, then a married man will be able to make a proposal to a second woman with a definite date for marriage. . . . If they introduce an amendment offering community property, I would accept the Bill. [Holland and Scandinavian countries have such provisions.]

A legal view came from an experienced divorce counsel:[13] 'If two people want a divorce now, nothing is easier. They just need to tell a few lies. The Bill is going to cloud the whole issue by trying to find out the truth of the situation.'

Sir Lionel Heald said that Clause 2(1)(e) offended 'against three of the fundamental maxims of British justice'.[14]

Mr Campbell, speaking in the Commons, expressed concern over the social consequences of the Bill: 'Every time that marriage is weakened and made a more precarious partnership, the family life of the nation is weakened.'[15]

The following headlines show how some other critics saw the problem of divorce reform. The *Daily Sketch*: 'Divorce—English style—where the man always comes off best'; the *Catholic Herald*: 'Polygamy on the State'; the *Sunday Telegraph*: 'Will girls give up marrying?'; and the *Sunday Express*: 'Who decided we wanted easy divorce?' The *Spectator* had a headline 'Towards a Bigamy Bill?'

On the whole, all the opponents' arguments tended to the conclusion that the Bill would cause a rise in the divorce-rate which might result in the weakening of the institution of marriage. In reply the reformers argued that divorce is merely an outcome of breakdown, not the disease itself. The most sophisticated view was presented by the Law Commission.[16] It had also posed the question of whether the rise in the divorce-rate should cause alarm. The answer it gave read as follows:

> The great increase in the number of divorces during this century is sometimes seen as evidence of a breakdown of English family life and a decline in moral standards. On this we would like to make three points: first, that an increased number of divorces is alarming only if it indicates an increase in the number of broken homes and not merely that a larger proportion of broken homes is leading to divorce; secondly, that even an increase in the number of broken homes might merely indicate that there were more marriages subject to the risk of breakdown; and thirdly, that, even if the proportion of marriages that did break down could be shown to have increased, it might merely be that the marriages were subjected to greater risks and not that there was any decline in respect for marriage and morality.[17]

As regards the first point, the Law Commission said that divorce is merely one of the possible outcomes, and not necessarily the most common one, of a marriage that has broken down. 'Until 1857 we had no divorce at all (except by Private Act of Parliament) but this certainly did not mean that there were no broken marriages. Marriage breakdowns are well known to occur in other countries, such as Italy, where divorce is not permitted.'[18]

As regards the second point, there has been a great increase in the number of marriages; the number of married women has more than doubled during this century. This is partly because of an increase in the total population, partly because a larger proportion of the population marry and

> . . . because we tend to marry earlier. The number of divorces has, of course, risen much more rapidly than the married population, but this, as already pointed out, is not necessarily an indication of an increase in the proportion of broken homes. It is almost certain that it is very largely due to the readier availability of divorce rather than to an increase in the proportion of marriages which break down.[19]

As regards the third, 'there are a number of reasons which might lead us to expect that a larger proportion of marriages would break down without necessarily indicating any deterioration of moral standards'.[20] The fact that people tend to marry at a younger age now and that people have a greater life expectancy than ever before means that the average duration of marriage has doubled since the nineteenth century. Thus the period which a union is exposed to risk has doubled as well. In addition the risks—such as the housing shortage[21]—to which marriages are subjected, have increased.

Despite all this, the Law Commission said, 'Marriage as an institution in present-day England is in a fairly healthy state as compared with the past.' As *The Field of Choice* pointed out, there is no conclusive evidence that the proportion of marriages which break down has increased during the century; nor, on the other hand, is there any evidence that it has not. Nevertheless, marriage remains a highly popular and universal institution; it would seem that in the long run it has a stronger appeal and a longer life expectancy than either the Church or the present system of the nation state. 'Marriage is the great safeguard against loneliness in our society. Few people I imagine contemplate divorce lightly.'[22]

Some people find it difficult to understand why divorce by consent[23] should be considered a 'most unfortunate phrase', while marriage by consent is so admirable. But the idea that divorce by consent is equally acceptable and can be as useful as an institution as marriage by consent is still quite foreign to the mentality of many sacramentalists, who have been conditioned to see marriage and divorce in terms of the Christian doctrine of marriage—the principle of indissolubility. However, divorce and remarriage have become more and more acceptable in recent years; the courts at least have recognized the necessity of divorce. The courts, or at any rate most judges, have increasingly taken the view that the interests of society are not served by the perpetuation of a marriage that has irretrievably broken down, nor the interests of the children of that marriage.[24]

Consequently, the social stigma so long attached to divorce is fast disappearing and the reaction of the general public towards the divorce issue, whether it be divorce by consent or divorce without consent, was relatively moderate. The strongest protests actually came from those who were concerned that innocent spouses, particularly wives and the children of the marriage, should be protected, rather than from 'indissolubilists'.

III. *The Special Character of Divorce Law Reform*

Obviously an issue as complex as that of divorce law reform involves religious, moral, sociological, legal and political questions, and it is not easy to distinguish clearly between the different aspects

H

of the problem. Nevertheless, it may be worth while to attempt to view the issue from a number of different angles.

So far as the welfare of wives and children is concerned, divorce is also a problem of financial consideration. As has already been pointed out, the most influential objection to divorce law reform was that put forward by people who were concerned about the financial protection of economically vulnerable wives and children. The financial provisions of the Act and the birth of the Matrimonial Proceedings and Property Act 1970 underlined the economic significance of the divorce issue.

Many people are concerned more with the welfare of children than with promiscuity or divorce itself. An important psychological aspect of the problem can be seen when the attachment between parents and children is examined. The marriage tie may last long and be a fulfilling social institution, but consanguinity—particularly the blood tie between parents and children—is a far stronger bond : marriage can be broken both in law and practice, but the blood tie between parents and children cannot be severed, although legally they can be separated. Some people may consider adultery and divorce, but few would desert or exchange their own children. The so-called 'love' between men and women is a changeable emotion and indeed many commit adultery, but even those who do commit adultery usually retain their paternal or maternal benevolence towards their own children.

There is a line of argument which maintains that religion and law have nothing in common : the law deals primarily with problems between men, whereas religion is concerned with an intangible link between men and God. The opposing view, put forward in a book by Mr Latey, maintains that 'without religion there can be no morality; and without morality there can be no law'.[25] However, it can be maintained that religion, morals and law are separable, although they are still very much dependent on, and indeed deeply entwined with, each other. In fact there can be morality and law without religion.

As has already been pointed out, Christian beliefs have been an integral part of English divorce law, and *Putting Asunder* was the result of the Church's concern over the issue. It was a difficult decision for the Church of England, which maintains the principle of indissolubility.[26] None the less, for the first time in history the Church group played a leading part in fostering divorce law reform.[27]

The divorce issue in any society is a theme of legal and moral debate. In England, the old system had few defenders and many of the most adamant opponents agreed to reform the law along the lines proposed by *Putting Asunder*. The great majority of vocal opinion was agreed on principle to the need for reform, but differences arose over the form it was to take. *Putting Asunder* followed all critics of the old law in attacking the concept of the matrimonial offence, and proposed substituting irretrievable breakdown of marriage as the only ground of divorce.

Sociological data and the views put forward by a number of sociologists also played an important role. The statistics collected from the public records clearly proved the weakness of a system which produced 28,000 applications for maintenance per year, by wives to the summary courts. Increasing numbers of illegitimate children gave the critics a further ground for urging reform. Although no economic or immediate political interests were involved, the divorce issue, like the abortion issue, gave rise to strong feeling, and each side made use of emotional references and appeals. Each claimed to have right on their side; while opponents justified their stand on moral and religious grounds, the reformers appealed to a sense of justice, pointing out the hypocrisy in the law; both supported their arguments by reference to statistical data.

A significant aspect of this legislation was that the law merely gave a formal recognition to the existing practice. Although it was a revolutionary change of legal concepts in divorce law, an actual change in the law had been made through the judicial interpretation which aimed to meet public demand. In practice, there already existed not only divorce by consent (collusion), but also unilateral divorce (by either cruelty or desertion). As *The Economist* pointed out,[28] most judges anyway had realized that the interests of society were not served by the perpetuation of a marriage that had irretrievably broken down; the courts made it clear that a broken marriage was often against the interests of the children and of the parties themselves. Therefore, it may be said that an important divorce law reform was made in the courts before Parliament gave official recognition to the judicial practice by this particular piece of legislation.

As soon as the reformers brought the question into Parliament, divorce law reform became an important public issue, irrespective of the amount or accuracy of the information available to ordinary people. Throughout the controversy it was asserted that divorce law reform was not a party political question, but an issue for a private member's bill. To some extent this was true. All the divisions taken in Parliament were on a free vote without whips and there was no real outcry from the Opposition benches on account of the divorce issue. Nevertheless, the debates on the Bill and the voting results of the divisions show politicians following reasonably clear party lines : most Labour and Liberal members in support and most Conservatives either not voting or voting against the Bill, although the leaders of the two major parties expressed no opinion publicly.

The ballot for a private member's bill and the attitude of the Government towards private members' bills also raise an interesting question which is peculiar to British politics : for which pieces of legislation can the Government be said to be responsible? If not responsible for private members' bills, it follows that it can be held responsible for only government bills. However, the anomaly remains : the Matrimonial Proceedings and Property Act, which was a by-product of the Divorce Reform Bill, was a government bill, while the Divorce Reform Bill, for which the Government claimed they were not responsible, was a private member's bill.[29]

In a democracy, the Government theoretically has the power to make public policy and the responsibility for shaping it,[30] but how should the decision be reached as to what issues are to be considered public policy and therefore the Government's responsibility? Some argue that policies primarily concerned with moral or social problems should be treated as non-party issues. At present, private members' bills offer a conventional way of dealing with such issues. However, this practice affords a double standard for dealing with political controversies and thus offers a way of escape from the responsibility which a democratic government ought to assume. As some of the opponents pointed out, a ruling party may well be able to have recourse to a private member's bill when it considers it safer for its own interests. On the other hand, if the Government thought that a certain private member's bill offered no party advantage or if it preferred some other Bill, it could determine the issue by providing Government time for the Bill which it favoured or refusing extra time for a Bill it disliked. Furthermore, if a government is to be responsible for 'public policy' it seems reasonable to argue that a law such as that on divorce and marriage, which affects potentially every family in the community, should be included in the term, and that the Government should take responsibility accordingly, rather than leave the issue to the luck of the ballot for private members' bills. It may be necessary to pay the price of changing a long-standing convention; for example, any private member's bill which completed the committee stage in the Commons might become the Government's responsibility, or the Government might at least be obliged to provide adequate time.[31]

The single most important characteristic of British government is the concentration of power in the hands of political leaders of the ruling party who form it. There is no separation of powers such as operates in the United States. The supremacy of the Government in the realms of administration and legislation is virtually unchallenged.[32] However, the Government did not assume a principal role in the divorce law reform legislation, and there was no single institutional or individual hero. It was the result of a combined effort on the part of all individuals[33] and groups concerned, including the opponents. The Government was reluctant to take responsibility for the reform and ostensibly remained neutral, claiming that this was a conventional attitude towards a social or religious issue. It had to bear in mind the coming election, and few democratic governments are willing to touch emotionally charged disputes such as divorce or abortion unless they are assured of public support. The Labour Government, as expected, provided extra time for the Bill, although this concession was only achieved after a long debate.[34]

The legal character of the controversy has already been pointed out.[35] But the existence of the Law Commission gave rise to a grave constitutional question. To what extent should the role of the Law Commission be extended? No one has yet offered an answer to the question, nor even publicly discussed it. The Law Commission emphasizes that it is established by statute[36] as an advisory body independent of either the Government or Parliament. In deciding what their advice to Parliament should be they are able to work in the open and fully to canvass legal and public opinion at all stages of their work. By circulating their working papers, they indicate the nature of the problem with which they are concerned, and express their views as to its possible solution.

This method of working in the open is, perhaps, the most useful contribution which we have made to the technique of law reform and it is interesting to note that it is beginning to be adopted by the law reform agencies. However, once our Final Report has been submitted the picture changes. It is to be doubted whether those responsible for the Act of 1965 envisaged that the Commission would have any further function to perform once the Report was submitted; thereafter it was up to Parliament and the Government. *In practice it has not worked out like that.* If the Government decides to introduce legislation on the lines that *we have recommended* it may, and *generally will, wish to consult us* about possible amendments or additions. While the legislation is in process of enactment the *promoter of the Bill may wish to seek our aid.* . . . *In fact we have been called upon to assist* in a variety of ways and have found it eminently desirable to respond. We have ensured, when requested, that members of our staff are present 'in the box', together with civil servants of the government department concerned, *especially at the Committee Stage* when the details, as opposed to the general policy, of the Bill are under scrutiny. *Thereby we have been able to help Parliament* to ensure that piecemeal amendments do not destroy the cohesion of the draft Bills for which we initially were responsible and that the wording of the ultimate Act maintains the clarity of drafting to which we aspire.[87]

The Report further stated that the Commissioners believe this role, although it may have been unforeseen, to be valuable to Parliament, the Government and the public. However, as has been pointed out earlier in Chapter 4, which dealt with the Law Commission, by presenting its proposals, giving advice, selecting evidence and sifting issues the Law Commission has taken over a considerable amount of work which traditionally belonged to the Lord Chancellor's Office and Parliament. Furthermore, the Commissioners made it clear that the above-mentioned methods of consultation during the legislative process may not suffice for mammoth measures of law reform, such as the codifications which are now beginning to show on the horizon. 'If a code's coherent structure is to be maintained and if Parliament is not to find it too indigestible, our assistance on a more formal basis may well be needed at all stages. The time has now come when thought should be given to this problem.'[38]

How far the Law Commission should be responsible for legislation is a grave constitutional issue, particularly as the Commissioners are not elected lawmakers; they are not subject to public scrutiny, or responsible to the electors.[39] When the Commissioners are wise and have no prejudice, no problem arises, but if even a few Commissioners were particularly interested in a certain reform, the consequence of their influence on legislation might be incalculable. However, the Commissioners have to be reappointed after every five-year term and the Government has the power[40] of veto. In any case, for the first time in England a divorce reform bill which was drafted by the Law Commission reached the Statute Book.

Were the reformers morally and socially justified? The answer is a difficult one; it will be necessary to await the decisions of the courts and to see what the impact of the Bill on the divorce-rate will be before making a judgment on the merits of the reform. There may be some unforeseen effects of the Act which could create a new situation. Moreover, a fresh generation whose attitudes have been shaped by this new social institution may well have a completely different outlook on divorce from our own.

Nevertheless, one thing is clear in the divorce controversy. Although each side claimed to be in the right, it is difficult, if not impossible, in a question of this kind to allocate moral praise or blame with any certainty.[41] Nor is it very profitable to speculate on what the outcome might have been had the opponents of reform had their way. Both the reformers and the opponents were concerned with the interests of society and hoped to strengthen the institution of marriage by reforming the law : their object was to promote a happy family life. They agreed as to the end of the divorce law, but disagreed as to the means to that end. Therefore, it may be said that several conflicting views, each claiming to represent the interests of society, struggled to reach the Statute Book through the so-called democratic legislative process. The outcome was a compromise. In this respect, the Divorce Reform Act 1969 was a rational product of the political settlement of an important social issue.

IV. *Social Change and the Reform*

Until 1968 it had been an uphill fight for the reformers against a variety of opponents. Traditional attachments to a long-standing social institution—marriage—and to the Christian teachings, in particular, together with the cautious attitude of lawmakers, were the most difficult obstacles to be overcome. A slowly but steadily rising divorce-rate and the fear of sudden change did not help the reformers. Their only clear advantage lay in the editorial support of most of the press and the results of the opinion polls. The role of the press in the reform movement, though not organized for the cause, in bringing persuasive articles into every home, can easily be underestimated.

Critics in turn blamed pressure groups and the 'permissive society' for the change, but there was no real pressure upon any Member of Parliament to vote for the Bill : no whip and no immediate political or economic interest was involved in the issue. Each member acted according to his own conscience. No one forced him to sit all night in the Chamber. An understanding of the motives which induced so many[42] members to turn out and vote for the Bill might illuminate the mainspring of the whole movement. Social change in a stable society rarely occurs suddenly without a large degree of consensus. There was no revolution, nor was there any emergency. But there had been gradual changes in the minds of the public, journalists, judges, clergy and Members of Parliament, although it is difficult to tell when and how they altered their opinions. What the reformers did was to create public concern and to mobilize something that may be called 'common consent', which if not already in existence was at least rapidly growing, by pointing out prevailing injustice and the defects of the law. Public and parliamentary opinion took a long time to change.

Some may not agree to this interpretation, arguing that there was no 'consent'. It is true that there was no referendum, nor are public opinion polls always accurate. However, there was at least a widespread indifference which often indicates tacit consent; there was no nation-wide outcry over the reform. There were many who supported the reform but still wished divorce were never necessary. It is also true that many people neither think nor care about this kind of problem at all. In the realm of political and legal activities there are always difficult questions which are mainly handled by a small group of professional people without proper understanding on the part of the general public. Divorce law reform was one of them.

Unlike the case of the capital punishment controversy, 'the technical competence'[43] in divorce reform legislation did have the effect, as it often does in politics, of reducing the size of the interested public and leaving the big decisions to the active few. Mr Christoph said that in the capital punishment controversy 'professional expertise was less in demand and less influential than it had been on other occasions'.[44] But in the divorce reform legislation, although the demand for reform of the law may originally have been voiced by a small group of citizens, the controversy was handled by a number of professional experts in the Church of England, the DLRU, the Law Commission and Parliament, and their views and activities were the key factors[45] throughout the process.

Nevertheless, there is a certain limit of flexibility in the attitude of any society, and if a change appears to exceed that limit, it cannot avoid facing formidable and widespread protest from the general public who believe that their criterion is right.[46] Had the reformers, or any one of them, openly denied the institution of marriage and monogamy or seriously preached polygamy, of course public reaction would have been quite different. The so-called silent majority would undoubtedly have joined with moralists and traditionalists to condemn the reformers.

On the other hand, since the English Parliament enjoys legislative supremacy, it is possible, both in theory and in practice, to make any law if a majority of lawmakers can be found to support it. For example, the abolition of capital punishment was carried despite the fact that the opinion polls reflected a majority of over 80 per cent against abolition. Does this not suggest that the importance of public opinion in so-called 'controversial' pieces of social legislation is in fact marginal? The point may, for example, be made with regard to divorce law reform, an issue which was met with greater public apathy than that of abortion or capital punishment. The favourable trend of the opinion polls was useful in persuading the Government to give extra parliamentary time to a private member's bill, and could be pointed to in debate as indicating public support for reform. M.P.s in addition always have to avoid outraging their constituents. But with these exceptions, public opinion counted for little. This raises the problem which underlies all legislation in a democratic country. Short of employing referenda on issues which are often too complex or specialized for the ordinary man to form a valid opinion about, it is difficult to see how the law can avoid reflecting the will of the lawmakers rather than the will of the people. Indeed the importance of a pressure group such as the DLRU lies in its impact on the opinion of an influential minority of lawmakers and journalists. Thus a nucleus of determined individuals can have an effect quite out of proportion to their numbers or position.

This is not to maintain that social trends are completely uninfluential in securing the passage of reform : the passage of an act embodying the terms of the 1969 Divorce Reform Act would have been unthinkable in 1937. The changing status of women, increasing permissiveness in social attitudes generally, the fact that divorce by consent was already in practice obtainable in the courts, all prepared the ground for reform. The attitude of the Archbishop's group as expressed in *Putting Asunder* was of particular importance as a barometer of conservative opinion. But the change in attitudes which mattered in legislative terms was that which occurred among the lawmakers in Parliament. The fact that the reformers failed to secure the whole-hearted support of a large number of women's organizations for the Bill was of surprisingly little practical significance. Members of Parliament were inundated with letters of protest against the Bill from women's organizations and religious groups, but it seems that these exerted a negligible influence on the attitudes of potential supporters of the Bill, nor did they have any noteworthy impact on the movement of the opposition. However, it appears that the direct approach of a few active sponsors of the Bill and members of the DLRU, who worked day and night inside Parliament, personally lobbying M.P.s, produced a remarkable result which may be an important exception in the history of British pressure groups' activities.[47] In short, although it was already apparent that there were quite a number of likely supporters of the Bill among the lawmakers, they were either still in a state of mere agreement or simply potential supporters whose will was yet to be expressed through casting their vote. The efforts of the reformers were undeniable contributory factors in rallying M.P.s into the Chamber, by a persistent campaign and personally lobbying Parliament, in contrast to those of the women's organizations and religious groups who merely wrote letters or sent petitions.

The factors which lead to success in securing the passage of specific legislative proposals are complex; timing and luck are often vital, and to attribute a reform to any one individual would be misleading. Nevertheless, a small number of reformers played a decisive part in shaping public and legislative opinion on the issue, and credit should perhaps be given to the men who had to take the blame when things went wrong. Above all, the Labour majority in Parliament was perhaps the most significant factor in the event, since all the available evidence indicates that the Bill would probably not have been passed under a Conservative Government.[48]

Both reformers and critics recognized the factors principally responsible for the change : the favourable attitude of the Government; general public opinion as expressed in the press and the opinion polls; the activities of a few M.P.s led by Mr Abse which provided an effective driving force; and the Mortimer group's report, *Putting Asunder,* which gave impetus to the reform movement. The Law Commission and the Lord Chancellor played an important role, and in particular *The Field of Choice* and the *Consensus* afforded the reformers strong support in mobilizing consent; the DLRU, led by Messrs Banks and Service, lobbied Parliament enthusiastically; the divided opponents mistimed their efforts and lacked a focus for resistance; and the reformers took advantage of a changing social mood and the intricacy of the subject.

V. *Myths*

The cause was bolstered by a number of political fictions. First, Leo Abse's so-called 'group' had in fact never existed. Mr Abse, having served a relatively long time in the House, had a good many friends among M.P.s, and his 'group' was no more than an informal discussion group which met on a number of occasions in the House when Mr Abse needed to demonstrate the existence of a considerable number of supporters for the cause. He pointed to it in attempting to persuade officials in the House and the Government, and it became a particularly effective weapon when press reports began to give credence to it. It was never more than an *ad hoc* group, existing in name only, but this masterly 'bluff' of Leo Abse's, like that by A. P. Herbert in 1936, apparently strengthened his hand in gathering official support for reform.

Secondly, to some extent the public was misled by the reformers' strategy. They defended their Bill by saying that opinion polls proved that the general public favoured the reform and argued that it was a necessary measure to relieve the plight of many unfortunate illegitimate children. However, as one of the opponents, Mr Percival, said, it was doubtful how many people who helped the pollsters actually understood the implications of the terms used in the polls; and as Mr Campbell pointed out,[49] improved legal status could be accorded to illegitimate children in another way, by altering the law relating to illegitimacy. Furthermore, the reformers had claimed that their Bill would make divorce more difficult, but would be a more humane and just law. This found sympathy with many an unsophisticated moralist and carried effective weight in countering the views brought by the opponents who claimed that the Bill would allow 'divorce at will'.

It seems incredible that no one has ever challenged the reformers with positive statistical evidence. Despite the reformers' claim, there is no real evidence of a *rapidly* increasing number of either illegitimate children[50] or broken marriages, although the divorce-rate has been steadily going up, and as noted in *The Field of Choice*,[51] there is no proof that the proportion of marriages which break down has not increased. Contrary to the claims put forward by the reformers and the opponents, there is no data proving that there were 'thousands of long-overdue marriages',[52] nor is there any evidence yet that the divorce-rate would destroy the institution of marriage. The opponents maintained that the rising divorce-rate under an easy divorce law would not only undermine the institution of marriage itself, but that it would also destroy the basic foundation of social life. However, as has already been pointed out, marriage has become more popular and the main causes of a rising divorce-rate are unlikely to be found in the law itself; other factors such as younger marriage, the longer duration of married life, circumstantial difficulties such as the housing shortage and the so-called mood of permissive society as a whole are equally important contributors to such rises in the divorce-rate as may occur. In short, the reasons for divorce and marital breakdown lie deep in the culture and the personalities society produces rather than in the substantial provisions of an Act of Parliament.

The next point is that although the DLRU had a list of members, the Union not only lacked any clear and simple slogan[53] and decisive driving force, but it had hardly any resources. Only a few committee members were active in holding public meetings, which rarely attracted an audience of more than a hundred at a time. Nor did anyone lobby Parliament until Mr Service joined the Union in 1967.

For a private member's bill such as this one, the attitudes of the

Government Chief Whip, the Lord Chancellor and the Law Commission were crucial; there was a series of understandings between them and the reformers behind the scenes. The agreement reached with these people, any one of whom could have placed major obstacles in the way of the Bill, was given little publicity, but was vital in securing its passage into law. Indeed the Lord Chancellor and a Commissioner, Mr Gower, had both been members of the DLRU;[54] Mr John Silkin, a solicitor who was then the Government Chief Whip, was a strong supporter of the Bill. Thus three most important positions were occupied by the reformers and their sympathizers during that period. Consequently these three lawyers, with Sir Leslie Scarman, played their part cautiously but effectively for the reform.

VI. *Future of the Act*

The following are the recent notable legislative developments in matrimonial law. The Matrimonial Causes Act 1967, giving County Courts jurisdiction in undefended causes, and the Matrimonial Homes Act 1967, giving one spouse protection in respect of a matrimonial home owned by the other spouse, came into operation in 1968; the Matrimonial Proceedings and Property Act 1970, abolishing restitution of conjugal rights and, at the same time, codifying the law applicable to matters ancillary to the main suit, the Law Reform (Miscellaneous Provisions) Act 1970, abolishing damages in matrimonial proceedings, and the Divorce Reform Act 1969, altering the law of divorce and judicial separation, all came into force on 1st January, 1971; and Part III of the Family Law Reform Act 1969, introducing a code for blood-tests to establish paternity, has come into force. Attention should also be drawn to section 1 of the Administration of Justice Act which transfers jurisdiction in matrimonial and related causes from the Probate, Divorce and Admiralty Division to a new Division, the Family Division. Another significant change has been effected in the jurisdiction of the Magistrates' Courts by the Maintenance Orders Act 1968, which removed the maximum limits on maintenance orders for spouses and children, leaving the court free to order such payments as it may think fit.

Among these notable legislative developments the outstanding landmark is undoubtedly the Divorce Reform Act 1969, which abolished the existing statutory absolute and discretionary bars in divorce and judicial separation and greatly simplified the law in these proceedings. The practical significance of the 1969 Act is that divorce is now available in two new circumstances—divorce by consent after two years' separation and divorce without consent after five years' separation, thus rejecting the old idea of matrimonial offence, although shades of the old concepts, such as adultery and desertion, will remain so long as they are used as evidence. None the less, the divorce law of England has entered a completely new era, which has been causing considerable anxiety and fear lest the divorce-rate increases too rapidly.

However, there is as yet no positive evidence of mass rushing to the Divorce Court, although the divorce proceedings[55] in the Principal Registry in the period from 1st January to the end of March 1971 indicated an increase of about 20 per cent over the corresponding period in 1970. Despite the fact that it had been claimed that there were thousands of broken marriages[56] which needed relief, the above-mentioned rise compares very favourably with the 40 per cent recorded in the State of California in 1970 after it had altered its divorce law. Although some lawyers claim that the present trends are counterbalanced by the potential effects of the new Maintenance Order 1968 and the financial provisions of the 1969 Act, the figures prove that there were not so many 'Casanovas' who had been awaiting the opportunity to get a divorce in spite of the warnings put forward by the opponents.

In conclusion, the following questions must be posed. What is the general view of the Act and how many people are going to take advantage of it? As to the first question, many may agree with the Archbishop of Canterbury who said : 'As usually happens in a compromise, it contains bits that are good, some I think very good, and bits that are bad. That is how I view the matter.' It is claimed, however, that contrary to Dr Ramsey's interpretation, Clause 2(1)(c) and (d) represent a definite improvement. On the other hand the justice of Clause 2(e), which allows divorce of a so-called innocent spouse after a five-year separation, is debatable.[57] An overall criticism would be the vagueness of some of the wording : phrases such as 'intolerable to live with the respondent' leave wide discretion to the judges, thus placing an additional burden on them. On the second question, Mr William Latey writes : 'One result of the Divorce Reform Act seems certain. The tide of divorce will rise rapidly and may overflow.'[58] Lord Denning states in his Foreword to Mr Latey's book : 'All good folk will hope that this prophecy will not come true. For the sake of our civilisation, we hope that the tide will turn.' Indeed, many expect a rise in the divorce-rate in the next few years, but no one can forecast with any certainty what will happen after that.[59] Since the law came into force on 1st January, 1971, its interpretation and application are firmly in the hands of judges. The fate of the new law will depend not only upon the people who bring their cases to the court, but upon the way in which they are handled there. For better or worse, every dissolution of marriage is subject to the Divorce Reform Act 1969 until it is repealed, and indeed it will affect the lives of many English people.

NOTES

1 It is tellingly illustrated by the conflicting approaches of Savigny and Bentham. For Savigny, a bitter opponent of the rationalizing and lawmaking tendencies spurred by the French Revolution, law was 'found', not made. By contrast, Bentham was a fervent believer in the efficacy of rationally constructed reforming laws. For a detailed account of their theories and Friedmann's illustration, see W. Friedmann, *Legal Theory* (5th ed. 1967), pp. 312 *et seq.* and pp. 210 *et seq.*

2 See W. Friedmann, *Law in a Changing Society* (1964), p. 19.

3 It also made cruelty or desertion for three years a ground for divorce in its own right.

4 pp. 3–4.

5 See p. 44, above.

6 See Winnett, *Divorce and Re-Marriage in Anglicanism*, p. 147; and *Putting Asunder*, p. 86.

7 He later voted against the Bill in the Lords.

8 A leaflet published by the Humanist lobby.

9 Ibid.

10 Printed by E. Ainsworth & Son, 15 Little Peter Street, Manchester 15.

11 In a leaflet published by the Humanist lobby.

12 Ibid.

13 Ibid.

14 *Sunday Post* (22nd Dec., 1968); see p. 125, above.

15 Hansard, Vol. 774, col. 2047.

16 See p. 70, above.

17 *The Field of Choice*, Cmd 3123, p. 6.

18 Ibid. But note that the first divorce law in Italy took effect on 18th December, 1970.

19 Ibid., p. 7.

20 Ibid.

21 Ibid.

22 Jean Sarjeant, 'The Decision of Divorce', *The Times* (14th Dec., 1970).

23 The problems of children and the distribution of justice in a unilateral divorce have been discussed already in Chap. 3 of the present volume, under the heading 'Putting Asunder'.

24 *The Economist* (24th May, 1969).

25 W. Latey, *The Tide of Divorce* (1970), p. 165.

26 See the Regulations Concerning Marriage and Divorce (Church of England), Clause 1(1).

27 See the discussion in Chap. 3. It should be noted in this respect that Catholics did not oppose the Bill vehemently.

28 24th May, 1969, p. 25.

29 But it is true that the Bill was aided by Government time.

30 See J. B. Christoph, *Capital Punishment and British Politics* (2nd imp. 1968), pp. 176 *et seq.*

31 For a useful discussion on this subject, see Richards, op. cit., pp. 197 *et seq.*

32 See Christoph, op. cit., p. 176.

33 Although Messrs Abse, Service, Gower and Lord Gardiner played key roles.

34 It may be necessary to point out that several supporters of Mr Jones's Bill were confident that they would be provided adequate time for the Bill, as a convention for providing time for social legislation such as the Abortion Bill had already been established.

35 The relationship between the law and the will of the people is discussed in the following section.

36 See pp. 61 *et seq.*, above.

37 Law Commission No. 36, *Fifth Annual Report 1969–70*, pp. 1–2. The italics are mine.

38 Ibid.

39 For a further relevant discussion, see Chap. 4.

40 See p. 65, above.

41 This view, however, is apparently not held by Keith Hindell and Madeleine Simms, authors of *Abortion Law Reformed*, in which they assume that there can be no serious doubt that ALRA had right on its side throughout the struggle, and in which the moral and technical objections of opponents are almost completely discounted.

42 An objection may be raised to this: only about 25 per cent of members attended! But how many private members' bills, one may well ask, have had more than 25 per cent attendance of the members?

43 See Christoph, op. cit., p. 172.

44 Ibid.

45 It is true that many other groups, including women's organizations, legal and religious groups also voiced their opinions, but these counted for little.

46 If one could compare the passages of the 1857 and the 1969 divorce reform bills with a passage of a future reform bill in the year 2000, one would be confronted with a fascinating study of the change that takes place in public attitudes toward social issues.

47 However, it should be noted that the impact of the DLRU on the divorce law reform movement was not as strong as that of ALRA on the abortion law reform campaign.

48 See Table 11, p. 168.

49 See pp. 120–21, above.

50 See Appendix 4, Table 31a.

51 '. . . recent sociological investigations seem to show that marriage as an institution in present-day England is in a fairly healthy state as compared with the past'. (p. 7)

52 If, over the decades, there had built up such a great backlog of divorces, there should in fact have been more positive sign of a rapidly increasing number of petitions for divorce than were seen in the recent past, although it is too early to predict conclusively as yet.

53 Until *Putting Asunder, The Field of Choice* and the *Consensus* were published.

54 In fact, Mr Gower never resigned from the Union, although before he became a Law Commissioner he had stopped being an active member following his resignation from the committee of the Union.

55 See Table 31, Appendix IV.

56 See pp. 163 and 184, above.

57 See also p. 51, above.

58 *The Tide of Divorce*, p. 168.

59 For recent statistics on petitions for divorce in the Principal Registry, see Table 31, Appendix IV.

Appendix 1

Divorce Reform Act 1969

CHAPTER 55

ARRANGEMENT OF SECTIONS

Section

1. Breakdown of marriage to be sole ground for divorce.
2. Proof of breakdown.
3. Provisions designed to encourage reconciliation.
4. Decree to be refused in certain circumstances.
5. Power to rescind decree nisi in certain cases.
6. Financial protection for respondent in certain cases.
7. Rules may enable certain agreements or arrangements to be referred to the court.
8. Judicial separation.
9. Consequential amendments, repeals and saving.
10. Saving for petitions presented before commencement of Act.
11. Short title, construction, commencement and extent.

Schedules:

Schedule 1—Consequential amendments of the Matrimonial Causes Act 1965.
Schedule 2—Repeals in the Matrimonial Causes Act 1965.

Divorce Reform Act 1969

ELIZABETH II

1969 CHAPTER 55

An Act to amend the grounds for divorce and judicial
separation; to facilitate reconciliation in matrimonial
causes; and for purposes connected with the matters
aforesaid.   [22nd October 1969]

B E IT ENACTED by the Queen's most Excellent Majesty,
by and with the advice and consent of the Lords
Spiritual and Temporal, and Commons, in this
present Parliament assembled, and by the authority of the
same, as follows:—

1.—After the commencement of this Act the sole ground
on which a petition for divorce may be presented to the
court by either party to a marriage shall be that the
marriage has broken down irretrievably.

Breakdown of marriage to be sole ground for divorce.

2.—(1) The court hearing a petition for divorce shall not
hold the marriage to have broken down irretrievably unless
the petitioner satisfies the court of one or more of the
following facts, that is to say—

Proof of breakdown.

    (*a*) that the respondent has committed adultery and
the petitioner finds it intolerable to live with the
respondent;

    (*b*) that the respondent has behaved in such a way
that the petitioner cannot reasonably be expected
to live with the respondent;

    (*c*) that the respondent has deserted the petitioner for
a continuous period of at least two years immediately preceding the presentation of the petition;

(*d*) that the parties to the marriage have lived apart for a continuous period of at least two years immediately preceding the presentation of the petition and the respondent consents to a decree being granted;

(*e*) that the parties to the marriage have lived apart for a continuous period of at least five years immediately preceding the presentation of the petition.

(2) On a petition for divorce it shall be the duty of the court to inquire, so far as it reasonably can, into the facts alleged by the petitioner and into any facts alleged by the respondent.

(3) If the court is satisfied on the evidence of any such fact as is mentioned in subsection (1) of this section, then, unless it is satisfied on all the evidence that the marriage has not broken down irretrievably, it shall, subject to section 4 of this Act and section 5(5) of the Matrimonial Causes Act 1965, grant a decree nisi of divorce.

1965 c. 72.

(4) For the purpose of subsection (1)(*c*) of this section the court may treat a period of desertion as having continued at a time when the deserting party was incapable of continuing the necessary intention if the evidence before the court is such that, had that party not been so incapable, the court would have inferred that his desertion continued at that time.

(5) For the purposes of this Act a husband and wife shall be treated as living apart unless they are living with each other in the same household.

(6) Provision shall be made by rules of court for the purpose of ensuring that where in pursuance of subsection (1)(*d*) of this section the petitioner alleges that the respondent consents to a decree being granted the respondent has been given such information as will enable him to understand the consequences to him of his consenting to a decree being granted and the steps which he must take to indicate that he consents to the grant of a decree.

Provisions designed to encourage reconciliation.

3.—(1) Provision shall be made by rules of court for requiring the solicitor acting for a petitioner for divorce to certify whether he has discussed with the petitioner the

possibility of a reconciliation and given him the names and
addresses of persons qualified to help effect a reconciliation
between parties to a marriage who have become estranged.

(2) If at any stage of proceedings for divorce it appears
to the court that there is a reasonable possibility of a
reconciliation between the parties to the marriage, the
court may adjourn the proceedings for such period as it
thinks fit to enable attempts to be made to effect such a
reconciliation.

The power conferred by the foregoing provision is additional to any other power of the court to adjourn
proceedings.

(3) Where the parties to the marriage have lived with
each other for any period or periods after it became known
to the petitioner that the respondent had, since the celebration of the marriage, committed adultery, then,—

    (a) if the length of that period or of those periods
        together was six months or less, their living with
        each other during that period or those periods shall
        be disregarded in determining for the purposes of
        section 2(1)(a) of this Act whether the petitioner
        finds it intolerable to live with the respondent;
        but

    (b) if the length of that period or of those periods
        together exceeded six months, the petitioner shall
        not be entitled to rely on that adultery for the
        purposes of the said section 2(1)(a).

(4) Where the petitioner alleges that the respondent has
behaved in such a way that the petitioner cannot reasonably be expected to live with him, but the parties to the
marriage have lived with each other for a period or periods
after the date of the occurrence of the final incident relied
on by the petitioner and held by the court to support his
allegation, that fact shall be disregarded in determining for
the purposes of section 2(1)(b) of this Act whether the
petitioner cannot reasonably be expected to live with the
respondent if the length of that period or of those periods
together was six months or less.

(5) In considering for the purposes of section 2(1) of
this Act whether the period for which the respondent has
deserted the petitioner or the period for which the parties

to a marriage have lived apart has been continuous, no account shall be taken of any one period (not exceeding six months) or of any two or more periods (not exceeding six months in all) during which the parties resumed living with each other, but no period during which the parties lived with each other shall count as part of the period of desertion or of the period for which the parties to the marriage lived apart, as the case may be.

(6) References in this section to the parties to a marriage living with each other shall be construed as references to their living with each other in the same household.

Decree to be refused in certain circumstances.

4.—(1) The respondent to a petition for divorce in which the petitioner alleges any such fact as is mentioned in paragraph (e) of section 2(1) of this Act may oppose the grant of a decree nisi on the ground that the dissolution of the marriage will result in grave financial or other hardship to him and that it would in all the circumstances be wrong to dissolve the marriage.

(2) Where the grant of a decree nisi is opposed by virtue of this section, then,—

(a) if the court is satisfied that the only fact mentioned in the said section 2(1) on which the petitioner is entitled to rely in support of his petition is that mentioned in the said paragraph (e), and

(b) if apart from this section it would grant a decree nisi, the court shall consider all the circumstances, including the conduct of the parties to the marriage and the interests of those parties and of any children or other persons concerned, and if the court is of opinion that the dissolution of the marriage will result in grave financial or other hardship to the respondent and that it would in all the circumstances be wrong to dissolve the marriage it shall dismiss the petition.

(3) For the purposes of this section hardship shall include the loss of the chance of acquiring any benefit which the respondent might acquire if the marriage were not dissolved.

5.—Where the court on granting a decree of divorce held that the only fact mentioned in section 2(1) of this Act on which the petitioner was entitled to rely in support of his petition was that mentioned in paragraph (*d*), it may, on an application made by the respondent at any time before the decree is made absolute, rescind the decree if it is satisfied that the petitioner misled the respondent (whether intentionally or unintentionally) about any matter which the respondent took into account in deciding to consent to the grant of a decree.

Power to rescind decree nisi in certain cases.

6.—(1) The following provisions of this section shall have effect where—

Financial protection for respondent in certain cases.

(*a*) the respondent to a petition for divorce in which the petitioner alleged any such fact as is mentioned in paragraph (*d*) or (*e*) of section 2(1) of this Act has applied to the court under this section for it to consider for the purposes of subsection (2) hereof the financial position of the respondent after the divorce; and

(*b*) a decree nisi of divorce has been granted on the petition and the court has held that the only fact mentioned in the said section 2(1) on which the petitioner was entitled to rely in support of his petition was that mentioned in the said paragraph (*d*) or (*e*).

(2) The court hearing an application by the respondent under this section shall consider all the circumstances, including the age, health, conduct, earning capacity, financial resources and financial obligations of each of the parties, and the financial position of the respondent as, having regard to the divorce, it is likely to be after the death of the petitioner should the petitioner die first; and notwithstanding anything in the foregoing provisions of this Act but subject to subsection (3) of this section, the court shall not make absolute the decree of divorce unless it is satisfied—

(*a*) that the petitioner should not be required to make any financial provision for the respondent, or

(*b*) that the financial provision made by the petitioner for the respondent is reasonable and fair or the best that can be made in the circumstances.

(3) The court may if it thinks fit proceed without observing the requirements of subsection (2) of this section if—

(*a*) it appears that there are circumstances making it desirable that the decree should be made absolute without delay, and

(*b*) the court has obtained a satisfactory undertaking from the petitioner that he will make such financial provision for the respondent as the court may approve.

Rules may enable certain agreements or arrangements to be referred to the court.

7.—(1) Provision may be made by rules of court for enabling the parties to a marriage, or either of them, on application made either before or after the presentation of a petition for divorce, to refer to the court any agreement or arrangement made or proposed to be made between them, being an agreement or arrangement which relates to, arises out of, or is connected with, the proceedings for divorce which are contemplated or, as the case may be, have begun, and for enabling the court to express an opinion, should it think it desirable to do so, as to the reasonableness of the agreement or arrangement and to give such directions, if any, in the matter as it thinks fit.

1967 c. 56.

(2) In section 3 of the Matrimonial Causes Act 1967 (consideration of agreements or arrangements by divorce county courts) after the word '1965' there shall be inserted the word 'or of section 7 of the Divorce Reform Act 1969'.

Judicial separation.

8.—(1) After the commencement of this Act the existence of any such fact as is mentioned in section 2(1) of this Act shall be a ground on which either party to a marriage may present a petition for judicial separation; and the ground for failure to comply with a decree for restitution of conjugal rights and any ground on which a decree of divorce a mensa et thoro might have been pronounced immediately before the commencement of the Matrimonial Causes Act of 1857 shall cease to be a ground on which such a petition may be presented.

1857 c. 85.

1965 c. 72.

(2) Accordingly for subsection (1) of section 12 of the Matrimonial Causes Act 1965 there shall be substituted the following subsection :—

'(1) A petition for judicial separation may be

presented to the court by either party to a marriage on the ground that any such fact as is mentioned in section 2(1) of the Divorce Reform Act
1969 exists, and sections 2(2), (4), (5) and (6), 3 and
7 of that Act and paragraph 2 of Schedule 1 to
this Act shall, with the necessary modifications
apply in relation to such a petition as they apply
in relation to a petition for divorce.'

(3) The court hearing a petition for judicial separation
shall not be concerned to consider whether the marriage
has broken down irretrievably, and if it is satisfied on the
evidence of any such fact as is mentioned in section 2(1)
of this Act, it shall, subject to section 33 of the Matrimonial
Causes Act 1965 (restrictions on decrees for dissolution or 1965 c. 72.
separation affecting children), grant a decree of judicial
separation.

9.—(1) The provisions of the Matrimonial Causes Act Consequential amendments,
1965 specified in Schedule 1 to this Act shall have effect repeals and
subject to the amendments set out in that Schedule, being saving.
amendments consequential on the foregoing provisions of
this Act.

(2) Each of the provisions of the Matrimonial Causes
Act 1965 specified in column 1 of Schedule 2 to this Act
is, to the extent specified in relation to it in column 2 of
that Schedule, hereby repealed.

(3) Without prejudice to any provision of this Act or of
the Matrimonial Causes Act 1965, as amended by this Act,
which empowers or requires the court to dismiss a petition
for divorce or judicial separation or to dismiss an application for a decree nisi of divorce to be made absolute,
nothing in section 32 of the Supreme Court of Judicature
(Consolidation) Act 1925 (rules as to exercise of jurisdic- 1925 c. 49.
tion) or in any rule of law shall be taken as empowering or
requiring the court to dismiss such a petition or application
on the ground of collusion between the parties in connection with the presentation or prosecution of the petition or
the obtaining of the decree nisi or on the ground of any Saving for
conduct on the part of the petitioner. petitions
presented
before com-
10.—This Act (including the repeals and amendments mencement of
made by it) shall not have effect in relation to any petition Act.

for divorce or judicial separation presented before the commencement of this Act.

Short title, construction, commencement and extent.

11.—(1) This Act may be cited as the Divorce Reform Act 1969.

(2) This Act shall be construed as one with the Matrimonial Causes Act 1965.

(3) This Act shall come into operation on 1st January 1971.

(4) This Act does not extend to Scotland or Northern Ireland.

SCHEDULES

SCHEDULE 1

Consequential Amendments of the Matrimonial Causes Act 1965

1. In section 3(1) after the word 'petitioner' there shall be inserted the words 'or respondent'.

2. In section 4(1) and (2) for the words 'on the ground of adultery' there shall be substituted the words 'in which adultery is alleged' and in section 4(1) for the words 'on that ground' there shall be substituted the words 'and alleging adultery'.

3. In section 5(6) for the words from 'opposes' to 'desertion' there shall be substituted the words 'alleges against the petitioner and proves any such fact as is mentioned in section 2(1) of the Divorce Reform Act 1969'.

4. In section 15(b) for the words 'on the ground of her husband's insanity' there shall be substituted the words 'and alleging any such fact as is mentioned in section 2(1)(e) of the Divorce Reform Act 1969 where the court is satisfied on proof of such facts as may be prescribed by rules of court that her husband is insane'.

5. In section 16(3) for the words from the beginning to 'insanity' there shall be substituted the words 'Where on a petition for divorce presented by a wife the court granted her a decree and held that the only fact mentioned in section 2(1) of the Divorce Reform Act 1969 on which she was entitled to rely was that mentioned in paragraph (e), then if the court is satisfied on proof of such facts as may be prescribed by rules of court that the husband is insane'.

6. In section 17(2) for the words from the beginning to 'she' there shall be substituted the words 'Where on a petition for divorce presented by the husband he satisfies the court of any such fact as is mentioned in section 2(1)(a), (b) or (c) of the Divorce Reform Act 1969 and the court grants him a decree of divorce, then if it appears to the court that the wife' and for the words 'innocent party' there shall be substituted the word 'husband'.

7. In section 20(1)(b) for the words 'on the ground of her husband's insanity' there shall be substituted the words 'and the court held that the only fact mentioned in section 2(1) of the Divorce Reform Act 1969 on which she was entitled to rely was that mentioned in paragraph (e) and the court is satisfied on proof of such facts as may be prescribed by rules of court that the husband is insane'.

8. In section 26(6), as amended by the Family Provision Act 1966, in the definition of 'court', after the word 'court', where first occurring, there shall be inserted the words 'means the High Court and'.

9. In section 30(2)—

    (a) in paragraph (a) for the words 'on the ground of her husband's insanity' there shall be substituted the words 'and the court is satisfied on proof of such facts as may be prescribed by rules of court that her husband is insane';

    (b) in paragraph (b) the word 'divorce' and the words 'or judicial separation' shall be omitted; and

    (c) after paragraph (a) there shall be inserted the following paragraph :—
    '(aa) a petition for divorce or judicial separation is presented by a husband and the court is satisfied on proof of such facts as may be prescribed by rules of court that his wife is insane; or'.

10. In section 34(3) for the words 'on the ground of the husband's insanity' there shall be substituted the words 'in favour of a wife where the court held that the only fact mentioned in section 2(1) of the Divorce Reform Act 1969 on which she was entitled to rely was that mentioned in paragraph (e) and the court is satisfied on proof of such facts as may be prescribed by rules of court that the husband is insane'.

11. In section 46(2) after the definition of 'adopted' there shall be inserted the following definition :—
    ' "the court" (except in sections 26, 27, 28 and 28A) means the High Court or, where a country court has jurisdiction by virtue of the Matrimonial Causes Act 1967, a county court; and'.

12. In Schedule 1. in paragraph 2 after the word 'Act' there shall be inserted the words 'or of section 2(1)(c) of the Divorce Reform Act 1969'.

SCHEDULE 2   Section 9(2).

REPEALS IN THE MATRIMONIAL CAUSES ACT 1965   1965 c. 72.

Provision	Extent of Repeal
Section 1 ...	The whole section.
Section 5 ...	Subsections (1), (2), (3) and (4).
Section 6 ...	In subsection (1), except as applied by section 10 or 14 of the said Act of 1965, paragraph (c).
Section 7 ...	In subsection (1), except as applied by the said section 10 or 14, the words from 'either' to 'collusion or'.
Section 30 ...	In subsection (2)(b), the word 'divorce' and the words 'or judicial separation'.
Section 42 ...	Subsections (1) and (3) so far as they apply in relation to proceedings for divorce or judicial separation. In subsection (2), the words 'this Act and'.

Appendix 2

Regulations Concerning

Marriage and Divorce

*Passed in the Upper House on 16 May 1956 and
23 May 1957 and in the Lower House on 21, 22
and 23 May 1957, and declared an Act of Convocation
by His Grace the Lord Archbishop of Canterbury
on 1 October 1957*

1. 'That this House reaffirms the following four Resolutions of 1938, and in place of Resolution 5 then provisionally adopted by the Upper House substitutes Resolution 2(A) below, which restates the procedure generally followed since 1938.

    (1) 'That this House affirms that according to God's will, declared by Our Lord, marriage is in its true principle, a personal union, for better or for worse, of one man with one woman, exclusive of all others on either side, and indissoluble save by death.'

    (2) 'That this House also affirms as a consequence that re-marriage after divorce during the lifetime of a former partner always involves departure from the true principle of marriage as declared by Our Lord.'

    (3) 'That in order to maintain the principle of lifelong obligation which is inherent in every legally contracted marriage and is expressed in the plainest terms in the Marriage Service, the Church should not allow the use of that Service in the case of anyone who has a former partner still living.'

    (4) 'That while affirming its adherence to our Lord's principle and standard of marriage as stated in the first and second of the above resolutions, this House recognizes that the actual discipline of particular Christian Communions in this matter has varied widely from time to time and place to place, and holds that the Church of England is competent

to enact such a discipline of its own in regard to marriage as may from time to time appear most salutary and efficacious. . . .'

2(A) 'Recognizing that the Church's pastoral care for all people includes those who during the lifetime of a former partner contract a second union, this House approves the following pastoral regulations as being the most salutary in present circumstances:

(a) When two persons have contracted a marriage in civil law during the lifetime of a former partner of either of them, and either or both desire to be baptized or confirmed or to partake of the Holy Communion, the incumbent or other priest having the cure of their souls shall refer the case to the Bishop of the diocese, with such information as he has and such recommendations as he may desire to make.

(b) The Bishop in considering the case shall give due weight to the preservation of the Church's witness to Our Lord's standard of marriage and to the pastoral care of those who have departed from it.

(c) If the Bishop is satisfied that the parties concerned are in good faith and that their receiving of the Sacraments would be for the good of their souls and ought not to be a cause of offence to the Church, he shall signify his approval thereof both to the priest and to the party or parties concerned : this approval shall be given in writing and shall be accepted as authoritative both in the particular diocese and in all other dioceses of the province.'

2(B) 'No public Service shall be held for those who have contracted a civil marriage after divorce. It is not within the competence of the Convocations to lay down what private prayers the curate in the exercise of his pastoral Ministry may say with the persons concerned, or to issue regulations as to where or when these prayers shall be said.'

2(C) 'Recognizing that pastoral care may well avert the danger of divorce if it comes into play before legal proceedings have been started, this House urges all clergy in their preparation of couples for marriage to tell them, both for their own sakes and for that of their friends, that the good offices of the clergy are always available.'

The following Resolution was passed by the Lower House of the Convocation of Canterbury on 2 October 1957 :

'This House desires to place on record its warm support of the action of His Grace the President in promulgating as an Act of Convocation the Resolutions of Convocation on Marriage and Divorce, and His Grace's statement which accompanied it; respectfully requests the President to ensure that this Act be made well known in each Diocese; and calls upon the clergy of the Province to give to the Act their loyal and unstinted allegiance in word and deed.'

Reprinted with permission

Appendix 3

The Consensus between the Church Group and the Law Commission[1]

In accordance with the wishes expressed during the Debate in the House of Lords on 23rd November 1966, the members of the Archbishop of Canterbury's Group on Divorce have had discussions with the Law Commission to see whether their view, expressed in 'Putting Asunder', that breakdown should become the sole and comprehensive ground of divorce could be reconciled with the view expressed by the Law Commission in 'Reform of the Grounds of Divorce—The Field of Choice' (Cmnd 3123) that the suggested inquest into the marriage was impracticable even if acceptable to public opinion. As a result of these discussions, the following proposals are put forward. They are supported by all the Group with the exception of one member who abstained. It will be seen that they fully maintain the principle (affirmed by the Church Assembly on 16th February) that breakdown should replace matrimonial offence and become the sole and comprehensive ground of divorce. But in place of the proposed inquest the court is directed to infer breakdown, in the absence of evidence to the contrary, on proof of the existence of certain matrimonial situations. The Law Commission is satisfied that these amended proposals would be practicable and could form the basis of a really worthwhile reform of the Divorce Law.

Proposals

1. Subject to the safeguards mentioned below, divorce should be available upon proof that the marriage had irretrievably broken down, and upon no other ground.

2. In accordance with the present law, no petition for divorce should be presented without leave within three years from the date of the marriage.

3. The solicitor acting for a petitioner should be required to certify whether or not he had discussed the possibility of a reconciliation being effected and had brought to the attention of the petitioner the names of appropriate persons and marriage guidance

organisations qualified to assist in effecting a reconciliation.

4. If at any stage in any case the court had reason to believe that a reconciliation might be effected, it should have power to adjourn the case for a period not exceeding three months to permit the possibility of reconciliation to be explored.

5.—(1) No marriage should be treated as having broken down irretrievably unless the court was satisfied that:—

    (a) the respondent had committed adultery and the petitioner found it intolerable to continue or resume cohabitation; or

    (b) the conduct of the respondent had been so intolerable that the petitioner could not reasonably be expected to continue or resume cohabitation; or

    (c) the parties had ceased to cohabit for a continuous period of at least two years and the respondent either
        (i) had deserted the petitioner; or
        (ii) did not object to the grant of a divorce; or

    (d) the parties had ceased to cohabit for a continuous period of not less than five years.

  (2) If the court was satisfied that any of the above situations existed, it should treat the marriage as having broken down irretrievably unless satisfied on all the evidence that the marriage had not broken down irretrievably.

6. There should be a procedure to ensure that a respondent's decision not to object to the grant of a divorce had been taken freely and with a full appreciation of the consequences (see the procedure suggested in paragraph 112 of 'The Field of Choice').

7. The court should be:—

    (a) *empowered* to refuse a divorce if the petitioner had attempted to deceive the court, and

    (b) *required* to do so if satisfied that, having regard to the conduct and interests of the parties and the interests of the children and other persons affected, it would be wrong to dissolve the marriage, notwithstanding the public interest in dissolving marriages which have irretrievably broken down.

8. The court should be *required* to refuse a divorce until satisfied :—

   (a) that satisfactory arrangements, or the best that could be devised in the circumstances, had been made for the care, upbringing and support of the children,

   (b) that, where the respondent had applied for financial relief, equitable financial arrangements (or the best that could be devised in the circumstances) had been made for the respondent, or that no such financial arrangements should be made.

Notes

1. It will be observed that all the existing 'matrimonial offences' disappear as individual grounds of divorce. On the other hand, many of them are elements of the various guide-posts on the basis of which the court is to infer breakdown in the absence of evidence to the contrary.

2. Under proposal 5(1)(a), if the respondent has committed adultery and the petitioner finds it intolerable to continue or to resume cohabitation, then, subject to proposals 7 and 8, he or she will be entitled to a divorce, unless there is positive evidence that, despite all this, the marriage has not irretrievably broken down. In the latter event, we envisage that the court would normally exercise its power to adjourn (proposal 4—a proposal to which we attach importance), rather than finally dismiss the petition. If both parties have committed adultery and each objects to the other obtaining a divorce, proposal 7(b) will be particularly relevant. We envisage that under this proposal the court will make the sort of assessment made by the President in the recent case of *Inglis v. Inglis & Baxter* (1967) 2 W.L.R. 488. There both parties had committed adultery. The husband petitioned for divorce; the wife for judicial separation. Although the President was satisfied that the husband was more responsible for the breakdown than the wife, he granted the former a divorce, after ensuring that financial arrangements had been made which would adequately compensate the wife for loss of her Army widow's pension, since to dissolve the marriage was in the best interests of the public and all the parties involved (including the child and woman named).

   It will be observed that, where adultery has been committed a divorce normally follows if the petitioner finds it intolerable to resume cohabitation. In this case, unlike 'cruelty' cases, it must, in our view, rest with the petitioner to say whether he or she is able to forgive and forget and not with the judge to say whether he or she ought to do so.

3. 'Cruelty' cases are subsumed under 5(1)(b). In effect, the test is the same as that at present required for cruelty, except that it is not necessary to prove actual or apprehended injury to health. In this case it must be for the judge, and not for the petitioner alone, to decide whether the conduct is sufficiently grave to make it unreasonable to expect the petitioner to endure it (otherwise mere incompatibility would be let in). On the other hand, as at present, in testing the gravity of the respondent's conduct, the judge must consider its effect on the particular petitioner and not on some hypothetical 'average reasonable husband or wife'.

A finding that the situation envisaged in 5(1)(b) is established will usually mean that the respondent is substantially responsible for the breakdown of the marriage and may be very relevant when maintenance is assessed. On the other hand, it will not operate as a finding that the respondent is solely to blame. A finding that 5(1)(a) is established need not in itself operate as any finding of responsibility for the breakdown. It will still be open to the respondent to prove if he or she can, that, despite his or her adultery, the beginning of the breakdown of the marriage was solely due to the petitioner. We think this difference is justified; if the marriage has broken down and if the respondent has committed adultery, the other spouse should normally be entitled to a divorce, even though the adultery is not the cause but rather the effect of the breakdown: cf. *Inglis v. Inglis & Baxter,* supra.

4. Desertion cases come within proposal 5(1)(c), the period being reduced from the present three years to two. In our view, it is unrealistic to suppose that normally a breakdown which has lasted for two years is retrievable. If, however, there is evidence that it is in fact retrievable, the court will be entitled to dismiss the petition or, preferably, to exercise the power to adjourn to explore the possibility of reconciliation. 5(1)(c) also covers the situation where there has been a consensual separation for two years and both parties want a divorce—a still clearer indication of irretrievable breakdown. In this case, proposal 6 is particularly relevant—the court must satisfy itself that the respondent's consent is genuine and informed. Both here and throughout we have used the expression 'ceased to cohabit', rather than 'lived separate and apart', to show that we mean a cessation of *consortium,* even though both parties continue to live under the same roof, which, under present housing conditions, they may be forced to do. Here and in proposal 5(1)(d), we have referred to

a 'continuous period' of two or five years' separation. We would, however, make it clear that, as under the present law, a short period of cohabitation with a view to effecting a permanent reconciliation should not operate to break the period. The wording of any legislation will require careful drafting; the present provisions (ss. 1(2) and 42(2) of the Matrimonial Causes Act 1965) are not wholly satisfactory.

5. Incurable unsoundness of mind is not specifically mentioned at all. Where, however, the conduct of the mentally disordered spouse has produced an intolerable situation for the petitioner, the latter could rely on 5(1)(b); this, in effect, preserves the present law. In other circumstances, the petitioner will normally have to rely on 5(1)(d) which will enable a divorce to be obtained after five years' separation without, as at present, having to prove that the insanity is 'incurable'—which involves an impossible forecast of the future state of medical science—or strict compliance with the highly technical existing rules about 'continuous care and attention'. The definition of 'cessation of cohabitation' will need to make it clear that it covers cases where the separation is not wilful but due to the fact that, for example, one spouse is in a mental home.

6. The bars in proposals 7 and 8 are intended to take the place of all the bars existing under the present law. Unreasonable delay, condonation, collusion, connivance, conduct conducing and the disclosed adultery of the petitioner all disappear as separate bars; they will be factors that the court may take into consideration in determining whether the marriage has irretrievably broken down, and in deciding whether even if it has broken down a divorce should be refused under proposal 7. Proposal 7(a) is intended to rationalise the present position, under which deceit of the court is a discretionary bar only if the court has a discretion on some other basis, for example, the petitioner's adultery. To make it workable the Rules will have to state clearly exactly what has to be stated in the petition.

7. Proposal 7(b) is not intended to make the grant of a divorce discretionary; that would be to introduce an impossibly wide area of uncertainty and would inevitably lead to wide variations of practice. It is intended as a 'long stop', requiring the court to refuse a divorce in defended cases if the overall justice of the case, including in particular the interests of the respondent and the children, appears to demand it. Where the interests of the respondent and the children can be properly protected, we do not intend that the court should refuse to dissolve the marriage on the ground that to penalize a petitioner who has shown

contempt of the sanctity of marriage in some way upholds the sanctity of marriage. *Inglis v. Inglis & Baxter*, to which we have already referred, affords a good example of circumstances in which the discretion would be relevant. If, as in that case, the respondent-wife could be adequately safeguarded in respect of her loss of widow's pension, the divorce should be granted to the petitioner. If she could not be adequately protected, it may well be that a divorce would be refused.

8. Proposal 8(*a*) is in accordance with the present law. 8(*b*) is new, but is, in our view, vital, especially in the light of proposal 5(1)(*d*). That latter proposal should not be implemented until the present provisions for financial relief have been reformed and, more especially, until both spouses have been afforded greater protection in respect of the home, on the lines proposed in the Matrimonial Homes Bill at present before Parliament. Under the present law, the rule embodied in proposal 8(*a*) is a bar on the granting of the decree absolute—not nisi. The Morton Commission found that there were administrative difficulties in making it a pre-condition to the grant of a decree nisi. We would much prefer that, if possible, the whole of proposal 8 should operate before decree nisi; and, having regard to the growing extent to which financial arrangements are settled in advance of the hearing under s. 5 of the Matrimonial Causes Act, we are not convinced that this would any longer be impracticable so long as the court had power to adjourn. If that could be done, it might well be possible to abolish the distinction between decree nisi and decree absolute—a distinction which wastes time and money, confuses the parties, especially those not legally represented, and can lead to premature (bigamous) marriages.

2nd June 1967.

NOTES

1 The actual heading is as follows: Reform of Grounds of Divorce. Result of Discussion between Archbishop's Group on Divorce and Law Commission. See Law Commission No. 15, *Third Annual Report 1967–68*, pp. 30 *et seq.*

Appendix 4

Statistics of Divorce and Illegitimacy

The statistics on divorce can be found in *Civil Judicial Statistics, Annual Abstract of Statistics*, the *Registrar General's Statistical Review* and *Social Trends; The Field of Choice* also provides the figures up to 1965. However, they are neither consolidated nor easily available in useful and convenient forms, although the *Registrar General's Statistical Review* is fairly comprehensive and may be found in university libraries.

The following are the figures on divorce, adapted from the above-mentioned sources and information supplied by the Law Commission.

TABLE 13

Total Number of Petitions Filed

Year	Petitions Filed	Increase/Decrease
1950	29,868	–
1951	38,551	+ 8,683
1952	34,753	– 3,798
1953	30,701	– 4,052
1954	29,184	– 1,517
1955	28,495	– 689
1956	28,640	+ 145
1957	28,062	– 578
1958	26,444	– 1,618
1959	26,561	+ 117
1960	28,790	+ 2,229
1961	32,152	+ 3,362
1962	34,892	+ 2,740
1963	37,548	+ 2,656
1964	41,789	+ 4,232
1965	43,255	+ 1,475
1966	46,890	+ 3,635
1967	51,269	+ 4,379
1968	55,256	+ 3,987
1969	60,134	+ 4,878

SOURCES : *Civil Judicial Statistics for England and Wales*, 1950–69; *Registrar General's Statistical Review*, 1968; *The Field of Choice;* and *Social Trends*, 1970.

The increase in 1951 is partly explained by the fact that the Legal Aid and Advice Act 1949 came into force in the autumn of 1950. The figures show a steady decrease 1952–8, with the exception of a small rise in 1956, but there has been a steady rise in the divorce-rate since 1959. The Legal Aid and Legal Advice Act 1960 also came into force in 1961.

TABLE 14

Petitions Filed 1954–68 by Suits

Year	Divorce	Nullity	Judicial Separation	Restitution
1954	28,347	689	104	44
1955	27,656	658	130	51
1956	27,753	673	153	61
1957	27,210	648	146	58
1958	25,584	658	158	47
1959	25,689	638	183	51
1960	27,870	672	200	48
1961	31,124	781	200	47
1962	33,818	807	215	52
1963	36,385	919	206	38
1964	40,621	847	253	59
1965	42,070	911	242	32
1966	45,610	999	242	39
1967	49,969	987	279	34
1968	54,036	971	233	16
1969	60,134	1,082	229	24

SOURCES : *Civil Judicial Statistics for England and Wales*, 1950–69; *Registrar General's Statistical Review*, 1968; *The Field of Choice;* and *Social Trends,* 1970.

As Professor McGregor said,[1] despite the emphasis placed by the Church of England on nullity, and its reiterated advice to its members to seek, whenever possible, annulments of marriage rather than divorce, the ratio of nullity to divorce has remained fairly constant.

TABLE 15

Petitions Legally Aided 1950–68

Year	Those Legally Aided	Decrease/Increase
1950	2,003	–
1951	24,865	+ 22,862
1952	21,076	— 3,789
1953	18,091	— 2,985
1954	15,805	— 2,286
1955	13,844	— 1,961
1956	12,981	— 863
1957	11,427	— 1,554
1958	9,936	— 1,491
1959	10,078	+ 142
1960	14,265	+ 4,187
1961	20,276	+ 6,011
1962	23,384	+ 3,108
1963	26,195	+ 2,811
1964	28,778	+ 2,583
1965	29,507	+ 729
1966	31,188	+ 1,681
1967	35,053	+ 3,865
1968	34,997	— 55

SOURCES : *Civil Judicial Statistics,* England and Wales, 1968, and *The Field of Choice.*

The decrease in the number of petitions receiving legal aid 1952–8, and the increase 1959–65, reflect changes in the total number of petitions filed (see Table 13). However, Table 16 shows a proportionate increase of about 50 per cent in the number of petitions which were legally aided between 1958 and 1965. A reasonable explanation of the increase would appear to be a greater awareness of the availability of the legal aid scheme.

TABLE 16

Comparative Table of Petitions and Legally Aided Petitioners

Year	Petitions	Legally Aided Petitioners	Legally Aided Petitioners as Proportion of all Petitioners
1950	29,868	2,003	6.7
1951	38,551	24,865	64.5
1952	34,753	21,076	60.6
1953	30,701	18,091	58.9
1954	29,184	15,805	54.2
1955	28,495	13,844	48.6
1956	28,640	12,981	45.3
1957	28,062	11,427	40.7
1958	26,444	9,936	37.6
1959	26,561	10,078	37.9
1960	28,790	14,265	49.5
1961	32,152	20,276	63.1
1962	34,892	23,384	67.0
1963	37,548	26,195	69.8
1964	41,780	28,778	68.9
1965	43,255	29,507	68.2
1966	46,890	31,188	66.5
1967	51,269	35,053	68.4
1968	55,256	34,997	63.3

SOURCES : *Civil Judicial Statistics*, England and Wales, 1968, and *The Field of Choice*.

TABLE 17

Those Legally Aided

Year	Husband	Wife	Total
1960	4,059	10,206	14,265
1961	6,565	13,711	20,276
1962	8,065	15,319	23,384
1963	8,784	17,411	26,195
1964	9,104	19,674	28,778
1965	8,760	20,747	29,507
1966	8,759	22,429	31,188
1967	9,473	25,580	35,053
1968	8,907	26,090	34,997

SOURCE : *Civil Judicial Statistics*, England and Wales, 1960–8.

The figures in Table 17 indicate that the number of wives getting legal aid is rapidly increasing. It is striking that nearly a threefold increase in the number of legally aided wives' petitions occurred in eight years.

TABLE 18

Dissolutions of Marriage Petitions Filed and Decrees Made Absolute,
1876–1944, England and Wales

Period	Petitions Filed Dissolutions*	Decrees Made Absolute Dissolutions*
1876–80	2,250	1,385†
1881–5	2,230	1,678†
1886–90	2,707	1,767†
1891–5	2,716	1,829†
1896–1900	3,254	2,450†
1901–5	3,936	2,732
1906–10	3,889	3,003
1911–15	4,995	3,178
1916–20	14,475	7,407
1921–5	13,826	13,365
1926–30	19,745	16,420
1931–5	23,226	19,545
1936	5,575	3,922
1937	5,750	4,735
1938	9,970	6,092
1939	8,517	7,793
1940	6,915	7,602
1941	8,079	6,234
1942	11,613	7,430
1943	14,887	9,778
1944	18,390	11,900

SOURCE: RGSR, 1968.   * Excluding annulments.   † Including annulments.

Note: From the twelfth to the seventeenth century under the ecclesiastical
courts, a valid marriage was indissoluble, except with the aid of the legislature. At the end of the seventeenth century a practice sprang up of
procuring divorces by private Act of Parliament. The following divorces
were granted by private Acts of Parliament: Lord de Ross in 1669; Duke of
Norfolk in 1692; before 1715 only 5 such bills were known; between 1715
and 1775 there were 60; between 1776 and 1800 there were 74; between
1801 and 1850 there were 90. See W. S. Holdsworth, *A History of English
Law*, p. 623; and House of Lords, MSS., 1699–1702. Sir William Holdsworth describes the role of ecclesiastical courts as follows: 'The ecclesiastical
courts had, certainly from the twelfth century, undisputed jurisdiction in
matrimonial causes. Questions as to the celebration of marriage, as to the
capacity of the parties to marry, as to the legitimacy of the issue, as to the
dissolution of marriage, were decided by the ecclesiastical courts administered by the canon law.' (op. cit., Vol 1, pp. 621 *et seq*.)

TABLE 19

Dissolutions and Annulments of Marriage: New Petitions Filed and Decrees Made Absolute 1945 to 1969, England and Wales

Year	Petitions Filed		Decrees Absolute Granted	
	Number	Per 1,000 married women aged 20–49	Number	Per 1,000 married women aged 20–49
1945	25,711	3.65	15,634	2.22
1946	43,163	6.09	29,829	4.21
1947	48,501	6.81	60,254	8.47
1948	37,919	5.28	43,698	6.08
1949	35,191	4.87	34,856	4.82
1950	29,729	4.09	30,870	4.24
1951	38,382	5.23	28,767	3.92
1952	34,567	4.69	33,922	4.60
1953	30,542	4.14	30,326	4.11
1954	29,036	3.93	28,027	3.79
1955	28,314	3.83	26,816	3.62
1956	28,426	3.83	26,265	3.54
1957	27,858	3.74	23,785	3.19
1958	26,239	3.52	22,654	3.04
1959	26,327	3.52	24,286	3.25
1960	28,542	3.80	23,868	3.18
1961	31,905	4.31	25,394	3.43
1962	34,625	4.66	28,935	3.89
1963	37,304	5.02	32,052	4.32
1964	41,468	5.58	34,868	4.70
1965	42,070	5.77	37,084	5.07
1966	45,610		38,352	
1967	49,969		42,378	
1968	54,036		45,036	
1969	60,134		50,581	
1970	70,575		57,421	

Sources: *Registrar General's Statistical Review* (RGSR) for 1970, Part II, Table 01, p. 65, *The Field of Choice*, p. 61, and *Social Trends*, 1970.

The figures for 1965–9 in Tables 18 and 19 show a steady increase in the number of decrees granted; the Matrimonial Causes Act 1967 appears to have had no significant impact. There were approximately four decrees of divorce made absolute in 1969 for every 1,000 married couples in England and Wales; a substantial proportion of divorced people marry again. Divorce is highest for girls marrying in their teens, the ratio being twice as high as for women aged 20 to 24 at marriage.[2]

TABLE 20

Divorce Proceedings: England and Wales(1)

Dissolution of marriage(2)	1961	1963	1965	1967	1968	1969
Petitions filed(3)	31,124	36,385	42,070	49,969	54,036	60,134
On grounds of:						
Adultery	13,876	16,972	19,847	23,655	26,011	29,891
Desertion	8,820	9,179	9,596	10,584	11,147	11,490
Cruelty	5,144	6,475	8,618	11,516	12,753	14,538
Adultery and desertion	1,395	1,540	1,621	1,647	1,478	1,397
Adultery and cruelty	717	902	974	1,171	1,212	1,397
Desertion and cruelty	752	894	939	1,055	1,046	1,064
Adultery, desertion and cruelty	100	85	110	91	100	92
Unsound mind	147	101	91	68	63	56
Presumed decease	100	120	111	62	109	75
Rape, etc.	12	15	33	19	8	15
Cruelty and rape, etc.	61	102	130	101	109	119
Decrees absolute granted	24,936	31,405	37,084	42,378	45,036	50,063

SOURCE: *Annual Abstract of Statistics,* No. 107 (1970), p. 84.

(1) Excluding proceedings for restitution of conjugal rights.
(2) Excluding petitions in which divorce is asked for in alternative to nullity.
(3) In the years preceding 1961, petitions based on two or more grounds were shown only under the first of these grounds.

Nearly 80 per cent of decrees granted were based on the three traditional grounds for divorce—namely, adultery, desertion and cruelty. Contrary to the expectations of critics, the Herbert Act 1937, making unsound mind a ground for divorce, was only used in a very small number of cases.[3]

As the Registrar General recognized, small fluctuations in figures from one year to another may be a reflection of changes in procedure designed to clear off accumulated arrears of suits awaiting hearing and from other administrative actions.

TABLE 21

Divorce-Rates per 1,000 Married Population by Age at Divorce 1950–1968, England and Wales

Year	Age at date of Decree Absolute								
	HUSBANDS All ages	Under 25	25–29	30–34	35–39	40–44	45–49	50–54	60 and over
1950–1954*	2.7	2.1	5.0	5.0	4.3	3.4	2.5	1.4	0.3
1955	2.4	2.0	4.2	4.4	3.7	3.0	2.3	1.3	0.3
1956	2.3	1.9	4.1	4.2	3.5	3.0	2.3	1.3	0.3
1957	2.1	1.1	3.6	3.7	3.3	2.6	2.2	1.3	0.3
1958	1.9	1.0	3.3	3.5	3.1	2.6	2.0	1.2	0.3
1959	2.1	1.1	3.6	3.9	3.2	2.9	2.1	1.3	0.3
1960	2.0	1.0	3.6	3.8	3.2	2.7	2.0	1.2	0.3
1961	2.1	1.4	4.0	4.2	3.4	2.8	2.1	1.3	0.3
1962	2.4	1.7	4.5	4.7	3.8	3.2	2.4	1.4	0.4
1963	2.7	2.0	5.2	5.2	4.2	3.4	2.6	1.5	0.4
1964	2.9	2.2	5.7	5.8	4.6	3.4	2.7	1.6	0.5
1965	3.1	2.5	6.4	6.1	4.9	3.8	2.9	1.7	0.5
1966	3.2	2.5	6.7	6.7	5.1	3.9	2.9	1.7	0.5
1967	3.5	3.0	7.6	7.3	5.5	4,2	3.3	1.9	0.5
1968	3.7	3.4	8.1	7.7	5.9	4.3	3.4	1.9	0.6
	WIVES								
1950–1954*	2.7	3.1	5.6	4.8	3.8	2.9	2,1	1.0	0.2
1955	2.3	3.0	4.6	4.2	3.2	2.6	2.0	0.9	0.2
1956	2.3	2.9	4.6	4.0	3.2	2.6	1.9	0.9	0.2
1957	2.0	2.0	4.1	3.6	2.9	2.3	1.8	0.9	0.2
1958	1.9	2.0	3.8	3.3	2.8	2.3	1.7	0.9	0.2
1959	2.1	2.1	4.1	3.7	2.9	2.5	1.8	1.0	0.2
1960	2.0	2.2	4.2	3.5	2.9	2.2	1.7	0.9	0.2
1961	2.1	2.4	4.6	3.9	3.0	2.4	1.8	1.0	0.2
1962	2.4	2.8	5.2	4.3	3.4	2.8	2.0	1.1	0.3
1963	2.7	3.2	5.9	4.8	3.7	2.9	2.3	1.2	0.3
1964	2.9	3.6	6.6	5.2	4.0	3.1	2.3	1.3	0.4
1965	3.1	4.0	7.2	5.6	4.3	3.4	2.5	1.3	0.3
1966	3.2	4.0	7.5	6.0	4.4	3.4	2.5	1.3	0.4
1967	3.5	4.7	8.3	6.5	4.8	3.7	2.7	1.4	0.4
1968	3.7	5.2	8.6	7.0	5.1	3.8	2.9	1.4	0.4

* Annual average.

SOURCE: RGSR, 1968, Table 02, p. 68.

This table shows that the highest incidence of divorce occurs in the age groups 25–39; within this group the most vulnerable age for both husbands and wives appears to be 25–29.

TABLE 22

Divorce-Rates per 1,000 Married Women: Great Britain

			1961	1966	1967	1968
Under 25 years	...	...	2.4	4.2	4.7	5.4
25–29	...	...	4.3	7.4	8.0	8.5
30–34	...	...	3.6	5.9	6.3	7.0
35–39	...	...	2.9	4.3	4.6	5.0
40–44	...	...	2.3	3.3	3.5	3.7
All ages	...	...	2.1	3.1	3.4	3.7

SOURCE: *Social Trends.*

This table shows little significant difference when compared with Table 21.

TABLE 23

Divorce-Rates per 1,000 Married Population: Great Britain

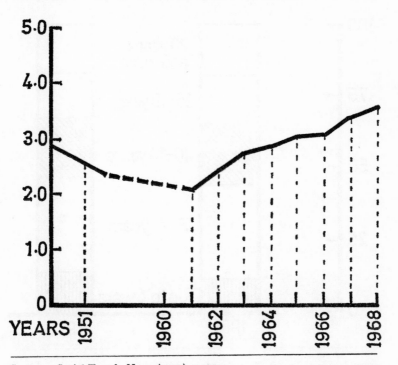

SOURCE: *Social Trends*, No. 1 (1970), p. 57.

TABLE 24

Percentage of Divorce by Duration of Marriage: Great Britain

		1961	1966	1967	1968
Up to 4 years ...	...	11.3	12.1	12.5	13.6
5 to 9 years	...	30.6	32.3	32.6	31.8
10 to 14 years ...	...	22.9	21.4	21.0	21.4
15 to 19 years	...	13.9	14.8	14.2	13.5
20 years and over	...	21.2	19.4	19.8	19.7

SOURCE: *Social Trends,* No. 1 (1970), p. 57.

According to this table, the most vulnerable duration of a marriage is one which has lasted between 5 and 9 years.
See also Tables 20, 21 and 22.

TABLE 25

Percentage of Divorce by Duration of Marriage: Great Britain

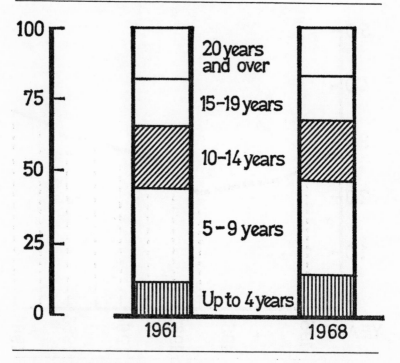

SOURCE: *Social Trends,* No. 1 (1970), p. 57.

TABLE 26

Estimated Total Population by Sex and Marital Condition, as at 30th June, 1968: England and Wales

All Ages	Total	Males				
		Total	Single	Married	Widowed	Divorced
	48.669.0	23.704.4	10.504.4	12.398.6	638.8	162.8
		Females				
		24.964.6	9.640.1	12.387.0	2.680.4	257.1

Source: RGSR, 1968.

TABLE 27

First Marriage-Rates by Sex: England and Wales

Year	Marriage-rate per 1,000 population over 15	
	Bachelors	Spinsters
1931	56.0	51.7
1938	64.8	61.4
1939–50	71.2	69.5
1951–55	70.8	71.9
1956–60	73.6	77.4
1961–65	68.5	76.1
1966	72.1	81.8
1967	72.1	82.5
1968	76.6	88.2

Source: RGSR, 1968, Part II, p. 57.

TABLE 28

Average Age at First Marriage: England and Wales

Period	Bachelors	Spinsters
1901–05	26.9	25.4
1911–15	27.5	25.8
1921–25	27.5	25.6
1931–35	27.4	25.5
1941–45	26.8	24.6
1951–55	26.5	24.2
1959–60	25.9	23.5
1961–65	25.4	22.9
1966	24.9	22.5
1967	24.8	22.5
1968	24.1	22.0

Source: RGSR, 1968, and Butler and Freeman, *British Political Facts 1900–1968* (1969).

This table shows that between 1901 and 1968 the average age at marriage had fallen, more notably for spinsters than for bachelors.

TABLE 29
Expectation of Life at Birth: England and Wales

Year	Males	Females
1838–1844	40.4	42.0
1891–1900	44.1	47.8
1920–1922	55.6	59.6
1930–1932	58.7	62.9
1950–1952	66.4	71.5
1960–1962	68.1	74.0
1963	67.8	73.8
1965	68.5	74.7
1966	68.4	74.7
1967	69.1	75.2
1968	68.6	74.8

SOURCE: RGSR, 1968, Part II, Table B2, p. 11.

This reflects the longer expectation of life in 1968 as compared with 1901, which in turn means a longer duration of marriage. Here is one factor adding to the risks to which marriages are subjected, as *The Field of Choice* indicates.

Over the past 30 years the proportion of the married population of Great Britain has risen from 42.1 per cent in 1938 to 50.7 per cent in 1969, while the proportion of single persons in the population over 15 years of age has fallen from 36.1 per cent to 18 per cent. This change has been due mainly to an increase in marriage-rates among men and women in their late teens and early twenties; whereas in 1938 only 25.4 per cent of young women aged 20 to 24 were married, in 1969 57.2 per cent of them were. Earlier marriage has led to a large increase in the number of children born to women under 30 years of age and in recent years has contributed to a substantial acceleration of the total flow of births into the population.[4]

TABLE 30
Remarriage-Rates by Sex: England and Wales

Year	Widowed and Divorced Men	Widowed and Divorced Women
1931	35.8	9.8
1938	38.1	10.2
1951–55	55.4	16.1
1961–65	51.4	13.3
1966	57.6	14.6
1967	59.5	15.0
1968	61.8	15.7

SOURCE: RGSR, 1968.

TABLE 31

Proceedings commenced in the Divorce Registry, Somerset House from 1st January, 1971 to 31st March, 1971 inclusive

COUNTY COURT—PETITIONS	Hus-band	Wife	Total	%
DISSOLUTION				
2 (1) (a) alone (adultery and intolerable)	254	330	584	15.7
2 (1) (b) alone (cannot reasonably be expected to live)	102	455	557	14.9
2 (1) (c) alone (desertion for two years or more)	174	136	310	8.3
2 (1) (a, b, c together)	5	2	7	
2 (1) (a, b together)	10	72	82	
2 (1) (a, c together)	18	19	37	
2 (1) (b, c together)	15	42	57	
2 (1) (d) either *alone* or with any combination of a, b and c. (d= divorce by consent)	284	268	552	14.8
2 (1) (d and e *together*) or with any				
2 (1) (e) either *alone* or with any combination of a, b and c or presumed decease (e=divorce without consent)	805	535	1340	35.9
combination of a, b and c	20	12	32	
Presumed decease *alone*				
NULLITY				
Incapacity	3	9	12	
Wilful Refusal	4	5	9	
Incapacity and Wilful Refusal (Alternatively)	13	14	27	
Invalidity	3	3	6	
Unsoundness of mind (Sec.9(1)(b) M.C.A. 1965)		1	1	
Pregnancy				
Venereal Disease				
JUDICIAL SEPARATION	1	15	16	
ORIGINATING APPLICATIONS				
MCA s.2	4	32	36	
DRA s.7	1	3	4	
MPPA s.6		9	9	
MPPA s.14		3	3	

Table 31—*continued*

HIGH COURT—PETITIONS	Husband	Wife	Total	%
Declaration of legitimacy	1		1	
Declaration of matrimonial status	2	2	4	
Originating Summonses				
MPPA s.15				
MCA s.26		9	9	
MWPA s.17	21	111	132	
MHA s.1	5	9	14	
RIIGA MCR 1968				
DIVISIONAL COURT	25	19	44	

Totals:

County Court: Petitions	3629	Originating applications	52
High Court: Petitions	5	Originating Summons	155
Divisional Court:	44	Transfers	114
Total proceedings to date	3885	(separate statistic).	

Total proceedings in corresponding period last year   3179.

SOURCE: Supplied by the Law Commission. This table relates only to petitions in the Principal Registry, but there is no reason to suppose the pattern in the district registries is any different.

As expected and has been pointed out, the statistics on the number of petitions for divorce in the first three months since the Act became effective indicate a considerable increase.[5] However, it seems that a little more than a 20 per cent increase in the Principal Registry during the first three months does not yet indicate that the Act is a 'Casanova's charter'. In this respect Mr Abse said '. . . despite jeremiads of those who prophesied that the Act would precipitate an avalanche of divorces, the increase in petitions over the number last year is very small'.[6]

As regards the grounds on which petitions have been filed, 1,340 petitions were filed on the ground 2(1)(*e*). As predicted, the number of petitions on the ground of Clause 2(1)(*e*) is greater than any other category. Of the 1,340 petitions involving marriages where the parties had been apart for five years or more, on the ground of Clause 2(1)(*e*) either alone or with any combination of (*a*), (*b*), and (*c*) or presumed decease, 805 were husbands' while 535 were wives'. 270 more men than wives filed petitions on this ground. 76 more wives (husbands 254, wives 330) out of a total of 584 petitions filed for divorce on the ground of Clause 2(1)(*a*) alone. As far as these figures are concerned, more wives claimed that they found it intolerable to live with their husbands, while more husbands brought forward petitions after a five-year separation. Many claim that if

the trend continued most marriages which came to an end would
dissolve by mutual consent and it would seem likely to be the case,
but at the moment petitions (husbands 284, wives 268) on that
ground—Clause 2(1)(d) either alone or with any combination of
(a), (b), and (c)—are in fact relatively lower than that of (a), (b), or
(e). However, the present trend seems more likely to be as a result
of the petitions filed by those who could now take advantage of
Clause 2(1)(e).

One interesting fact that has come to light which was not fore-
seen before the legislation is that, in cases reported by a solicitor, a
number of husbands were unwilling to proceed with a divorce in
view of the financial responsibility to be borne by the respondent.
If this were to be the general case, one of the supposed contribu-
tions of the Act—to reduce the number of illegitimate children—
would be very slight in practice.

There are several points to be made in view of these statistics.
First, until 1970, petitions filed on grounds of matrimonial offence
—namely adultery, cruelty and desertion—occupied nearly 90 per
cent of the total, but according to the figures for the first three
months of 1971, petitions filed on the ground of unilateral divorce
took over the highest position formerly occupied by adultery. Then
the ground (a)—the respondent has committed adultery and the
petitioner finds it intolerable to live with the respondent—and (b)
—the respondent has behaved in such a way that the petitioner can
not reasonably be expected to live with the respondent—took over
the positions occupied, until 1970, by the grounds of cruelty and
desertion. Secondly, contrary to the 'nervousness and anxiety'
expressed by the critics of the Act, the law is unlikely to be the
major cause of the rising divorce-rate, although in the short term
it will be a contributory factor because of the accumulated arrears
and eased accessibility to the dissolution of marriage, namely Clause
2(1)(e) and (d). Nevertheless, even if the present trend continues,
the number of petitions filed would be unlikely to show a 100 per
cent increase. Thirdly, the Legal Aid and Legal Advice Act 1949
had the strongest impact on the number of petitions filed[7] of any
divorce legislation in England. Even if, under the present Act, the
total number of petitions had reached 100,000 in 1971, the percentage would have remained within a 50 per cent increase over the
total number of petitions filed in 1969.

TABLE 31A

Illegitimate maternities and pre-maritally conceived legitimate maternities, 1938–1960; illegitimate live births and pre-maritally conceived legitimate live births, 1961–1968: England and Wales

Year	Illegitimate maternities/ live births	Pre-maritally conceived legitimate maternities/ live births*†	Total maternities/ live births conceived extra-maritally*		Percentage of extra-maritally conceived maternities/ live births legitimated by marriage of parents before birth of child
			Numbers	Percentage of all maternities/ live births	
		MATERNITIES			
1938	27,440	64,530	91,970	14.4	70.2
1939	26,569	60,346	86,915	13.8	69.4
1940–1944**	39,542	43,146	82,688	12.4	52.2
1945–1949**	49,466	52,557	102,023	13.0	51.5
1950	35,816	54,188	90,004	12.8	60.2
1951	33,444	50,477	83,921	12.3	60.1
1952	33,088	44,239	77,327	11.4	57.2
1953	33,083	43,988	77,071	11.2	57.1
1954	32,128	44,319	76,447	11.2	58.0
1955	31,649	43,601	75,250	11.1	57.9
1956	34,113	47,377	81,490	11.5	58.1
1957	35,098	48,611	83,709	11.5	58.1
1958	36,787	49,775	86,562	11.6	57.5
1959	38,792	50,871	89,663	11.9	56.7
1960	43,281	54,576	97,857	12.4	55.8
		LIVE BIRTHS			
1961	48,490	59,115	107,605	13.3	54.9
1962	55,376	62,455	117,831	14.0	53.0
1963	59,104	64,427	123,531	14.5	52.2
1964	63,340	67,933	131,273	15.0	51.7
1965	66,249	70,457	136,706	15.8	51.5
1966	67,056	71,648	138,704	16.3	51.7
1967	69,928	73,667	143,595	17.3	51.3
1968	69,806	74,531	144,337	17.6	51.6

* From 1952 onwards the figures relate to women married once only.
† Marriage durations under 8½ months up to 1951, under 8 months thereafter.
** Annual averages.
SOURCE: RGSR, 1968.

ILLEGITIMATE MATERNITIES/LIVE BIRTHS

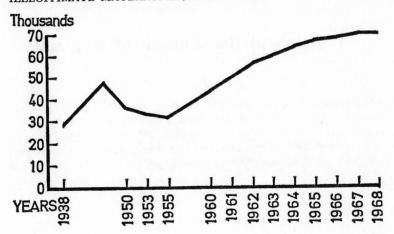

NOTES

1 *Divorce in England,* p. 41.
2 *Britain 1971* An official handbook, 1971, p. 10.
3 The number of petitions filed on the ground of unsound mind (lunacy) since 1938 were: 326 in 1938; 205 in 1958; 162 in 1960; 96 in 1962; 92 in 1964; 87 in 1966.
4 *Britain 1971.*
5 706 increase, from 3,179 in the corresponding period of 1970 to 3,885 petitions presented in the London area.
6 *The Times* (27th Apr., 1971).
7 Over 30 per cent increase—from 29,868 in 1950 to 38,551 in 1951. This represents an increase of 8,683.

Appendix 5

Statistics of the Church of England

As has been seen, the impact of the religious teachings on marriage and divorce in England[1] has been immense, although there are clear signs that the influence is waning. Nevertheless, the following tables show the link between the Church and marriage and divorce, as well as the dominant numerical position of the Church of England.

TABLE 32

Population England and Wales

Year	Total	Males	Females	Divorce
1801	8,892.5	4,254.7	4,637.8	n.a.
1851	17,927.6	8,781.2	9,146.4	n.a.
1901	32,527.8	15,728.6	16,799.2	(1901/1905)
1911	36,670.5	17,445.6	18,624.9	2,732 (1911–1915)
1921	37,886.7	18,075.2	19,811.5	3,178 (1921–1925)
1931	39,952.4	19,133.0	20,819.4	13,365 (1931–1935)
1936	–	–	–	19,545
1937	–	–	–	3,922
1938	–	–	–	4,735
1939	–	–	–	6,092
1951	43,757.9	21,015.6	22,742.3	7,793 28,265
1961	46,104.5	22,303.8	23,800.7	24,936
1968	48,669.0	23,704.4	24,964.6	45,036
1969	48,826.8	23,852.0	25,074.8	50,063

SOURCE: RGSR, 1968, Part II, Table A1, pp. 2–5.

TABLE 33

The Church of England Principal Degrees of Membership for the Provinces of Canterbury and York

Year	Home Population of the two Provinces (ooo's)	Estimated baptized membership		Estimated confirmed membership		
		(ooo's)	Per 1,000 home pop.	(ooo's)	Per 1,000 pop. aged 13 and over	Per 1,000 pop. all ages
1901	30,673	n.a.		n.a.		
1911	33,807	n.a.		n.a.		
1931	37,511	23,800	634	9,000	302	
1951	41,330	25,800	624	9,400	284	
1960	43,296	27,323	631	9,792	281	226
1964	44,893	27,500	613	9,730	270	217
1966	45,547	27,658	607	9,694	n.a.	213
1968	46,047	27,756	603	9,691	n.a.	210

SOURCES: R. F. Neuss (ed.), *Facts and Figures about the Church of England*, No. 3 (1965); D. E. Butler and J. Freeman, *British Political Facts 1900–1968* (1969); and with figures for 1966–8 supplied by the Church of England.

This table shows a fall in membership both per 1,000 home population and per 1,000 population aged 13 and over, although the home population and the estimated baptized membership are increasing. None the less, the increase has not kept pace with the increase in the total population : this gap indicates the decline of the Church's influence.

TABLE 34

Marriages in England and Wales, 1844–1967: Manner of Solemnization

Year	Number of marriages					
	Total marriages	Ch. of Eng. and Ch. in Wales	Roman Catholic	Other Christian denominations	Jews	Civil ceremonies
1844	132,249	120,009	2,280	6,339	175	3,446
1854	151,727	134,109	7,813	9,925	287	7,593
1864	180,387	141,083	8,659	15,685	349	14,611
1874	202,010	150,819	8,179	21,300	456	21,256
1884	204,301	144,344	8,783	23,787	601	26,786
1894	226,449	155,352	9,453	26,965	1,129	33,550
1904	257,856	165,519	10,450	33,825	1,815	46,247
1914	194,401	171,700	13,729	36,119	1,973	70,880
1924	296,416	171,480	16,286	36,074	1,972	97,120
1934	342,307	183,123	22,323	37,508	2,233	97,120

TABLE 34—*continued*

Number of marriages

Year	Total marriages	Ch. of Eng. and Ch. in Wales	Roman Catholic	Other Christian denomi- nations	Jews	Civil cere- monies
1952	349,308	173,282	33,050	34,323	1,876	106,777
1957	346,903	172,010	39,136	36,136	1,713	97,084
1962	347,732	164,707	42,788	35,586	1,549	103,102
1967	386,052	173,278	43,305	36,191	1,557	131,721

SOURCE: R. F. Neuss (ed.), *Facts and Figures about the Church of England*, No. 3 (1965), with figures for 1967 supplied by the Church of England.

Note: Figures are not available for 1941–7.

TABLE 35

Marriages in England and Wales, 1844–1967: Manner of Solemnization

Proportions per 1,000 total marriages

Years	Ch. of Eng. and Ch. in Wales	Roman Catholic	Other Christian denomina- tions	Jews	Civil marriage
1844	907	17	49	1	26
1854	840	49	61	2	48
1864	782	48	87	2	81
1874	747	40	106	2	105
1884	707	43	116	3	131
1894	686	42	119	5	148
1904	642	41	131	7	179
1914	583	47	122	7	241
1924	578	55	122	7	238
1934	535	65	109	7	284
1952	496	74	99	5	306
1957	496	115	104	5	280
1962	474	123	102	5	296
1967	449	112	94	4	341

SOURCE: Neuss, op cit., with figures for 1967 supplied by the Church of England.

Note: The trends in this table show that within a few years, if not already, for the first time in England there will be more civil marriages than marriages in the Church of England. See Table 36.

TABLE 36

Manner of Solemnization per 1,000 Marriages 1844–1967

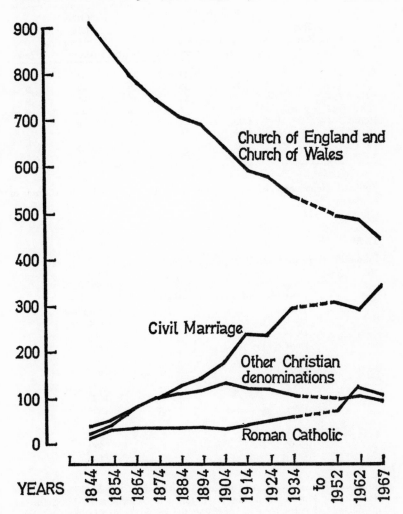

SOURCE : Ibid. Statistics are not available between 1934–52.

TABLE 37

Proportions per 1,000 Marriages with Religious Ceremonies

Years	Ch. of Eng and Ch. in Wales	Roman Catholic	Metho-dist	Congre-gational	Baptist	Other Christian denomina-tions	Jews
1919	776	67	73	31	25	21	7
1924	759	72	79	33	26	22	9
1929	756	80	76	31	25	23	9
1934	747	91	73	30	25	25	9
1952	714	136	69	29	22	22	8
1957	688	160	69	26	24	26	7
1962	673	175	69	27	25	25	6
1967	681	170	69	26	22	26	6

SOURCE: Neuss, op. cit., with figures for 1967 supplied by the Church of England.

TABLE 38

Infant Baptisms at Church of England Fonts per 1,000 Live Births, 1902–1968

Years	Number
1902	658
1910	689
1920	678
1930	699
1940	641
1950	672
1958	579
1960	554
1962	531
1964	526
1966	511
1968	490

SOURCES: Neuss, op cit., and the manscript of the *Church of England Year Book,* 1971, I must thank Mr V. A. James of Westminster Abbey, Church of England, for his help in providing the recent figures in this and other relevant tables.

TABLE 39

Infant Baptisms at Church of England Fonts per 1,000 Live Births, 1902–1968

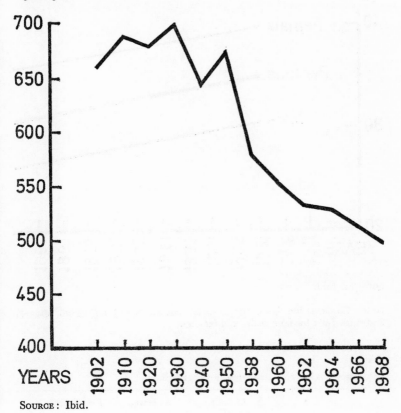

SOURCE: Ibid.

TABLE 40

Confirmations, Males and Females, per 1,000 population aged 12–20, 1911–1964

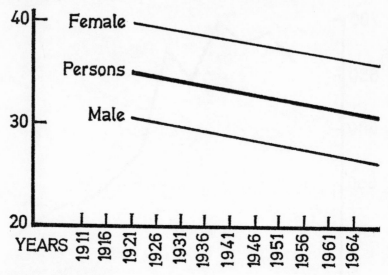

Source: Ibid.

Note: Confirmation figures for males are not available for 1915–20, 1941–7, and since 1964 for both males and females.

TABLE 41

Frequency of Church Attendance in Great Britain

	At least once a month	At least once a year	Less than once a year	%
Church of England	16%	40	44	100
Church of Scotland	39%	27	34	100
Non-Conformist	45%	32	23	100
Roman Catholic	73%	11	16	100

Source: D. E. Butler and D. Stokes, *Political Change in Britain* (1969), p. 125.

The frequency of church attendance clearly indicates the changing attitude towards the Church, although the Roman Catholic Church retains a relatively strong hold on its congregation. 'Among Anglicans the proportion claiming to attend church at least once a week was less than a tenth; among Roman Catholics, fully two-thirds.'[2]

TABLE 42

Religious Preference in Great Britain

Church of England	64%	Baptist	2%
Church of Scotland,		Other non-conformist	4%
Presbyterian	9%	Jewish	1%
Methodist	7%	Other	1%
Catholic	9%	No preference	3%

SOURCE: Ibid., p. 124.

The figures in Tables 38, 41 and 42 indicate the way in which the Church of England retains its dominance. In England, the proportion favouring the Church of England rises to 71 per cent. Tables 37 and 38 show that despite the decline in religious observance almost half the marriages in Britain take place in an Anglican church and about half the babies are christened in an Anglican font. Thus the Church still enjoys its legacy of privilege not only in respect of marriages but also with regard to most new-born babies.

NOTES

1 I must record my thanks to the Central Board of Finance of the Church of England for permission to reproduce the useful data in the preceding pages from the works, *Church of England Year Book* for 1971 and the *Facts and Figures about the Church of England* (No. 3, 1965).
2 Butler and Stokes, op. cit., below.

Selected Bibliography

Note : As there has been no book specifically devoted to the passage of divorce legislation apart from Sir Alan Herbert's *The Ayes Have It,* published in 1937, the main sources were the official government publications, such as Parliamentary debates and the Royal Commissions' Reports; these were supplemented by the press reports, articles, and particularly by the memories of politicians and civil servants who took part in the legislation, however uncertain and subjective they may be. Above all, the most important sources were many private papers which were kindly offered for use in confidence.

I. GOVERNMENT PUBLICATIONS

Parliamentary Debates, Official Report, Hansard, 5th Series.

Parliamentary Papers : Bills and Proceedings of Standing Committees.

The Matrimonial Causes Acts 1857–1967, the Divorce Reform Act 1969, and the Law Commissions Act 1965.

Royal Commissions' Reports on Marriage and Divorce : C. 1604/ 1853; Cd 6478/1912; and Cmd 9678/1956.

Law Commission's Reports and Command Papers :

Law Com. No. 1/1965 : First Programme of the Law Commission.

Law Com. No. 4/1966 : First Annual Report.

Law Com. No. 6/1966 : Reform of the Grounds of Divorce : The Field of Choice (Cmnd 3123).

Law Com. No. 12/1967 : Second Annual Report.

Law Com. No. 14/1968 : Second Programme of Law Reform.

Law Com. No. 15/1968 : Third Annual Report.

Law Com. No. 25/1969 : Family Law. Report on Financial Provision in Matrimonial Proceedings.

Law Com. No. 27/1969 : Fourth Annual Report.

Law Com. No. 36/1970 : Fifth Annual Report.

Civil Judicial Statistics for England and Wales 1950–68.

Registrar General's Statistical Review for 1963–70.

Social Trends, No. 1, 1970.

2. BOOKS

Allen, C. K., *Law in the Making*, Oxford, 7th ed., 1966.

Barnett, M. J., *The Politics of Legislation—The Rent Act 1957*, London, 1969.

Beer, S. H., *Modern British Politics,* London, 1969.

Bentham, J., *The Principles of Morals and Legislation*, Hafner Library Classics, New York, 2nd print., 1961.

Bird, J. W. and Bird, L. F., *The Freedom of Sexual Love*, London, 1968.

Bromhead, P. A., *Private Members' Bills in the British Parliament*, London, 1956.

Butler, D. E., and Freeman, J., *British Political Facts 1900–1968*, London, 1969.

Butler, D. E., and Stokes, D., *Political Change in Britain*, London, 1969.

Butt, R., *The Power of Parliament*, London, 2nd ed., 1969.

Campion, G., *et al.* (eds), *Parliament: A Survey*, London, 4th imp., 1965.

Christoph, J. B., *Capital Punishment and British Politics*, Chicago, 2nd imp., 1968.

Cockain, D., *Divorce and Matrimonial Causes*, London, 1966.

Cole, M. I., *Marriage Past and Present*, London, 1939.

Corry, J. A. and Abraham, H. J., *Elements of Democratic Government*, Oxford, 4th ed., 1964.

Crick, B. (ed.), *Essays on Reform*, Oxford, 1967.

Davidson, R., and Benham, W., *Life of Archibald Campbell Tait*, London, 1891.

Denning, A., *The Changing Law*, London, 1953.

Dent, H. A., *The Education Act 1944*, London, 12th ed., 1968.

Dominian, J., *Marital Breakdown*, Harmondsworth, Middx, 1967.

Ellis, T. P., *Welsh Tribal Law and Custom in the Middle Ages*, Oxford, 1926.

Engels, F., *The Origin of the Family, Private Property and the State*, Moscow, 7th print., 1968.

Finer, S. E., *Anonymous Empire*, London, 1966.

K

Fisher, G. F., *Problems of Marriage and Divorce*, London, 1955.

Fletcher, R., *The Family and Marriage in Britain: An Analysis and Moral Assessment*, London, 1966.

Flood, D. P., *The Dissolution of Marriage*, London, 1961.

Folson, J. K., *The Family and Democratic Society*, London, 1948.

Fox, R., *Kinship and Marriage*, Harmondsworth, Middx, 1967.

Friedmann, W., *Law in a Changing Society*, Harmondsworth, Middx, 1964.

——, *Legal Theory*, London, 5th ed., 1967.

Gardiner, G., and Martin, A. (eds), *Law Reform Now*, London, 1963.

Gore, C., *The Sermon on the Mount*, London, 1895.

——, *The Question of Divorce*, London, 1911.

Harris, C., *The Family*, London, 1969.

Herbert, A. P., *The Ayes Have It—the Story of the Marriage Bill*, London, 1937.

——, *Holy Deadlock*, London, 1937.

Hindell, K., and Simms, M., *Abortion Law Reformed*, London, 1971.

Holdsworth, W. S., *A History of English Law*, 2 vols, London, 3rd ed., 1922–3.

Hollis, C., *The Homicide Act*, London, 1964.

Howells, W., *Mankind in the Making*, Harmondsworth, Middx, 1959.

Hynes, S. L., *The Edwardian Turn of Mind*, London, 1968.

Jennings, I., *Parliament*, Cambridge, 2nd ed., 1969.

Kidd, B. J. (ed.), *Selected Letters of William Bright*, London, 1903.

Kirk, K. E., *Marriage and Divorce*, London, 1948.

Krader, L. (ed.), *Anthropology and Early Law*, New York, 1966.

Lacey, T. A., revised and supplemented by R. C. Mortimer, *Marriage in Church and State*, London, 1947.

Latey, W., *The Tide of Divorce*, London, 1970.

Lathbury, D. C. (ed.), *Letters of Church and State*, 1910.

Lowie, R., *Primitive Society*, London, 3rd imp., 1949.

——, *The Origin of the State*, New York, 1962.

Lubbock, J., *The Origin of Civilisation and the Primitive Condition of Man: Mental and Social Condition of Savages*, London, 5th ed., 1889.

McGregor, O. R., *Divorce in England*, London, 1957.

McGregor, O. R., Blom-Cooper, L., and Gibson, C., *Separated Spouses*, London, 1971.

McLennan, J. F., *Primitive Marriage*, Edinburgh, 1865.

——, *Studies in Ancient History*, London, 1896.

Macmillan, A. T., *Legal Aspects of Marriage*, London, 1951.

Maine, H. S., *Ancient Law*, London, repr. 1950.

Mill, J. S., *Considerations on Representative Government*, London, 1861.

Morgan, L. H., *Systems of Consanguinity and Affinity of the Human Family*, Washington, 1871.

Morris, D., *The End of Marriage*, London, 1971.

Morrison, H., *Government and Parliament*, Oxford, 1960.

Novak, M. (ed.), *The Experience of Marriage: The Testimony of a Catholic Layman*, London, 1965.

Passingham, B., *The Divorce Reform Act 1969*, London, 1970.

Piper, O., *The Biblical View of Sex and Marriage*, Welwyn, 1960.

Pollard, R. S. W., *The Problem of Divorce*, London, 1958.

Puxon, M., *The Family and the Law*, London, 1967.

Rayden, W., *Rayden on Divorce*, edited by Jackson *et al.*, London, 11th ed., 1971.

Richards, P. G., *Parliament and Conscience*, London, 1970.

Rigby, F. F., *What Christian Marriage Means: A Commentary on the Marriage*, London, 1950.

Russell, G. W. E., *Edward King* (60th Bishop of Lincoln), London, 1912.

Scarman, L., *Law Reform: The New Pattern*, London, 1968.

Smith, J. M., *The Theory of Evolution*, Harmondsworth, Middx, 1966.

Stewart, J. D., *British Pressure Groups*, Oxford, 1958.

Tolstoy, D., *Divorce and Matrimonial Causes*, London, 7th ed., 1971.

Travers, R. L., *Husband and Wife in English Law*, London, 1956.

Walkland, S. A., *The Legislative Process in Great Britain*, 1968.

Westermarck, E., *The History of Human Marriage*, London, 5th ed., 1921.

——, *A Short History of Marriage*, London, 1926.

Wheare, K. C., *Legislation*, Oxford, 2nd ed., 1968.

Wilberforce, R. G., *Life of Bishop Wilberforce*, 3 vols, London, 1880–2; 3rd rev. ed. in 1 vol., 1888.

Wilson, H. H., *Pressure Group*, London, 1961.

Winnett, A. R., *Divorce and Re-Marriage in Anglicanism*, London, 1958.

——, *The Church and Divorce*, London, 1968.

Wordsworth, C., *Occasional Sermons*, Series IV, London, 1850–9.

Yardley, D. C. M., *The Future of the Law*, London, 1964.

3. ARTICLES, LECTURES, PAMPHLETS, REPORTS, ETC.

The Church Assembly Board for Social Responsibility, 'Fatherless by Law?', London, 1966.

The Church Assembly, Report of Proceedings, 1967.

The Church of England Moral Welfare Council, 'Marriage, Divorce and the Royal Commission' (a study outline of the Report of the Royal Commission on Marriage and Divorce 1951–1955), London, 1956.

DLRU, 'Divorce in a Modern Society', 1968.

——, 'Just Cause' : 1965–1971.

Gardiner, G., 'The Lord Chancellor's Speech at the Annual Conference of the National Marriage Guidance Council' (5th May, 1967).

Herbert, A. P., 'The Birth of an Act' (unpublished), deposited in the Senate Library, University of London.

Kahn-Freund, O., 'Divorce Law Reform', *Modern Law Review*, 19 (1956).

McKenna, B., 'Divorce by Consent and Divorce for Breakdown of Marriage', *Modern Law Review*, 30 (1967).

MacKenzie, W. J. M., 'Pressure Groups in British Government', *British Journal of Sociology* (July 1955).

Mortimer group, *Putting Asunder: A Divorce Law for Contemporary Society*, London, 1966.

Paulsen, M. G., 'Divorce—Canterbury Style', *New Society* (4th Aug., 1966).

Perkins, D., 'Husbands and Wives' (a survey of recent changes in the law), London, 1962.

Pollard, R. S. W., 'The Need for an Inquiry into Divorce', *Contemporary Review* (Jan. 1951).

Report of the Joint Committee of the Convocations of Canterbury and York : The Church and Marriage, 1935.

Scarman, L., 'Family Law and Law Reform', public lecture in the University of Bristol (18th March, 1966).

——, 'The Law', *The Times* (3rd Oct., 1970).

Simon, J., 'With All My Worldly Goods . . .', presidential address to the Holdworth Club in the University of Birmingham, 1964.

——, 'Recent Developments in the Matrimonial Law', the Riddell Lecture 1970, in Lincoln's Inn New Hall (19th Feb., 1970).

Stone, O. M., 'Royal Commission on Marriage and Divorce: Family Dependents and Their Maintenance', *Modern Law Review,* 19 (1956).

4. POLLS

Gallup Poll; National Opinion Poll.

5. NEWSPAPERS, MAGAZINES, PERIODICALS

For this study most national newspapers and magazines, particularly *The Times* and *The Economist,* were thoroughly researched. The dates of the sources are omitted, as these are clearly indicated where reference is made to them in the text.

Birmingham Post; Catholic Herald; Christian and Christianity Today; Church Times; Daily Mail; Daily Mirror; Daily Sketch; Daily Telegraph; The Economist; Evening Echo; Evening Standard; Guardian; Illustrated London News; Law Society's Gazette; Methodist Recorder; New Law Journal; New Society; Observer; People; Scottish Daily Express; Solicitors' Journal; Spectator; Sun; Sunday Post; Sunday Times; The Times; Tribune.

Index